D0146431

What Is Political Philosophy?

LEO STRAUSS

What Is Political Philosophy?

AND OTHER STUDIES

GREENWOOD PRESS, PUBLISHERS
WESTPORT, CONNECTICUT

RMU LIBRARY

The Library of Congress has catalogued this publication as follows:

Library of Congress Cataloging in Publication Data

Strauss, Leo.
    What is political philosophy?

    Reprint of the ed. published by Free Press, New
York.
    1. Political science—Addresses, essays, lectures
I. Title.
⌐JA71.S795 1973⌐   320'.01   73-1408
ISBN 0-8371-6802-3

All rights reserved. No part of this book may be reproduced o
transmitted in any form or by any means, electronic or mechanica
including photocopying, recording, or by any information storag
and retrieval system, without permission in writing from th
Publisher.

Copyright © 1959 by The Free Press, a Corporation

Originally published in 1959
by The Free Press, New York

This edition is reprinted by arrangement with The Free Press
A Division of The Macmillan Company

First Greenwood Reprinting 1973

Library of Congress Catalogue Card Number 73-1408

ISBN 0-8371-6802-3

Printed in the United States of America

PREFACE

The matter collected in this volume has all been published before,
but not all of it in the English original. "What is Political Philosophy?" is a revised version of the Judah L. Magnes Lectures, which
I delivered at the Hebrew University, Jerusalem, in December 1954
and January 1955; a Hebrew translation with an English summary
was published in *Iyyun*, April 1955; the first lecture was published
in Italian translation in *Il Politico*, 1956, No. 2; a part of the essay
was published in the *Journal of Politics*, August 1957. "Political
Philosophy and History" was published in the *Journal of the History
of Ideas*, January 1949. "On Classical Political Philosophy" was
published in *Social Research*, February 1945, and republished in
Karl de Schweinitz, Jr. and Kenneth W. Thompson, *Man and
Modern Society* (New York: Holt, 1953). "Restatement" was published in French translation in *De La Tyrannie*, *Les Essais*, LXIX
(Paris: Gallimard, 1954). "How Fārābī read Plato's *Laws*" was
published in the third volume of *Mélanges Louis Massignon*, Da-
mascus, 1957. "Maimonides' Statement on Political Science" was
published in the *Proceedings of the American Academy for Jewish
Research*, 1953. "On the Basis of Hobbes's Political Philosophy"
was published in French translation in *Critique*, April 1954. "Locke's
Doctrine of Natural Law" was published in *The American Political
Science Review*, June 1958. "On a Forgotten Kind of Writing"
was published in the *Chicago Review*, Winter-Spring 1954. "Kurt
Riezler" is an enlarged version of a memorial lecture delivered at
the Graduate Faculty of the New School for Social Research in

New York City; it was published in *Social Research*, Spring 1956. All the notes on books were published in *Social Research*, 1941-1950, with the exception of the notes on Chrimes' *Fortescue* (*Columbia Law Review*, September 1943), on Gough's *Locke* (*The American Political Science Review*, September 1950) and Simon's *Democratic Government* (*The New Scholasticism*, July 1952).

I wish to thank the editors and proprietors of the above-mentioned works or periodicals for their kind permission to reprint.

L. S.

CONTENTS

I

WHAT IS
POLITICAL
PHILOSOPHY?

1. The Problem
of Political Philosophy

It is a great honor, and at the same time a challenge to accept a
task of particular difficulty, to be asked to speak about political
philosophy in Jerusalem. In this city, and in this land, the theme
of political philosophy—"the city of righteousness, the faithful city"
—has been taken more seriously than anywhere else on earth. Nowhere else has the longing for justice and the just city filled the
purest hearts and the loftiest souls with such zeal as on this sacred
soil. I know all too well that I am utterly unable to convey to you
what in the best possible case, in the case of any man, would be no
more than a faint reproduction or a weak imitation of our prophets'
vision. I shall even be compelled to lead you into a region where
the dimmest recollection of that vision is on the point of vanishing
altogether—where the Kingdom of God is derisively called an imagined principality—to say here nothing of the region which was never

illumined by it. But while being compelled, or compelling myself, to wander far away from our sacred heritage, or to be silent about it, I shall not for a moment forget what Jerusalem stands for.

The meaning of political philosophy and its meaningful character is as evident today as it always has been since the time when political philosophy came to light in Athens. All political action aims at either preservation or change. When desiring to preserve, we wish to prevent a change to the worse; when desiring to change, we wish to bring about something better. All political action is then guided by some thought of better and worse. But thought of better or worse implies thought of the good. The awareness of the good which guides all our actions has the character of opinion: it is no longer questioned but, on reflection, it proves to be questionable. The very fact that we can question it directs us towards such a thought of the good as is no longer questionable—towards a thought which is no longer opinion but knowledge. All political action has then in itself a directedness towards knowledge of the good: of the good life, or of the good society. For the good society is the complete political good.

If this directedness becomes explicit, if men make it their explicit goal to acquire knowledge of the good life and of the good society, political philosophy emerges. By calling this pursuit political philosophy, we imply that it forms a part of a larger whole: of philosophy; or that political philosophy is a branch of philosophy. In the expression "political philosophy," "philosophy" indicates the manner of treatment: a treatment which both goes to the roots and is comprehensive; "political" indicates both the subject matter and the function: political philosophy deals with political matters in a manner that is meant to be relevant for political life; therefore its subject must be identical with the goal, the ultimate goal of political action. The theme of political philosophy is mankind's great objectives, freedom and government or empire—objectives which are capable of lifting all men beyond their poor selves. Political philosophy is that branch of philosophy which is closest to political life, to non-philosophic life, to human life. Only in his *Politics* does Aristotle make use of oaths—the almost inevitable accompaniment of passionate speech.

Since political philosophy is a branch of philosophy, even the most provisional explanation of what political philosophy is cannot dispense with an explanation, however provisional, of what philosophy is. Philosophy, as quest for wisdom, is quest for universal knowledge, for knowledge of the whole. The quest would not be necessary if such knowledge were immediately available. The absence of knowledge of the whole does not mean, however, that men do not have thoughts about the whole: philosophy is necessarily preceded by opinions about the whole. It is, therefore, the attempt to replace opinions about the whole by knowledge of the whole. Instead of "the whole" the philosophers also say "all things": the whole is not a pure ether or an unrelieved darkness in which one cannot distinguish one part from the other, or in which one cannot discern anything. Quest for knowledge of "all things" means quest for knowledge of God, the world, and man—or rather quest for knowledge of the natures of all things: the natures in their totality are "the whole."

Philosophy is essentially not possession of the truth, but quest for the truth. The distinctive trait of the philosopher is that "he knows that he knows nothing," and that his insight into our ignorance concerning the most important things induces him to strive with all his power for knowledge. He would cease to be a philosopher by evading the questions concerning these things or by disregarding them because they cannot be answered. It may be that as regards the possible answers to these questions, the pros and cons will always be in a more or less even balance, and therefore that philosophy will never go beyond the stage of discussion or disputation and will never reach the stage of decision. This would not make philosophy futile. For the clear grasp of a fundamental question requires understanding of the nature of the subject matter with which the question is concerned. Genuine knowledge of a fundamental question, thorough understanding of it, is better than blindness to it, or indifference to it, be that indifference or blindness accompanied by knowledge of the answers to a vast number of peripheral or ephemeral questions or not. *Minimum quod potest haberi de cognitione rerum altissimarum, desiderabilius est quam certissima cognitio quae habetur de minimis rebus.* (Thomas Aquinas, *Summa Theologica,* I, qu. 1a.5)

Of philosophy thus understood, political philosophy is a branch. Political philosophy will then be the attempt to replace opinion about the nature of political things by knowledge of the nature of political things. Political things are by their nature subject to approval and disapproval, to choice and rejection, to praise and blame. It is of their essence not to be neutral but to raise a claim to men's obedience, allegiance, decision or judgment. One does not understand them as what they are, as political things, if one does not take seriously their explicit or implicit claim to be judged in terms of goodness or badness, of justice or injustice, i.e., if one does not measure them by some standard of goodness or justice. To judge soundly one must know the true standards. If political philosophy wishes to do justice to its subject matter, it must strive for genuine knowledge of these standards. Political philosophy is the attempt truly to know both the nature of political things and the right, or the good, political order.

Political philosophy ought to be distinguished from political thought in general. In our times, they are frequently identified. People have gone so far in debasing the name of philosophy as to speak of the philosophies of vulgar impostors. By political thought we understand the reflection on, or the exposition of, political ideas; and by a political idea we may understand any politically significant "phantasm, notion, species, or whatever it is about which the mind can be employed in thinking" concerning the political fundamentals. Hence, all political philosophy is political thought but not all political thought is political philosophy. Political thought is, as such, indifferent to the distinction between opinion and knowledge; but political philosophy is the conscious, coherent and relentless effort to replace opinions about the political fundamentals by knowledge regarding them. Political thought may not be more, and may not even intend to be more, than the expounding or the defense of a firmly held conviction or of an invigorating myth; but it is essential to political philosophy to be set in motion, and be kept in motion, by the disquieting awareness of the fundamental difference between conviction, or belief, and knowledge. A political thinker who is not a philosopher is primarily interested in, or attached to, a specific order or policy; the political philosopher is primarily interested in, or attached to, the truth. Political thought which is not political philosophy finds its adequate expression in laws and codes, in poems and stories, in tracts and public speeches *inter alia;* the proper form of presenting political philosophy is the treatise. Political thought is as old as the human race; the first man who uttered a word like "father" or an expression like "thou shalt not . . ." was the first political thinker; but political philosophy appeared at a knowable time in the recorded past.

By political theory, people frequently understand today comprehensive reflections on the political situation which lead up to the suggestion of a broad policy. Such reflections appeal in the last resort to principles accepted by public opinion or a considerable part of it; i.e., they dogmatically assume principles which can well be questioned. Works of political theory in this sense would be Pinsker's *Autoemancipation* and Herzl's *Judenstaat*. Pinsker's *Autoemancipation* carries as its motto the words: "If I am not for myself, who will be for me? And if not now, when?" It omits the words: "And if I am only for myself, what am I?" Pinsker's silent rejection of the thought expressed in the omitted words is a crucial premise of the argument developed in his tract. Pinsker does not justify this rejection. For a justification, one would have to turn to the 3rd and 16th chapters of Spinoza's *Tractatus theologico-politicus*, to a work of a political pholosopher.

We are compelled to distinguish political philosophy from political theology. By political theology we understand political teachings which are based on divine revelation. Political philosophy is limited to what is accessible to the unassisted human mind. As regards social philosophy, it has the same subject matter as political philosophy, but it regards it from a different point of view. Political philosophy rests on the premise that the political association—one's country or one's nation—is the most comprehensive or the most authoritative association, whereas social philosophy conceives of the political association as a part of a larger whole which it designates by the term "society."

Finally, we must discuss the relation of political philosophy to political science. "Political science" is an ambiguous term: it designates such investigations of political things as are guided by the model of natural science, and it designates the work which is being done by the members of political science departments. As regards the former, or what we may call "scientific" political science, it conceives of itself as *the* way towards genuine knowledge of political things. Just as genuine knowledge of natural things began when people turned from sterile and vain speculation to empirical and experimental study, the genuine knowledge of political things will begin when political philosophy will have given way completely to the scientific study of politics. Just as natural science stands on its own feet, and at most supplies unintentionally materials for the speculations of natural philosophers, political science stands on its own feet, and at most supplies unintentionally materials for the speculations of political philosophers. Considering the contrast between the solidity of the one pursuit and the pitiful pretentiousness characteristic of the other, it is however more reasonable to dismiss the vague and inane speculations of political philosophy altogether than to go on paying lip service to a wholly discredited and decrepit tradition. The sciences, both natural and political, are frankly non-philosophic. They need philosophy of a kind: methodology or logic. But these philosophic disciplines have obviously nothing in common with political philosophy. "Scientific" political science is in fact incompatible with political philosophy.

The useful work done by the men called political scientists is independent of any aspiration towards "scientific" political science. It consists of careful and judicious collections and analyses of politically relevant data. To understand the meaning of this work, we remind ourselves of our provisional definition of political philosophy. Political philosophy is the attempt to understand the nature of political things. Before one can even think of attempting to understand the nature of political things, one must know political things: one must possess political knowledge. At least every sane adult possesses political knowledge to some degree. Everyone knows something of taxes, police, law, jails, war, peace, armistice. Everyone knows that the aim of war is victory, that war demands the supreme sacrifice and many other deprivations, that bravery deserves praise and cowardice deserves blame. Everyone knows that buying a shirt, as distinguished from casting a vote, is not in itself a political action. The man in the street is supposed to possess less political knowledge than the men who make it their business to supply him with information and guidance regarding political things. He certainly possesses less political knowledge than very intelligent men of long and varied political experience. At the top of the ladder we find the great statesman who possesses political knowledge, political understanding, political wisdom, political skill in the highest degree: political science (*politikē epistēmē*) in the original meaning of the term.

All political knowledge is surrounded by political opinion and interspersed with it. By political opinion we understand here opinion as distinguished from knowledge of political things: errors, guesses, beliefs, prejudices, forecasts, and so on. It is of the essence of political life to be guided by a mixture of political knowledge and political opinion. Hence, all political life is accompanied by more or less coherent and more or less strenuous efforts to replace political opinion by political knowledge. Even governments which lay claim to more than human knowledge are known to employ spies.

The character of political knowledge and of the demands made on it has been profoundly affected by a fairly recent change in the character of society. In former epochs, intelligent men could acquire the political knowledge, the political understanding they needed, by listening to wise old men or, which is the same thing, by reading good historians, as well as by looking around and by devoting themselves to public affairs. These ways of acquiring political knowledge are no longer sufficient because we live in "dynamic mass societies," i.e., in societies which are characterized by both immense complexity and rapid change. Political knowledge is more difficult to come by and it becomes obsolete more rapidly than in former times. Under these conditions it becomes necessary that a number of men should devote themselves entirely to the task of collecting and digesting knowledge of political things. It is this activity which today is frequently called political science. It does not emerge if it has not been realized among other things that even such political matters as have no bearing on the situation of the day deserve to be studied, and that their study must be carried on with the greatest possible care: a specific care which is designed to counteract the specific fallacies to which our judgment on political things is exposed. Furthermore, the men we speak of invest much toil in giving political knowledge the form of teachings which can be transmitted in classrooms. Moreover, while even the most unscrupulous politician must constantly try to replace in his own mind political opinion by political knowledge in order to be successful, the scholarly student of political things will go beyond this by trying to state the results of his investigations in public without any concealment and without any partisanship: he will act the part of the enlightened and patriotic citizen who has no axe of his own to grind. Or, differently expressed, the scholarly quest for political knowledge is essentially animated by a moral impulse, the love of truth. But however one may conceive of the difference between the scholarly and the non-scholarly quest for political knowledge, and however important these differences may be, the scholarly and the non-scholarly quest for political knowledge are identical in the decisive respect: their center of reference is the given political situation, and even in most cases the given political situation in the individual's own country. It is true that a botanist in Israel pays special attention to the flora of Israel, whereas the botanist in Canada pays special attention to the flora of Canada. But this difference, which is not more than the outcome of a convenient and even indispensable division of labor, has an entirely different character than the only apparently similar difference between the preoccupation of the Israeli political scientist and the Canadian political scientist. It is only when the Here and Now ceases to be the center of reference that a philosophic or scientific approach to politics can emerge.

All knowledge of political things implies assumptions concerning the nature of political things; i.e., assumptions which concern not merely the given political situation, but political life or human life as such. One cannot know anything about a war going on at a given time without having some notion, however dim and hazy, of war as such and its place within human life as such. One cannot see a policeman as a policeman without having made an assumption about law and government as such. The assumptions concerning the nature of political things, which are implied in all knowledge of political things, have the character of opinions. It is only when these assumptions are made the theme of critical and coherent analysis that a philosophic or scientific approach to politics emerges.

The cognitive status of political knowledge is not different from that of the knowledge possessed by the shepherd, the husband, the general, or the cook. Yet the pursuits of these types of man do not give rise to a pastoral, marital, military, or culinary philosophy because their ultimate goals are sufficiently clear and unambiguous. The ultimate political goal, on the other hand, urgently calls for coherent reflection. The goal of the general is victory, whereas the goal of the statesman is the common good. What victory means is not essentially controversial, but the meaning of the common good is essentially controversial. The ambiguity of the political goal is due to its comprehensive character. Thus the temptation arises to deny, or to evade, the comprehensive character of politics and to treat politics as one compartment among many. But this temptation must be resisted if it is necessary to face our situation as human beings, i.e., the whole situation.

Political philosophy as we have tried to circumscribe it has been cultivated since its beginnings almost without any interruption until a relatively short time ago. Today, political philosophy is in a state of decay and perhaps of putrefaction, if it has not vanished altogether. Not only is there complete disagreement regarding its subject matter, its methods, and its function; its very possibility in any form has become questionable. The only point regarding which academic teachers of political science still agree, concerns the usefulness of studying the history of political philosophy. As regards the philosophers, it is sufficient to contrast the work of the four greatest philosophers of the last forty years—Bergson, Whitehead, Husserl, and Heidegger—with the work of Hermann Cohen in order to see how rapidly and thoroughly political philosophy has become discredited. We may describe the present situation as follows. Originally political philosophy was identical with political science, and it was the all-embracing study of human affairs. Today, we find it cut into pieces which behave as if they were parts of a worm. In the first place, one has applied the distinction between philosophy and science to the study of human affairs, and accordingly one makes a distinction between a non-philosophic political science and a non-scientific political philosophy, a distinction which under present conditions takes away all dignity, all honesty from political philosophy. Furthermore, large segments of what formerly belonged to political philosophy or political science have become emancipated under the names of economics, sociology, and social psychology. The pitiable rump for which honest social scientists do not care is left as prey to philosophers of history and to people who amuse themselves more than others with professions of faith. We hardly exaggerate when we say that today political philosophy does not exist any more, except as matter for burial, i.e., for historical research, or else as a theme of weak and unconvincing protestations.

If we inquire into the reasons for this great change, we receive these answers: political philosophy is unscientific, or it is unhistorical, or it is both. Science and History, those two great powers of the modern world, have finally succeeded in destroying the very possibility of political philosophy.

The rejection of political philosophy as unscientific is characteristic of present-day positivism. Positivism is no longer what it desired to be when Auguste Comte originated it. It still agrees with Comte by maintaining that modern science is the highest form of knowledge, precisely because it aims no longer, as theology and metaphysics did, at absolute knowledge of the Why, but only at relative knowledge of the How. But after having been modified by utilitarianism, evolutionism, and neo-Kantianism, it has abandoned completely Comte's hope that a social science modeled on modern natural science would be able to overcome the intellectual anarchy of modern society. In about the last decade of the 19th century, social science positivism reached its final form by realizing or decreeing that there is a fundamental difference between facts and values, and that only factual judgments are within the competence of science: scientific social science is incompetent to pronounce value judgments, and must avoid value judgments altogether. As for the meaning of the term "value" in statements of this kind, we can hardly say more than that "values" mean both things preferred and principles of preference.

A discussion of the tenets of social science positivism is today indispensable for explaining the meaning of political philosophy. We reconsider especially the practical consequences of this positivism. Positivistic social science is "value-free" or "ethically neutral": it is neutral in the conflict between good and evil, however good and evil may be understood. This means that the ground which is common to all social scientists, the ground on which they carry on their investigations and discussions, can only be reached through a process of emancipation from moral judgments, or of abstracting from moral judgments: moral obtuseness is the necessary condition for scientific analysis. For to the extent to which we are not yet completely insensitive to moral distinctions, we are forced to make value judgments. The habit of looking at social or human phenomena without making value judgments has a corroding influence on any preferences. The more serious we are as social scientists, the more completely we develop within ourselves a state of indifference to any goal, or of aimlessness and drifting, a state which may be called nihilism. The social scientist is not immune to preferences; his activity is a constant fight against the preferences he has as a human being and a citizen and which threaten to overcome his scientific detachment. He derives the power to counteract these dangerous influences by his dedication to one and only one value—to truth. But according to his principles, truth is not a value which it is necessary to choose: one may reject it as well as choose it. The scientist as scientist must indeed have chosen it. But neither scientists nor science are simply necessary. Social science cannot pronounce on the question of whether social science itself is good. It is then compelled to teach that society can with equal right and with equal reason favor social science as well as suppress it as disturbing, subversive, corrosive, nihilistic. But strangely enough we find social scientists very anxious to "sell" social science, i.e., to prove that social science is necessary. They will argue as follows. Regardless of what our preferences or ends may be, we wish to achieve our ends; to achieve our ends, we must know which means are conducive to our ends; but adequate knowledge of the means conducive to any social ends is the sole function of social science and only of social science; hence social science is necessary for any society or any social movement; social science is then simply necessary; it is a value from every point of view. But once we grant this we are seriously tempted to wonder if there are not a few other things which must be values from every point of view or for every thinking human being. To avoid this inconvenience the social scientist will scorn all considerations of public relations or of private advancement, and take refuge in the virtuous contention that he does not know, but merely believes that quest for truth is good: other men may believe with equal right that quest for truth is bad. But what does he mean by this contention? Either he makes a distinction between noble and ignoble objectives or he refuses to make such a distinction. If he makes a distinction between noble and ignoble objectives he will say there is a variety of noble objectives or of ideals, and that there is no ideal which is compatible with all other ideals: if one chooses truth as one's ideal, one necessarily rejects other ideals; this being the case, there cannot be a necessity, an evident necessity for noble men to choose truth in preference to other ideals. But as long as the social scientist speaks of ideals, and thus makes a distinction between noble and not noble objectives, or between idealistic integrity and petty egoism, he makes a value judgment which according to his fundamental contention is, as such, no longer necessary. He must then say that it is as legitimate to make the pursuit of safety, income, deference one's sole aim in life as it is to make the quest for truth one's chief aim. He thus lays himself open to the suspicion that his activity as a social scientist serves no other purpose than to increase his safety, his income, and his prestige, or that his competence as a social scientist is a skill which he is prepared to sell to the highest bidder. Honest citizens will begin to wonder whether such a man can be trusted, or whether he can be loyal, especially since he must maintain that it is as defensible to choose loyalty as one's value as it is to reject it. In a word, he will get entangled in the predicament which leads to the downfall of Thrasymachus and his taming by Socrates in the first book of Plato's *Republic*.

It goes without saying that while our social scientist may be confused, he is very far from being disloyal and from lacking integrity. His assertion that integrity and quest for truth are values which one can with equal right choose or reject is a mere movement of his lips and his tongue, to which nothing corresponds in his heart or mind. I have never met any scientific social scientist who apart from being dedicated to truth and integrity was not also wholeheartedly devoted to democracy. When he says that democracy is a value which is not evidently superior to the opposite value, he does not mean that he is impressed by the alternative which he rejects, or that his heart or his mind is torn between alternatives which in themselves are equally attractive. His "ethical neutrality" is so far from being nihilism or a road to nihilism that it is not more than an alibi for thoughtlessness and vulgarity: by saying that democracy and truth are values, he says in effect that one does not have to think about the reasons why these things are good, and that he may bow as well as anyone else to the values that are adopted and respected by his society. Social science positivism fosters not so much nihilism as conformism and philistinism.

It is not necessary to enter here and now into a discussion of the theoretical weaknesses of social science positivism. It suffices to allude to the considerations which speak decisively against this school. (1) It is impossible to study social phenomena, i.e., all important social phenomena, without making value judgments. A man who sees no reason for not despising people whose horizon is limited to their consumption of food and their digestion may be a tolerable econometrist; he cannot say anything relevant about the character of a human society. A man who refuses to distinguish between great statesmen, mediocrities, and insane impostors may be a good bibliographer; he cannot say anything relevant about politics and political history. A man who cannot distinguish between a profound religious thought and a languishing superstition may be a good statistician; he cannot say anything relevant about the sociology of religion. Generally speaking, it is impossible to understand thought or action or work without evaluating it. If we are unable to evaluate adequately, as we very frequently are, we have not yet succeeded in understanding adequately. The value judgments which are forbidden to enter through the front door of political science, sociology or economics, enter these disciplines through the back door; they come from that annex of present-day social science which is called psychopathology. Social scientists see themselves compelled to speak of unbalanced, neurotic, maladjusted people. But these value judgments are distinguished from those used by the great historians, not by greater clarity or certainty, but merely by their poverty: a slick operator is as well adjusted as, he may be better adjusted than, a good man or a good citizen. Finally, we must not overlook the invisible value judgments which are concealed from undiscerning eyes but nevertheless most powerfully present in allegedly purely descriptive concepts. For example, when social scientists distinguish between democratic and authoritarian habits or types of human beings, what they call "authoritarian" is in all cases known to me a caricature of everything of which they, as good democrats of a certain kind, disapprove. Or when they speak of three principles of legitimacy, rational, traditional, and charismatic, their very expression "routinization of charisma" betrays a Protestant or liberal preference which no conservative Jew and no Catholic would accept: in the light of the notion of "routinization of charisma," the genesis of the Halakah out of Biblical prophesy on the one hand, and the genesis of the Catholic Church out of the New Testament teaching, necessarily appear as cases of "routinization of charisma." If the objection should be made that value judgments are indeed inevitable in social science but have a merely conditional character, I would reply as follows: are the conditions in question not necessarily fulfilled when we are interested in social phenomena? must the social scientist not necessarily make the assumption that a healthy social life in this world is good, just as medicine necessarily makes the assumption that health and a healthy long life are good? And also are not all factual assertions based on conditions, or assumptions, which however do not become questionable as long as we deal with facts qua facts (e.g., that there are "facts," that events have causes)?

The impossibility of a "value-free" political science can be shown most simply as follows. Political science presupposes a distinction between political things and things which are not political; it presupposes therefore some answer to the question "what is political?" In order to be truly scientific, political science would have to raise this question and to answer it explicitly and adequately. But it is impossible to define the political, i.e., that which is related in a relevant way to the *polis*, the "country" or the "state," without answering the question of what constitutes this kind of society. Now, a society cannot be defined without reference to its purpose. The most well known attempt to define "the state" without regard to its purpose admittedly led to a definition which was derived from "the modern type of state" and which is fully applicable only to that type; it was an attempt to define the modern state without having first defined the state. But by defining the state, or rather civil society, with reference to its purpose, one admits a standard in the light of which one must judge political actions and institutions: the purpose of civil society necessarily functions as a standard for judging of civil societies.

(2) The rejection of value judgments is based on the assumption that the conflicts between different values or value-systems are essentially insoluble for human reason. But this assumption, while generally taken to be sufficiently established, has never been proven. Its proof would require an effort of the magnitude of that which went into the conception and elaboration of the *Critique of Pure Reason;* it would require a comprehensive critique of evaluating reason. What we find in fact are sketchy observations which pretend to prove that this or that specific value conflict is insoluble. It is prudent to grant that there are value conflicts which cannot

in fact be settled by human reason. But if we cannot decide which of two mountains whose peaks are hidden by clouds is higher than the other, cannot we decide that a mountain is higher than a mole-hill? If we cannot decide, regarding a war between two neighboring nations which have been fighting each other for centuries, which nation's cause is more just, cannot we decide that Jezebel's action against Naboth was inexcusable? The greatest representative of social science positivism, Max Weber, has postulated the insolu-bility of all value conflicts, because his soul craved a universe in which failure, that bastard of forceful sinning accompanied by still more forceful faith, instead of felicity and serenity, was to be the mark of human nobility. The belief that value judgments are not subject, in the last analysis, to rational control, encourages the inclination to make irresponsible assertions regarding right and wrong or good and bad. One evades serious discussion of serious issues by the simple device of passing them off as value problems. One even creates the impression that all important human conflicts are value conflicts, whereas, to say the least, many of these con-flicts arise out of men's very agreement regarding values.

(3) The belief that scientific knowledge, i.e., the kind of knowl-edge possessed or aspired to by modern science, is the highest form of human knowledge, implies a depreciation of pre-scientific knowledge. If one takes into consideration the contrast between scientific knowledge of the world and pre-scientific knowledge of the world, one realizes that positivism preserves in a scarcely dis-guised manner Descartes' universal doubt of pre-scientific knowl-edge and his radical break with it. It certainly distrusts pre-scientific knowledge, which it likes to compare to folklore. This superstition fosters all sorts of sterile investigations or complicated idiocies. Things which every ten-year-old child of normal intelligence knows are regarded as being in need of scientific proof in order to be-come acceptable as facts. And this scientific proof, which is not only not necessary, is not even possible. To illustrate this by the simplest example: all studies in social science presuppose that its devotees can tell human beings from other beings; this most funda-mental knowledge was not acquired by them in classrooms; and this knowledge is not transformed by social science into scientific knowledge, but retains its initial status without any modification throughout. If this pre-scientific knowledge is not knowledge, all

scientific studies, which stand or fall with it, lack the character of knowledge. The preoccupation with scientific proof of things which everyone knows well enough, and better, without scientific proof, leads to the neglect of that thinking, or that reflection, which must precede all scientific studies if these studies are to be relevant. The scientific study of politics is often presented as ascending from the ascertainment of political "facts," i.e., of what has happened hitherto in politics, to the formulation of "laws" whose knowledge would permit the prediction of future political events. This goal is taken as a matter of course without a previous investigation as to whether the subject matter with which political science deals admits of adequate understanding in terms of "laws" or whether the universals through which political things can be understood as what they are must not be conceived of in entirely different terms. Scientific concern with political facts, relations of political facts, recurrent relations of political facts, or laws of political behavior, requires isolation of the phenomena which it is studying. But if this isolation is not to lead to irrelevant or misleading results, one must see the phenomena in question within the whole to which they belong, and one must clarify that whole, i.e., the whole political or politico-social order. One cannot arrive, e.g., at a kind of knowledge of "group politics" which deserves to be called scientific if one does not reflect on what genus of political orders is presupposed if there is to be "group politics" at all, and what kind of political order is presupposed by the specific "group politics" which one is studying. But one cannot clarify the character of a specific democracy, e.g., or of democracy in general, without having a clear understanding of the alternatives to democracy. Scientific political scientists are inclined to leave it at the distinction between democracy and authoritarianism, i.e., they absolutize the given political order by remaining within a horizon which is defined by the given political order and its opposite. The scientific approach tends to lead to the neglect of the primary or fundamental questions and therewith to thoughtless acceptance of received opinion. As regards these fundamental questions our friends of scientific exactness are strangely unexacting. To refer again to the most simple and at the same time decisive example, political science requires clarification of what distinguishes political things from things which are not political; it requires that the question be raised and answered "what is political?" This question cannot be dealt with scientifically but only dialectically. And dialectical treatment necessarily begins from pre-scientific knowledge and takes it most seriously. Pre-scientific knowledge, or "common sense" knowledge, is thought to be discredited by Copernicus and the succeeding natural science. But the fact that what we may call telescopic-microscopic knowledge is very fruitful in certain areas does not entitle one to deny that there are things which can only be seen as what they are if they are seen with the unarmed eye; or, more precisely, if they are seen in the perspective of the citizen, as distinguished from the perspective of the scientific observer. If one denies this, one will repeat the experience of Gulliver with the nurse in Brobdingnag and become entangled in the kind of research projects by which he was amazed in Laputa.

(4) Positivism necessarily transforms itself into historicism. By virtue of its orientation by the model of natural science, social science is in danger of mistaking peculiarities of, say, mid-twentieth century United States, or more generally of modern western society, for the essential character of human society. To avoid this danger, it is compelled to engage in "cross-cultural research," in the study of other cultures, both present and past. But in making this effort, it misses the meaning of those other cultures, because it interprets them through a conceptual scheme which originates in modern western society, which reflects that particular society, and which fits at best only that particular society. To avoid this danger, social science must attempt to understand those cultures as they understand or understood themselves: the understanding primarily required of the social scientist is historical understanding. Historical understanding becomes the basis of a truly empirical science of society. But if one considers the infinity of the task of historical understanding, one begins to wonder whether historical understanding does not take the place of the scientific study of society. Furthermore, social science is said to be a body of true propositions about social phenomena. The propositions are answers to questions. What valid answers, objectively valid answers, are, may be determined by the rules or principles of logic. But the questions depend on one's direction of interest, and hence on one's values, i.e., on subjective principles. Now it is the direction of interests, and not logic, which supplies the fundamental concepts.

NMU LIBRARY

It is therefore not possible to divorce from each other the subjective and objective elements of social science: the objective answers receive their meaning from the subjective questions. If one does not relapse into the decayed Platonism which is underlying the notion of timeless values, one must conceive of the values embodied in a given social science as dependent on the society to which the social science in question belongs, i.e., on history. Not only is social science superseded by historical studies; social science itself proves to be "historical." Reflection on social science as a historical phenomenon leads to the relativization of social science and ultimately of modern science generally. As a consequence, modern science comes to be viewed as one historically relative way of understanding things which is not in principle superior to alternative ways of understanding.

It is only at this point that we come face to face with the serious antagonist of political philosophy: historicism. After having reached its full growth historicism is distinguished from positivism by the following characteristics. (1) It abandons the distinction between facts and values, because every understanding, however theoretical, implies specific evaluations. (2) It denies the authoritative character of modern science, which appears as only one form among many of man's thinking orientation in the world. (3) It refuses to regard the historical process as fundamentally progressive, or, more generally stated, as reasonable. (4) It denies the relevance of the evolutionist thesis by contending that the evolution of man out of non-man cannot make intelligible man's humanity. Historicism rejects the question of the good society, that is to say, of *the* good society, because of the essentially historical character of society and of human thought: there is no essential necessity for raising the question of the good society; this question is not in principle coeval with man; its very possibility is the outcome of a mysterious dispensation of fate. The crucial issue concerns the status of those permanent characteristics of humanity, such as the distinction between the noble and the base, which are admitted by the thoughtful historicists: can these permanencies be used as criteria for distinguishing between good and bad dispensations of fate? The historicist answers this question in the negative. He looks down on the permanencies in question because of their objective, common, superficial and rudimentary character:

to become relevant, they would have to be completed, and their completion is no longer common but historical. It was the contempt for these permanencies which permitted the most radical historicist in 1933 to submit to, or rather to welcome, as a dispensation of fate, the verdict of the least wise and least moderate part of his nation while it was in its least wise and least moderate mood, and at the same time to speak of wisdom and moderation. The biggest event of 1933 would rather seem to have proved, if such proof was necessary, that man cannot abandon the question of the good society, and that he cannot free himself from the responsibility for answering it by deferring to History or to any other power different from his own reason.

II. *The Classical Solution*

When we describe the political philosophy of Plato and of Aristotle as classical political philosophy, we imply that it is the classic form of political philosophy. The classic was once said to be characterized by noble simplicity and quiet grandeur. This suggestion guides us in the right direction. It is an attempt to articulate what was formerly also called the "natural" character of classical thought. "Natural" is here understood in contradistinction to what is merely human, all too human. A human being is said to be natural if he is guided by nature rather than by convention, or by inherited opinion, or by tradition, to say nothing of mere whims. Classical political philosophy is non-traditional, because it belongs to the fertile moment when all political traditions were shaken, and there was not yet in existence a tradition of political philosophy. In all later epochs, the philosophers' study of political things was mediated by a tradition of political philosophy which acted like a screen between the philosopher and political things, regardless of whether the individual philosopher cherished or rejected that tradition. From this it follows that the classical philosophers see the political things with a freshness and directness which have never been equalled. They look at political things in the perspective of the enlightened citizen or statesman. They see things clearly which the enlightened citizens or statesmen do not see clearly, or do not see at all. But this has no other reason but the fact that they look further afield in the same direction as the enlightened citizens or statesmen. They do not look at political things from the outside, as spectators of political life. They speak the language of the citizens or statesmen: they hardly use a single term which is not familiar to the market place. Hence their political philosophy is comprehensive; it is both political theory and political skill; it is as open minded to the legal and institutional aspects of political life as it is to that which transcends the legal and institutional; it is equally free from the narrowness of the lawyer, the brutality of the technician, the vagaries of the visionary, and the baseness of the opportunist. It reproduces, and raises to its perfection, the magnanimous flexibility of the true statesman, who crushes the insolent and spares the vanquished. It is free from all fanaticism because it knows that evil cannot be eradicated and therefore that one's expectations from politics must be moderate. The spirit which animates it may be described as serenity or sublime sobriety.

Compared with classical political philosophy, all later political thought, whatever else its merits may be, and in particular modern political thought, has a derivative character. This means that in later times there has occurred an estrangement from the simple and primary issues. This has given to political philosophy the character of "abstractness," and has therefore engendered the view that the philosophic movement must be a movement, not from opinion to knowledge, not from the here and now to what is always or eternal, but from the abstract towards the concrete. It was thought that by virtue of this movement towards the concrete, recent philosophy has overcome the limitations not only of modern political philosophy, but of classical political philosophy as well. It was overlooked, however, that this change of orientation perpetuated the original defect of modern philosophy because it accepted abstractions as its starting point, and that the concrete at which one eventually arrived was not at all the truly concrete, but still an abstraction.

One example must suffice here. Today it is held in certain circles that the basic task of political or social science is to understand the most concrete human relation, and that relation is called the I—Thou—We relation. It is obvious that the Thou and the We are supplements to Descartes' Ego; the question is whether the fundamental inadequacy of Descartes' Ego can be disposed of by any supplements, and whether it is not necessary to return to a more fundamental beginning, or to the natural beginning. The phenomenon which is now called the I—Thou—We relation was known to the classics by the name of friendship. When speaking to a friend I address him in the second person. But philosophic or scientific analysis is not speaking to a friend, i.e., to this individual here and now, but speaking to anyone concerned with such analysis. Such analysis cannot be meant to be a substitute for living together as friends; it can at best only point to such living together or arouse a desire for it. When speaking about someone with whom I have a close relation I call him my friend. I do not call him my Thou. Adequate "speaking about" in analytical or objective speech must be grounded in and continue the manner of "speaking about" which is inherent in human life. By speaking of "the Thou" instead of "the friend," I am trying to preserve in objective speech what cannot be preserved in objective speech; I am trying to objectify something that is incapable of being objectified. I am trying to preserve in "speaking about" what can be actual only in "speaking to." Hence I do injustice to the phenomena; I am untrue to the phenomena; I miss the concrete. While attempting to lay a foundation for genuine human communication, I preserve an incapacity for genuine human communication.

The character of classical political philosophy appears with the greatest clarity from Plato's *Laws*, which is his political work *par excellence*. The *Laws* is a conversation about law, and political things in general, between an old Athenian stranger, an old Cretan, and an old Spartan. The conversation takes place on the island of Crete. At the beginning one receives the impression that the Athenian has come to Crete in order to study there the best laws. For if it is true that the good is identical with the ancestral, the best laws for a Greek would be the oldest Greek laws, and these are the Cretan laws. But the equation of the good with the ancestral is not tenable if the first ancestors were not gods, or sons of gods, or pupils of gods. Hence, the Cretans believed that their laws were originated by Zeus, who instructed his son Minos, the Cretan legislator. The *Laws* opens with an expression of this belief. It appears immediately afterwards that this belief has no other ground, no better ground, than a saying of Homer—and the poets are of questionable veracity—as well as what the Cretans say—and the

Cretans were famous for their lack of veracity. However this may be, very shortly after its beginning, the conversation shifts from the question of the origins of the Cretan laws and the Spartan laws to the question of their intrinsic worth: a code given by a god, by a being of superhuman excellence, must be unqualifiedly good. Very slowly, very circumspectly does the Athenian approach this grave question. To begin with he limits his criticism of the principle underlying the Cretan and the Spartan codes by criticizing not these codes, but a poet, a man without authority and, in addition, an expatriate, who had praised the same principle. In the sequel, the philosopher attacks not yet the Cretan and the Spartan codes, but the interpretation of these codes which had been set forth by his two interlocutors. He does not begin to criticize these venerable codes explicitly until he has appealed to a presumed Cretan and Spartan law which permits such criticism under certain conditions—under conditions which are fulfilled, to some extent, in the present conversation. According to that law, all must say with one voice and with one mouth that all the laws of Crete, or of Sparta, are good because they are god-given, and no one is suffered to say something different; but an old citizen may utter a criticism of an allegedly divine law before a magistrate of his own age if no young men are present. By this time it has become clear to the reader that the Athenian has not come to Crete in order to study there the best laws, but rather in order to introduce into Crete new laws and institutions, truly good laws and institutions. These laws and institutions will prove to be, to a considerable extent, of Athenian origin. It seems that the Athenian, being the son of a highly civilized society, has embarked on the venture of civilizing a rather uncivilized society. Therefore he has to apprehend that his suggestions will be odious, not only as innovations, but above all as foreign, as Athenian: deep-seated, old animosities and suspicions will be aroused by his recommendations. He begins his explicit criticism with a remark about the probable connection between certain Cretan and Spartan institutions and the practice of homosexuality in these cities. The Spartan, rising in defense of his fatherland, does not, indeed, defend homosexuality, but, turning to the offensive, rebukes the Athenians for their excessive drinking. The Athenian is thus given a perfect excuse for recommending the introduction of the Athenian institution of banquets: he is compelled to defend that institution; by defending it he acts the part, not of a civilizing philosopher who, being a philosopher, is a philanthropist, but of the patriot. He acts in a way which is perfectly understandable to his interlocutors and perfectly respectable in their opinion. He attempts to show that wine-drinking, and even drunkenness, if it is practiced in well-presided banquets, is conducive to education in temperance or moderation. This speech about wine forms the bulk of the first two books of the *Laws*. Only after the speech about wine has been brought to its conclusion does the Athenian turn to the question of the beginning of political life, to a question which is the true beginning of his political theme. The speech about wine appears to be *the* introduction to political philosophy.

Why does *the* Platonic dialogue about politics and laws begin with such an extensive conversation about wine? What is the artistic or logographic necessity demanding this? The proper interlocutors in a conversation about laws are old citizens of communities famous for their laws, for their obedience and allegiance to their old laws. Such men understand best what living under laws, living in laws, means. They are the perfect incarnation of the spirit of laws: of lawfulness, of law-abidingness. But their very virtue becomes a defect if there is no longer a question of preserving old laws, but of seeking the best laws or introducing new and better ones. Their habits and their competence make these men impervious to suggestions for improvement. The Athenian induces them to participate in a conversation about wine-drinking, about a pleasure that is forbidden to them by their old laws. The talk about wine-drinking is a kind of vicarious enjoyment of wine, especially since wine-drinking is a forbidden pleasure. Perhaps the talk reminds the two old interlocutors of secret and pleasurable transgressions of their own. The effect of the talk about wine is therefore similar to the effect of actual wine-drinking; it loosens their tongues; it makes them young; it makes them bold, daring, willing to innovate. They must not actually drink wine, since this would impair their judgment. They must drink wine, not in deed, but in speech.

But this means that wine-drinking educates to boldness, to courage, and not to moderation, and yet wine-drinking was said to be conducive to moderation. Let us therefore consider the other partner in the conversation, the Athenian philosopher. To doubt the sacredness of the ancestral means to appeal from the ancestral to the natural. It means to transcend all human traditions, nay, the whole dimension of the merely human. It means to learn to look down on the human as something inferior or to leave the cave. But by leaving the cave one loses sight of the city, of the whole political sphere. If the philosopher is to give political guidance, he must return to the cave: from the light of the sun to the world of shadows; his perception must be dimmed; his mind must undergo an obfuscation. The vicarious enjoyment of wine through a conversation about wine, which enlarges the horizon of the law-bred old citizens, limits the horizon of the philosopher. But this obfuscation, this acceptance of the political perspective, this adoption of the language of political man, this achievement of harmony between the excellence of man and the excellence of the citizen, or between wisdom and law-abidingness is, it seems, the most noble exercise of the virtue of moderation: wine-drinking educates to moderation. For moderation is not a virtue of thought: Plato likens philosophy to madness, the very opposite of sobriety or moderation; thought must be not moderate, but fearless, not to say shameless. But moderation is a virtue controlling the philosopher's speech.

We have suggested that the Athenian stranger had gone to Crete in order to civilize an uncivilized society, and that he had done this out of philanthropy. But does not philanthropy begin at home? Did he not have more pressing duties to perform at home? What kind of man is the Athenian stranger? The *Laws* begins with the word "God": it is the only Platonic dialogue which begins in that manner. There is one and only one Platonic dialogue which ends with the word "God": the *Apology of Socrates*. In the *Apology of Socrates* an old Athenian philosopher, Socrates, defends himself against the charge of impiety, of not believing that the gods worshiped by the city of Athens exist. It seems that there is a conflict between philosophy and accepting the gods of the city. In the *Laws* an old Athenian philosopher recommends a law about impiety which renders impossible the conflict between philosophy and the city, or which brings about harmony between philosophy and the city. The gods whose existence is to be admitted by every citizen of the city of the *Laws* are beings whose existence can be demonstrated. That old Athenian philosopher of the *Apology of Socrates* was condemned to death by the city of Athens. He was given an opportunity to escape from prison: he refused to avail himself of this opportunity. His refusal was not based on an appeal to a categorical imperative demanding passive obedience, without if's and but's. His refusal was based on a deliberation, on a prudential consideration of what was the right thing to do in the circumstances. One of the circumstances was Socrates' old age: we are forced to wonder how Socrates would have decided if he had been 30 or 40 years old instead of 70. Another circumstance was the unavailability of a proper place of exile: where should he flee? He seems to have a choice between law-abiding cities nearby, where his life would be unbearable, since he would be known as a fugitive from justice, and a lawless country far away, where the prevailing lack of order would make his life miserable. The disjunction is obviously incomplete: there were law-abiding cities far away, for instance on Crete, which is mentioned as a law-abiding place in the very deliberation in question. We are entitled to infer that if Socrates had fled, he would have gone to Crete. The *Laws* tells us what he would have done in Crete after his arrival: he would have brought the blessings of Athens, Athenian laws, Athenian institutions, banquets, and philosophy to Crete. (When Aristotle speaks about Plato's *Laws*, he takes it for granted that the chief character of the *Laws* is Socrates.) Escaping to Crete, living in Crete, was the alternative to dying in Athens. But Socrates chose to die in Athens. Socrates preferred to sacrifice his life in order to preserve philosophy in Athens rather than to preserve his life in order to introduce philosophy into Crete. If the danger to the future of philosophy in Athens had been less great, he might have chosen to flee to Crete. His choice was a political choice of the highest order. It did not consist in the simple subsumption of his case under a simple, universal, and unalterable rule.

But let us return after this long story to the beginning of Plato's *Laws*. If the originator of the Cretan laws, or any other laws, is not a god, the cause of laws must be human beings, the human legislator. There is a variety of types of human legislators: the legislator has a different character in a democracy, in an oligarchy, in a monarchy. The legislator is the governing body, and the character of the governing body depends on the whole social and political order, the *politeia*, the regime. The cause of the laws is the regime. Therefore the guiding theme of political philosophy is the regime rather than the laws. Regime becomes the guiding theme of political thought when the derivative or questionable character of laws has been realized. There are a number of Biblical terms which can be properly translated by "law"; there is no Biblical equivalent to "regime."

Regime is the order, the form, which gives society its character. Regime is therefore a specific manner of life. Regime is the form of life as living together, the manner of living of society and in society, since this manner depends decisively on the predominance of human beings of a certain type, on the manifest domination of society by human beings of a certain type. Regime means that whole, which we today are in the habit of viewing primarily in a fragmentized form: regime means simultaneously the form of life of a society, its style of life, its moral taste, form of society, form of state, form of government, spirit of laws. We may try to articulate the simple and unitary thought, that expresses itself in the term *politeia*, as follows: life is activity which is directed towards some goal; social life is an activity which is directed towards such a goal as can be pursued only by society; but in order to pursue a specific goal, as its comprehensive goal, society must be organized, ordered, constructed, constituted in a manner which is in accordance with that goal; this, however, means that the authoritative human beings must be akin to that goal.

There is a variety of regimes. Each regime raises a claim, explicitly or implicitly, which extends beyond the boundaries of any given society. These claims conflict, therefore, with each other. There is a variety of conflicting regimes. Thus the regimes themselves, and not any preoccupation of mere bystanders, force us to wonder which of the given conflicting regimes is better, and ultimately, which regime is the best regime. Classical political philosophy is guided by the question of the best regime.

The actualization of the best regime depends on the coming together, on the coincidence of, things which have a natural tendency to move away from each other (e.g., on the coincidence of philosophy and political power); its actualization depends therefore on chance. Human nature is enslaved in so many ways that it is almost a miracle if an individual achieves the highest: what can one expect of society! The peculiar manner of being of the best regime —namely, its lacking actuality while being superior to all actual regimes—has its ultimate reason in the dual nature of man, in the fact that man is the in-between being: in between brutes and gods.

The practical meaning of the notion of the best regime appears most clearly, when one considers the ambiguity of the term "good citizen." Aristotle suggests two entirely different definitions of the good citizen. In his more popular *Constitution of Athens* he suggests that the good citizen is a man who serves his country well, without any regard to the difference of regimes—who serves his country well in fundamental indifference to the change of regimes. The good citizen, in a word, is the patriotic citizen, the man whose loyalty belongs first and last to his fatherland. In his less popular *Politics*, Aristotle says that there is not *the* good citizen without qualification. For what it means to be a good citizen depends entirely on the regime. A good citizen in Hitler's Germany would be a bad citizen elsewhere. But whereas good citizen is relative to the regime, good man does not have such a relativity. The meaning of good man is always and everywhere the same. The good man is identical with the good citizen only in one case—in the case of the best regime. For only in the best regime is the good of the regime and the good of the good man identical, that goal being virtue. This amounts to saying that in his *Politics* Aristotle questions the proposition that patriotism is enough. From the point of view of the patriot, the fatherland is more important than any difference of regimes. From the point of view of the patriot, he who prefers any regime to the fatherland is a partisan, if not a traitor. Aristotle says in effect that the partisan sees deeper than the patriot but that only one kind of partisan is superior to the patriot; this is the partisan of virtue. One can express Aristotle's thought as follows: patriotism is not enough for the same reason that the most doting mother is happier if her child is good than if he is bad. A mother loves her child because he is her own; she loves what is her own. But she also loves the good. All human love is subject to the law that it be both love of one's own and love of the good, and there is necessarily a tension between one's own and the good, a tension which may well lead to a break, be it only the breaking of a heart. The relation between one's own and the good finds its political expression in the relation between the father-

land and the regime. In the language of classical metaphysics, the
fatherland or the nation is the matter whereas the regime is the
form. The classics held the view that the form is higher in dignity
than the matter. One may call this view "idealism." The practical
meaning of this idealism is that the good is of higher dignity than
one's own, or that the best regime is a higher consideration than the
fatherland. The Jewish equivalent of this relation might be said to
be the relation between the Torah and Israel.

Classical political philosophy is today exposed to two very common objections, the raising of which requires neither originality
nor intelligence, nor even erudition. The objections are these: (1)
classical political philosophy is anti-democratic and hence bad;
(2) classical political philosophy is based on classical natural philosophy or on classical cosmology, and this basis has been proven to
be untrue by the success of modern natural science.

To speak first of the classics' attitude towards democracy, the
premises: "the classics are good," and "democracy is good" do not
validate the conclusion "hence the classics were good democrats."
It would be silly to deny that the classics rejected democracy as an
inferior kind of regime. They were not blind to its advantages. The
severest indictment of democracy that ever was written occurs in
the eighth book of Plato's *Republic*. But even there, and precisely
there, Plato makes it clear—by coordinating his arrangement of
regimes with Hesiod's arrangement of the ages of the world—that
democracy is, in a very important respect, equal to the best regime,
which corresponds to Hesiod's golden age: since the principle of
democracy is freedom, all human types can develop freely in a
democracy, and hence in particular the best human type. It is true
that Socrates was killed by a democracy; but he was killed when
he was 70; he was permitted to live for 70 long years. Yet Plato
did not regard this consideration as decisive. For he was concerned not only with the possibility of philosophy, but likewise
with a stable political order that would be congenial to moderate
political courses; and such an order, he thought, depends on the
predominance of old families. More generally, the classics rejected
democracy because they thought that the aim of human life, and
hence of social life, is not freedom but virtue. Freedom as a goal is
ambiguous, because it is freedom for evil as well as for good. Virtue
emerges normally only through education, that is to say, through

the formation of character, through habituation, and this requires leisure on the part of both parents and children. But leisure in its turn requires some degree of wealth—more specifically a kind of wealth whose acquisition or administration is compatible with leisure. Now, as regards wealth, it so happens, as Aristotle observes, that there is always a minority of well-to-do people and a majority of the poor, and this strange coincidence will last forever because there is a kind of natural scarcity. "For the poor shall never cease out of the land." It is for this reason that democracy, or rule of the majority, is government by the uneducated. And no one in his senses would wish to live under such a government. This classical argument would not be stringent if men did not need education in order to acquire a firm adhesion to virtue. It is no accident that it was Jean-Jacques Rousseau who taught that all knowledge which men need in order to live virtuously is supplied by the conscience, the preserve of the simple souls rather than of other men: man is sufficiently equipped by nature for the good life; man is by nature good. But the same Rousseau was compelled to develop a scheme of education which very few people could financially afford. On the whole the view has prevailed that democracy must become rule by the educated, and this goal will be achieved by universal education. But universal education presupposes that the economy of scarcity has given way to an economy of plenty. And the economy of plenty presupposes the emancipation of technology from moral and political control. The essential difference between our view and the classical view consists then, not in a difference regarding moral principle, not in a different understanding of justice: we, too, even our communist coexistents, think that it is just to give equal things to equal people and unequal things to people of unequal merit. The difference between the classics and us with regard to democracy consists exclusively in a different estimate of the virtues of technology. But we are not entitled to say that the classical view has been refuted. Their implicit prophecy that the emancipation of technology, of the arts, from moral and political control would lead to disaster or to the dehumanization of man has not yet been refuted.

Nor can we say that democracy has found a solution to the problem of education. In the first place, what is today called education, very frequently does not mean education proper, i.e., the formation of character, but rather instruction and training. Secondly, to the extent to which the formation of character is indeed intended, there exists a very dangerous tendency to identify the good man with the good sport, the cooperative fellow, the "regular guy," i.e., an overemphasis on a certain part of social virtue and a corresponding neglect of those virtues which mature, if they do not flourish, in privacy, not to say in solitude: by educating people to cooperate with each other in a friendly spirit, one does not yet educate non-conformists, people who are prepared to stand alone, to fight alone, "rugged individualists." Democracy has not yet found a defense against the creeping conformism and the ever-increasing invasion of privacy which it fosters. Beings who look down on us from a star might find that the difference between democracy and communism is not quite as great as it appears to be when one considers exclusively the doubtless very important question of civil and political liberties, although only people of exceptional levity or irresponsibility say that the difference between communism and democracy is negligible in the last analysis. Now to the extent to which democracy is aware of these dangers, to the same extent it sees itself compelled to think of elevating its level and its possibilities by a return to the classics' notions of education: a kind of education which can never be thought of as mass-education, but only as higher and highest education of those who are by nature fit for it. It would be an understatement to call it royal education.

Yet granted that there are no valid moral or political objections to classical political philosophy—is that political philosophy not bound up with an antiquated cosmology? Does not the very question of the nature of man point to the question of the nature of the whole, and therewith to one or the other specific cosmology? Whatever the significance of modern natural science may be, it cannot affect our understanding of what is human in man. To understand man in the light of the whole means for modern natural science to understand man in the light of the sub-human. But in that light man as man is wholly unintelligible. Classical political philosophy viewed man in a different light. It was originated by Socrates. And Socrates was so far from being committed to a specific cosmology that his knowledge was knowledge of ignorance. Knowledge of ignorance is not ignorance. It is knowledge of the elusive character of the truth, of the whole. Socrates, then, viewed man in the light of the mysterious character of the whole. He held therefore that we are more familiar with the situation of man as man than with the ultimate causes of that situation. We may also say he viewed man in the light of the unchangeable ideas, i.e., of the fundamental and permanent problems. For to articulate the situation of man means to articulate man's openness to the whole. This understanding of the situation of man which includes, then, the quest for cosmology rather than a solution to the cosmological problem, was the foundation of classical political philosophy.

To articulate the problem of cosmology means to answer the question of what philosophy is or what a philosopher is. Plato refrained from entrusting the thematic discussion of this question to Socrates. He entrusted it to a stranger from Elea. But even that stranger from Elea did not discuss explicitly what a philosopher is. He discussed explicitly two kinds of men which are easily mistaken for the philosopher, the sophist and the statesman: by understanding both sophistry (in its highest as well as in its lower meaning) and statesmanship, one will understand what philosophy is. Philosophy strives for knowledge of the whole. The whole is the totality of the parts. The whole eludes us but we know parts: we possess partial knowledge of parts. The knowledge which we possess is characterized by a fundamental dualism which has never been overcome. At one pole we find knowledge of homogeneity: above all in arithmetic, but also in the other branches of mathematics, and derivatively in all productive arts or crafts. At the opposite pole we find knowledge of heterogeneity, and in particular of heterogeneous ends; the highest form of this kind of knowledge is the art of the statesman and of the educator. The latter kind of knowledge is superior to the former for this reason. As knowledge of the ends of human life, it is knowledge of what makes human life complete or whole; it is therefore knowledge of a whole. Knowledge of the ends of man implies knowledge of the human soul; and the human soul is the only part of the whole which is open to the whole and therefore more akin to the whole than anything else is. But this knowledge—the political art in the highest sense—is not knowledge of *the* whole. It seems that knowledge of the whole would have to combine somehow political knowledge in the highest sense with knowledge of homogeneity. And this combination is not at our disposal. Men are therefore constantly tempted to force the issue by imposing unity on the phenomena, by absolutizing either knowledge of homogeneity or knowledge of ends. Men are constantly attracted and deluded by two opposite charms: the charm of competence which is engendered by mathematics and everything akin to mathematics, and the charm of humble awe, which is engendered by meditation on the human soul and its experiences. Philosophy is characterized by the gentle, if firm, refusal to succumb to either charm. It is the highest form of the mating of courage and moderation. In spite of its highness or nobility, it could appear as Sisyphean or ugly, when one contrasts its achievement with its goal. Yet it is necessarily accompanied, sustained and elevated by *eros*. It is graced by nature's grace.

III. The Modern Solutions

It was possible to speak of the classical solution to the problem of political philosophy because there is a fundamental and at the same time specific agreement among all classical political philosophers: the goal of political life is virtue, and the order most conducive to virtue is the aristocratic republic, or else the mixed regime. But in modern times, we find a great variety of fundamentally different political philosophies. Nevertheless, all modern political philosophies belong together because they have a fundamental principle in common. This principle can best be stated negatively: rejection of the classical scheme as unrealistic. The positive principle animating modern political philosophy has undergone a great variety of fundamental changes. This fact, and its reason, can be shown best if we proceed in a somewhat more narrative way than we have done hitherto.

The founder of modern political philosophy is Machiavelli. He tried to effect, and he did effect, a break with the whole tradition of political philosophy. He compared his achievement to that of men like Columbus. He claimed to have discovered a new moral continent. His claim is well founded; his political teaching is "wholly new." The only question is whether the new continent is fit for human habitation.

In his *Florentine Histories* he tells the following story: Cosimo de Medici once said that men cannot maintain power with paternosters in their hands. This gave occasion to Cosimo's enemies to slander him as a man who loved himself more than his fatherland and who loved this world more than the next. Cosimo was then said to be somewhat immoral and somewhat irreligious. Machiavelli himself is open to the same charge. His work is based on a critique of religion and a critique of morality.

His critique of religion, chiefly of Biblical religion, but also of paganism, is not original. It amounts to a restatement of the teaching of pagan philosophers, as well as of that medieval school which goes by the name of Averroism and which gave rise to the notion of the three impostors. Machiavelli's originality in this field is limited to the fact that he was a great master of blasphemy. The charm and gracefulness of his blasphemies will however be less strongly felt by us than their shocking character. Let us then keep them under the veil under which he has hidden them. I hasten to his critique of morality which is identical with his critique of classical political philosophy. One can state the main point as follows: there is something fundamentally wrong with an approach to politics which culminates in a utopia, in the description of a best regime whose actualization is highly improbable. Let us then cease to take our bearings by virtue, the highest objective which a society might choose; let us begin to take our bearings by the objectives which are actually pursued by all societies. Machiavelli consciously lowers the standards of social action. His lowering of the standards is meant to lead to a higher probability of actualization of that scheme which is constructed in accordance with the lowered standards. Thus, the dependence on chance is reduced: chance will be conquered.

The traditional approach was based on the assumption that morality is something substantial: that it is a force in the soul of man, however ineffective it may be especially in the affairs of states and kingdoms. Against this assumption Machiavelli argues as follows: virtue can be practiced only within society; man must be habituated to virtue by laws, customs and so forth. Men must be educated to virtue by human beings. But to quote that Machiavellian, Karl Marx, the educators themselves must be educated. The original educators, the founders of society, cannot have been educated to virtue: the founder of Rome was a fratricide. Morality is possible only within a context which cannot be created by morality, for morality cannot create itself. The context within which morality is possible is created by immorality. Morality rests on immorality, justice rests on injustice, just as all legitimacy ultimately rests on revolutionary foundations. Man is not by nature directed toward virtue. If he were, pangs of conscience would be the greatest evil for him; but in fact we find that the pangs of disappointment are at least as strong as the pangs of guilt. In other words, one cannot define the good of society, the common good, in terms of virtue, but one must define virtue in terms of the common good. It is this understanding of virtue which in fact determines the life of societies. By the common good we must understand the objectives actually pursued by all societies. These objectives are: freedom from foreign domination, stability or rule of law, prosperity, glory or empire. Virtue in the effectual sense of the word is the sum of habits which are required for or conducive to this end. It is this end, and this end alone, which makes our actions virtuous. Everything done effectively for the sake of this end is good. This end justifies every means. Virtue is nothing but civic virtue, patriotism or devotion to collective selfishness.

Machiavelli cannot leave it at this. Devotion to the fatherland is itself dependent on education. This means that patriotism is not natural. Just as man is not by nature directed toward virtue, he is not by nature directed toward society. By nature man is radically selfish. Yet while men are by nature selfish, and nothing but selfish, hence bad, they can become social, public spirited, or good. This transformation requires compulsion. The success of this compulsion is due to the fact that man is amazingly malleable: much more so than had hitherto been thought. For if man is not by nature ordered toward virtue or perfection, if there is no natural end of man, man can set for himself almost any end he desires: man is almost infinitely malleable. The power of man is much greater, and the power of nature and chance is correspondingly much smaller, than the ancients thought.

Men are bad; they must be compelled to be good. But this compulsion must be the work of badness, of selfishness, of selfish passion. Which passion will induce a bad man to be passionately concerned with compelling other bad men to become good and to remain good? Which passion will educate the educator of men? The passion in question is the desire for glory. The highest form of the desire for glory is the desire to be a new prince in the fullest sense of the term, a wholly new prince: a discoverer of a new type of social order, a molder of many generations of men. The founder of society has a selfish interest in the preservation of society, of his work. He has therefore a selfish interest in the members of his society being and remaining sociable, and hence good. The desire for glory is the link between badness and goodness. It makes possible the transformation of badness into goodness. The wholly new prince of the highest kind is animated by nothing but selfish ambition. The great public tasks which he undertakes are for him only opportunities for coloring his design. He is distinguished from great criminals merely by the fact that the criminals lack a defensible opportunity; the moral motivation is the same.

It is not possible here to show how Machiavelli succeeds in building on this basis a political teaching which does full justice to all possible requirements of any policy of blood and iron, and which is at the same time most favorable to political liberty and the rule of law. I must limit myself to indicating how easy it is, after a few centuries of Machiavellianization of Western thought, to give Machiavelli's teaching an air of perfect respectability. He can be presented as arguing as follows: you want justice? I am going to show you how you can get it. You will not get it by preaching, by hortatory speeches. You will get it only by making injustice utterly unprofitable. What you need is not so much formation of character and moral appeal, as the right kind of institutions, institutions with teeth in them. The shift from formation of character to the trust in institutions is the characteristic corollary of the belief in the almost infinite malleability of man.

In Machiavelli's teaching we have the first example of a spectacle which has renewed itself in almost every generation since. A fearless thinker seems to have opened up a depth from which the classics, in their noble simplicity, recoiled. As a matter of fact, there is in the whole work of Machiavelli not a single true observation regarding the nature of man and of human affairs with which the classics were not thoroughly familiar. An amazing contraction of the horizon presents itself as an amazing enlargement of the horizon. How can we account for this delusion? By Machiavelli's time the classical tradition had undergone profound changes. The contemplative life had found its home in monasteries. Moral virtue had been transfigured into Christian charity. Through this, man's responsibility to his fellow men and for his fellow men, his fellow creatures, had been infinitely increased. Concern with the salvation of men's immortal souls seemed to permit, nay, to require courses of action which would have appeared to the classics, and which did appear to Machiavelli, to be inhuman and cruel: Machiavelli speaks of the pious cruelty of Ferdinand of Aragon, and by implication of the inquisition, in expelling the Marannos from Spain. Machiavelli was the only non-Jew of his age who expressed this view. He seems to have diagnosed the great evils of religious persecution as a necessary consequence of the Christian principle, and ultimately of the Biblical principle. He tended to believe that a considerable increase in man's inhumanity was the unintended but not surprising consequence of man's aiming too high. Let us lower our goals so that we shall not be forced to commit any bestialities which are not evidently required for the preservation of society and of freedom. Let us replace charity by calculation, by a kind of utilitarianism *avant la lettre*. Let us revise all traditional goals from this point of view. I would then suggest that the narrowing of the horizon which Machiavelli was the first to effect, was caused, or at least facilitated, by anti-theological ire—a passion which we can understand but of which we cannot approve.

Machiavelli radically changed, not only the substance of the political teaching, but its mode as well. The substance of his political teaching may be said to be the wholly new teaching regarding the wholly new prince, i.e., regarding the essential inherence of immorality in the foundation of society and hence in the structure of society. The discoverer of such a teaching is necessarily a bringer of a new moral code, of a new Decalogue. He is a wholly new prince in the highest possible sense of the term, a new Moses, a prophet. Concerning prophets, Machiavelli teaches that all armed prophets have conquered and all unarmed prophets have failed. The greatest example of an armed prophet is Moses. The greatest example of an unarmed prophet is Jesus. But can Machiavelli reasonably say that Jesus has failed? Or to put the same question in a different form, is not Machiavelli himself an unarmed prophet? How can he possibly hope for the success of his more than daring venture if unarmed founders necessarily fail?

Jesus failed insofar as he was crucified. He did not fail insofar as the new modes and orders found by him have become accepted by many generations of many nations. This victory of Christianity was due to propaganda: the unarmed prophet conquered posthumously by virtue of propaganda. Machiavelli, being himself an unarmed prophet, has no other hope of conquest except through propaganda. The only element of Christianity which Machiavelli took over was the idea of propaganda. This idea is the only link between his thought and Christianity. He attempted to destroy Christianity by the same means by which Christianity was originally established. He desired to imitate, not Moses, the armed prophet, but Jesus. It goes without saying that Machiavelli's *imitatio Christi* is limited to this point. In particular, the author of *Mandragola* avoided the cross in more than one sense by not publishing his great works during his lifetime.

Machiavelli assumed that every religion or "sect" has a lifespan of between 1,666 and 3,000 years. He was then uncertain as to whether the end of Christianity would come about a century after his death or whether Christianity might still last for another millenium and a half. Machiavelli thought and wrote in this perspective: that he himself might be preparing a radical change of modes and orders, a change which would be consummated in a not too distant future, but that it is equally possible that his enterprise would fail completely. He certainly reckoned with the possibility that the destruction of the Christian Church was imminent. As for the way in which Christianity might be superseded by a new social order, he saw this alternative. One possibility was the irruption of barbarian hordes from the East, from what is now Russia: it was this region which he regarded as the pool from which the human race rejuvenates itself periodically. The alternative was a radical change within the civilized world. It was of course only the latter kind of change for which he was anxious, and which he did everything in his power to prepare. He conceived of this preparation as of a war, a spiritual war. He desired to bring about a change of opinion which in due time would precipitate a change in political power. He did not expect more than the conversion of very few men, but he counted on influencing many. These many were those who, in case of conflict between their fatherland and their souls, the salvation of their souls, would prefer their fatherland; these many were the lukewarm Christians. He expected these many to be sympathetic

to his enterprise, which was infinitely more favorable to the earthly
fatherland than to the heavenly fatherland of the Christians. These
many would not be able to understand the full meaning of his
undertaking, but they could be counted upon to guarantee that his
books would get some hearing. They would make his books publicly defensible. However, they would not be reliable allies in his
war to the finish. His long range success depended on the full
conversion of some men, of very few. They would provide the
vital center which would gradually inspire, in favorable circumstances, the formation of a new ruling class, a new kind of princes,
comparable to the patriciate of ancient Rome. Machiavelli's warfare
has the character of propaganda. No earlier philosopher had thought
of guaranteeing the posthumous success of his teaching by developing a specific strategy and tactics for this purpose. The earlier
philosophers of all persuasions were resigned to the fact that their
teaching, the true teaching, would never supersede what they
regarded as false teachings, but would coexist with them. They
offered their teachings to their contemporaries and above all to
posterity, without even dreaming of controlling the future fate of
human thought in general. And if they were political philosophers,
and had arrived at definite conclusions regarding the right political
order, they would have been vicious, and hence not philosophers,
if they had not been willing to help their fellow men in ordering
their common affairs in the best possible way. But they did not for
one moment believe that the true political teaching is, or is likely
to be, the political teaching of the future. Machiavelli is the first
philosopher who attempted to force chance, to control the future
by embarking on a campaign, a campaign of propaganda. This
propaganda is at the opposite pole of what is now called propaganda,
high-pressure salesmanship and hold-up of captive audiences. Machiavelli desires to convince, not merely to persuade or to bully. He
was the first of a long series of modern thinkers who hoped to
bring about the establishment of new modes and orders by means
of enlightenment. The enlightenment—*lucus a non lucendo*—begins
with Machiavelli.

In order to realize the magnitude of Machiavelli's success it is
necessary that one should have a clear grasp of his principle. This
principle, to repeat, is this: one must lower the standards in order
to make probable, if not certain, the actualization of the right or

desirable social order or in order to conquer chance; one must effect a shift of emphasis from moral character to institutions. The right order, as Machiavelli himself conceived of it, was the hard-headed republic, which was modelled on ancient Rome, but which was meant to be an improvement on ancient Rome. For what the Romans had done haphazardly or instinctively can now be done consciously and deliberately: now—after Machiavelli has understood the reasons of the success of the Romans. Republicanism in the Roman style, as interpreted by Machiavelli, became one of the most powerful trends of modern political thought. We observe its presence in the works of Harrington, Spinoza, Algernon Sydney, Montesquieu, Rousseau, and in *The Federalist*, and among those upper class Frenchmen who favored the French revolution out of concern for the status of France as a great power. But this posthumous success of Machiavelli is not comparable in importance to that which came about through the transformation of his scheme —a transformation which was inspired by his own principle.

Machiavelli's scheme was open to serious theoretical difficulties. The theoretical or cosmological basis of his political teaching was a kind of decayed Aristotelianism. This means that he assumed, but did not demonstrate, the untenable character of teleological natural science. He rejected the view that man must take his bearings by virtue, by his perfection, by his natural end; but this rejection required a criticism of the notion of natural ends. This proof was supplied, or was thought to be supplied, by the new natural science of the 17th century. There is a hidden kinship between Machiavelli's political science and the new natural science. The classics had taken their bearings by the normal case as distinguished from the exception; Machiavelli effects his radical change in the understanding of political things by taking his bearings by the exception, by the extreme case. As appears from Bacon, there is a close connection between Machiavelli's orientation and the notion of torturing nature, i.e., of the controlled experiment.

But the main reason why Machiavelli's scheme had to be modified was its revolting character. The man who mitigated Machiavelli's scheme in a manner which was almost sufficient to guarantee the success of Machiavelli's primary intention was Hobbes. One could think for a moment that Hobbes's correction of Machiavelli consists in a masterpiece of prestidigitation. Machiavelli wrote a book called *On The Prince;* Hobbes wrote a book called *On The Citizen;* i.e., Hobbes chose as his theme, not the practices of kingdoms and states, but rather the duties of subjects; hence what Hobbes did teach sounds much more innocent than what Machiavelli had taught, without necessarily contradicting Machiavelli's teaching. But it is both more charitable and more correct to say that Hobbes was an honest and plain-spoken Englishman who lacked the fine Italian hand of his master. Or if you wish, you may compare Hobbes to Sherlock Holmes and Machiavelli to Professor Moriarty. For certainly Hobbes took justice much more seriously than Machiavelli had done. He may even be said to have defended the cause of justice: he denies that it is of the essence of civil society to be founded on crime. To refute Machiavelli's fundamental contention may be said to be the chief purpose of Hobbes's famous doctrine about the state of nature. He accepted the traditional notion that justice is not merely the work of society but that there is a natural right. But he also accepted Machiavelli's critique of traditional political philosophy: traditional political philosophy aimed too high. Hence he demanded that natural right be derived from the beginnings: the elementary wants or urges, which effectively determine all men most of the time and not from man's perfection or end, the desire for which effectively determines only a few men, and by no means most of the time. These primary urges are of course selfish; they can be reduced to one principle: the desire for self-preservation, or negatively expressed, the fear of violent death. This means that not the glitter and glamour of glory—or pride—but the terror of fear of death stands at the cradle of civil society: not heroes, if fratricidal and incestuous heroes, but naked, shivering poor devils were the founders of civilization. The appearance of the diabolical vanishes completely. But let us not be too rash. Once government has been established, the fear of violent death turns into fear of government. And the desire for self-preservation expands into the desire for comfortable self-preservation. Machiavelli's glory is indeed deflated; it stands now revealed as mere, unsubstantial, petty, ridiculous vanity. That glory does not however give way to justice or human excellence, but to concern with solid comfort, with practical, pedestrian hedonism. Glory survives only in the form of competition. In other words, whereas the pivot of Machiavelli's political teaching was glory, the pivot of Hobbes's political teaching is power. Power is infinitely more businesslike than glory. Far from being the goal of a lofty or demonic longing, it is required by, or the expression of, a cold objective necessity. Power is morally neutral. Or, what is the same thing, it is ambiguous if of concealed ambiguity. Power, and the concern with power lack the direct human appeal of glory and the concern with glory. It emerges through an estrangement from man's primary motivation. It has an air of senility. It becomes visible in grey eminences rather than in Scipios and Hannibals. Respectable, pedestrian hedonism, sobriety without sublimity and subtlety, protected or made possible by "power politics"—this is the meaning of Hobbes's correction of Machiavelli.

Hobbes's teaching was still much too bold to be acceptable. It, too, was in need of mitigation. The mitigation was the work of Locke. Locke took over the fundamental scheme of Hobbes and changed it only in one point. He realized that what man primarily needs for his self-preservation is less a gun than food, or more generally, property. Thus the desire for self-preservation turns into the desire for property, for acquisition, and the right to self-preservation becomes the right to unlimited acquisition. The practical consequences of this small change are enormous. Locke's political teaching is the prosaic version of what in Hobbes still had a certain poetic quality. It is, precisely on Hobbes's premises, more reasonable than Hobbes's own political teaching. With a view to the resounding success of Locke, as contrasted with the apparent failure of Hobbes, especially in the Anglo-Saxon world, we can say that Machiavelli's discovery or invention of the need for an immoral or amoral substitute for morality, became victorious through Locke's discovery or invention that that substitute is acquisitiveness. Here we have an utterly selfish passion whose satisfaction does not require the spilling of any blood and whose effect is the improvement of the lot of all. In other words, the solution of the political problem by economic means is the most elegant solution, once one accepts Machiavelli's premise: economism is Machiavellianism come of age. No one understood this more profoundly than Montesquieu. His *Esprit des Lois* reads as if it were nothing but the document of an incessant fight, an unresolved conflict, between two social or political ideals: the Roman republic, whose principle is virtue, and England, whose principle is political liberty. But in fact Montesquieu decides eventually in favor of England. The superiority of England is based in his view on the fact that the English had found a substitute for stern, republican, Roman virtue; that substitute is trade and finance. The ancient republics based on virtue, needed pure manners; the modern system which replaces virtue by trade, is productive of gentle manners, of *humanité*. In Montesquieu's work we observe a last resurgence of the poetry underlying modern prose. There are only two books of the *Esprit des Lois* which are prefaced with poems: the book dealing with population is prefaced with Lucretius' verses in praise of Venus; the first book dealing with commerce is prefaced with a prose poem which is the work of Montesquieu himself.

This serpentine wisdom, which corrupted by charming and charmed by corrupting, this degradation of man, called forth Jean Jacques Rousseau's passionate and still unforgettable protest. With Rousseau there begins what we may call the second wave of modernity: the wave which bore both German idealistic philosophy and the romanticism of all ranks in all countries. This great and complex counter-movement consisted in the first place in a return from the world of modernity to pre-modern ways of thinking. Rousseau returned from the world of finance, from what he was the first to call the world of the *bourgeois*, to the world of virtue and the city, to the world of the *citoyen*. Kant returned from Descartes' and Locke's notion of ideas to the Platonic notion. Hegel returned from the philosophy of reflection to the "higher vitality" of Plato and Aristotle. And romanticism as a whole is primarily a movement of return to the origins. Yet in all these cases, the return to pre-modern thought was only the initial step of a movement which led, consciously or unconsciously, to a much more radical form of modernity—to a form of modernity which was still more alien to classical thought than the thought of the 17th and 18th centuries had been.

Rousseau returned from the modern state as it had developed by his time to the classical city. But he interpreted the classical city in the light of Hobbes's scheme. For according to Rousseau too, the root of civil society is the right of self-preservation. But deviating from Hobbes and from Locke, he declares that this fundamental right points to a social order which is closely akin to the classical city. The reason for this deviation from Hobbes and Locke is identical with the primary motivation of modern political philosophy in general. In Hobbes's and Locke's schemes, the fundamental right of man had retained its original status even within civil society: natural law remained the standard for positive law; there remained the possibility of appealing from positive law to natural law. This appeal was of course, generally speaking, ineffective; it certainly did not carry with itself the guarantee of its being effective. Rousseau drew from this the conclusion that civil society must be so constructed as to make the appeal from positive law to natural law utterly superfluous; a civil society properly constructed in accordance with natural law will automatically produce just positive law. Rousseau expresses this thought as follows: the general will, the will of a society, in which everyone subject to the law must have had a say in the making of the law, cannot err. The general will, the will immanent in societies of a certain kind, replaces the transcendent natural right. One cannot emphasize too strongly that Rousseau would have abhorred the totalitarianism of our day. He favored, indeed, the totalitarianism of a free society, but he rejected in the clearest possible language any possible totalitarianism of government. The difficulty into which Rousseau leads us lies deeper. If the ultimate criterion of justice becomes the general will, i.e., the will of a free society, cannibalism is as just as its opposite. Every institution hallowed by a folk-mind has to be regarded as sacred.

Rousseau's thought marks a decisive step in the secular movement which tries to guarantee the actualization of the ideal, or to prove the necessary coincidence of the rational and the real, or to get rid of that which essentially transcends every possible human reality. The assumption of such a transcendence had permitted earlier men to make a tenable distinction between liberty and license. License consists in doing what one lists; liberty consists in doing in the right manner the good only; and our knowledge of the good must come from a higher principle, from above. These men acknowledged a limitation of license which comes from above, a vertical limitation. On the basis of Rousseau, the limitation of license is effected horizontally by the license of other men. I am just if I grant to every other man the same rights which I claim for myself, regardless of what these rights may be. The horizontal limitation is preferred to the vertical limitation because it seems to be more realistic: the horizontal limitation, the limitation of my claim by the claims of others is self enforcing.

One might say that Rousseau's doctrine of the general will is a juridical, not a moral doctrine, and that the law is necessarily more lax than morality. One might illustrate this distinction by referring to Kant who declared in his moral teaching that every lie, the saying of any untruth, is immoral, whereas he declared in his juridical teaching that the right of freedom of speech is as much the right to lie as the right to say the truth. But one may very well wonder whether the separation of law and morality of which German legal philosophy was so proud, is in itself a sound suggestion. Above all, the moral teaching of Rousseau does not dispose of the difficulty indicated. The place occupied in his juridical teaching by the right of self preservation is occupied in his moral teaching by the right or duty of self legislation. "Material" ethics gives way to "formal" ethics with the result that it becomes impossible ever to establish clear substantive principles and that one is compelled to borrow substantive principles from the "general will" or from what came to be called History.

Rousseau was not unaware of these difficulties. They had been caused by the exinanition of the notion of human nature and ultimately by the turn from man's end to man's beginning. Rousseau had accepted Hobbes's anti-teleological principle. By following it more consistently than Hobbes himself had done, he was compelled to reject Hobbes's scheme or to demand that the state of nature—man's primitive and pre-social condition—be understood as perfect, i.e., as not pointing beyond itself toward society. He was compelled to demand that the state of nature, man's beginning, become the goal for social man: only because man has drifted away from his beginnings, because he has thus become corrupted, does he need an end. That end is primarily the just society. The just society is distinguished from the unjust society by the fact that it comes as close to the state of nature as a society possibly can: the desire determining man in the state of nature, the desire for self-preservation, is the root of the just society and determines its end. This fundamental desire which is at the same time the fundamental right, animates the juridical as distinguished from the moral: society is so far from being based on morality that it is the basis of morality;

the end of society must therefore be defined in juridical, not in moral terms; and there cannot be an obligation to enter society (or the social contract cannot bind "the body of the people"). Whatever the meaning and the status of morality may be, it certainly presupposes society, and society, even the just society, is bondage or alienation from nature. Man ought therefore to transcend the whole social and moral dimension and to return to the wholeness and sincerity of the state of nature. Since the concern with self-preservation compels man to enter society, man ought to go back beyond self-preservation to the root of self-preservation. This root, the absolute beginning, is the feeling of existence, the feeling of the sweetness of mere existence. By giving himself to the sole feeling of his present existence without any thought of the future, by thus living in blessed oblivion of every care and fear, the individual senses the sweetness of all existence: he has returned to nature. It is the feeling of one's existence which gives rise to the desire for the preservation of one's existence. This desire compels man to devote himself entirely to action and thought, to a life of care and duty and misery, and therewith cuts him off from the bliss which is buried in his depth or origin. Only very few men are capable of finding the way back to nature. The tension between the desire for the preservation of existence and the feeling of existence expresses itself therefore in the insoluble antagonism between the large majority who in the best case will be good citizens and the minority of solitary dreamers who are the salt of the earth. Rousseau left it at that antagonism. The German philosophers who took up his problem thought that a reconciliation is possible, and that reconciliation can be brought about, or has already been brought about, by History.

German idealistic philosophy claimed to have restored, and more than restored, the high level of classical political philosophy while fighting against the debasement caused by the first wave of modernity. But to say nothing of the replacement of Virtue by Freedom, the political philosophy belonging to the second wave of modernity is inseparable from philosophy of history, and there is no philosophy of history in classical political philosophy. For what is the meaning of the philosophy of history? Philosophy of history shows the essential necessity of the actualization of the right order. There is no chance in the decisive respect, i.e., the same realistic tendency which led to the lowering of the standards in the first wave led to philosophy of history in the second wave. Nor was the introduction of philosophy of history a genuine remedy for the lowering of the standards. The actualization of the right order is achieved by blind selfish passion: the right order is the unintended by-product of human activities which are in no way directed toward the right order. The right order may have been as loftily conceived by Hegel as it was by Plato, which one may doubt. It certainly was thought by Hegel to be established in the Machiavellian way, not in the Platonic way: it was thought to be established in a manner which contradicts the right order itself. The delusions of communism are already the delusions of Hegel and even of Kant.

The difficulties to which German idealism was exposed gave rise to the third wave of modernity—of the wave that bears us today. This last epoch was inaugurated by Nietzsche. Nietzsche retained what appeared to him to be the insight due to the historical consciousness of the 19th century. But he rejected the view that the historical process is rational as well as the premise that a harmony between the genuine individual and the modern state is possible. He may be said to have returned, on the level of the historical consciousness, from Hegel's reconciliation to Rousseau's antinomy. He taught then that all human life and human thought ultimately rests on horizon-forming creations which are not susceptible of rational legitimization. The creators are great individuals. The solitary creator who gives a new law unto himself and who subjects himself to all its rigors takes the place of Rousseau's solitary dreamer. For Nature has ceased to appear as lawful and merciful. The fundamental experience of existence is therefore the experience, not of bliss, but of suffering, of emptiness, of an abyss. Nietzsche's creative call to creativity was addressed to individuals who should revolutionize their own lives, not to society or to his nation. But he expected or hoped that his call, at once stern and imploring, questioning and desirous to be questioned, would tempt the best men of the generations after him to become true selves and thus to form a new nobility which would be able to rule the planet. He opposed the possibility of a planetary aristocracy to the alleged necessity of a universal classless and stateless society. Being certain of the tameness of modern western man, he preached the sacred right of "merciless extinction" of large masses of men with as little restraint as his great antagonist had done. He used much of his unsurpassable and inexhaustible power of passionate and fascinating speech for making his readers loathe, not only socialism and communism, but conservatism, nationalism and democracy as well. After having taken upon himself this great political responsibility, he could not show his readers a way toward political responsibility. He left them no choice except that between irresponsible indifference to politics and irresponsible political options. He thus prepared a regime which, as long as it lasted, made discredited democracy look again like the golden age. He tried to articulate his understanding both of the modern situation and of human life as such by his doctrine of the will to power. The difficulty inherent in the philosophy of the will to power led after Nietzsche to the explicit renunciation of the very notion of eternity. Modern thought reaches its culmination, its highest self-consciousness, in the most radical historicism, i.e., in explicitly condemning to oblivion the notion of eternity. For oblivion of eternity, or, in other words, estrangement from man's deepest desire and therewith from the primary issues, is the price which modern man had to pay, from the very beginning, for attempting to be absolutely sovereign, to become the master and owner of nature, to conquer chance.

II

POLITICAL
PHILOSOPHY
AND HISTORY

Political philosophy is not a historical discipline. The philosophic questions of the nature of political things and of the best, or the just, political order are fundamentally different from historical questions, which always concern individuals: individual groups, individual human beings, individual achievements, individual "civilizations," the one individual "process" of human civilization from its beginning to the present, and so on. In particular, political philosophy is fundamentally different from the history of political philosophy itself. The question of the nature of political things and the answer to it cannot possibly be mistaken for the question of how this or that philosopher or all philosophers have approached, discussed or answered the philosophic question mentioned. This does not mean that political philosophy is absolutely independent of history. Without the experience of the variety of political institutions and convictions in different countries and at different times, the questions of the nature of political things and of the best, or the just, political order could never have been raised. And after they have been raised, only historical knowledge can prevent one from mistaking the specific features of the political life of one's time and one's country for the nature of political things. Similar considerations apply to the history of political thought and the history of political philosophy. But however important historical knowledge may be for political philosophy, it is only preliminary and auxiliary to political philosophy; it does not form an integral part of it.

This view of the relation of political philosophy to history was unquestionably predominant at least up to the end of the eighteenth century. In our time it is frequently rejected in favor of "historicism," *i.e.*, of the assertion that the fundamental distinction between philosophic and historical questions cannot in the last analysis be maintained. Historicism may therefore be said to question the possibility of political philosophy. At any rate it challenges a premise that was common to the whole tradition of political philosophy and apparently never doubted by it. It thus seems to go deeper to the roots, or to be more philosophic, than the political philosophy of the past. It certainly casts a doubt on the very questions of the nature of political things and of the best, or the just, political order. Thus it creates an entirely new situation for political philosophy. The question that it raises is today the most urgent question for political philosophy.

It may well be doubted whether the fusion of philosophy and history, as advocated by historicism, has ever been achieved, or even whether it can be achieved. Nevertheless that fusion appears to be, as it were, the natural goal toward which the victorious trends of nineteenth- and early twentieth-century thought converge. At any rate, historicism is not just one philosophic school among many, but a most powerful agent that affects more or less all present-day thought. As far as we can speak at all of the spirit of a time, we can assert with confidence that the spirit of our time is historicism.

Never before has man devoted such an intensive and such a comprehensive interest to his whole past, and to all aspects of his past, as he does today. The number of historical disciplines, the range of each, and the interdependence of them all are increasing almost constantly. Nor are these historical studies, carried on by thousands of ever more specialized students, considered merely instrumental, and without value in themselves: we take it for granted that historical knowledge forms an integral part of the highest kind of learning. To see this fact in the proper perspective, we need only look back to the past. When Plato sketched in his *Republic* a plan of studies he mentioned arithmetic, geometry, astronomy, and so on: he did not even allude to history. We cannot recall too often the saying of Aristotle (who was responsible for much of the most outstanding historical research done in classical antiquity) that poetry is more philosophic than history. This attitude was characteristic of all the classical philosophers and of all the philosophers of the Middle Ages. History was praised most highly not by the philosophers but by the rhetoricians. The history of philosophy in particular was not considered a philosophic discipline: it was left to antiquarians rather than to philosophers.

A fundamental change began to make itself felt only in the sixteenth century. The opposition then offered to all earlier philosophy, and especially to all earlier political philosophy, was marked from the outset by a novel emphasis on history. That early turn toward history was literally absorbed by the "unhistorical" teachings of the Age of Reason. The "rationalism" of the seventeenth and eighteenth centuries was fundamentally much more "historical" than the "rationalism" of pre-modern times. From the seventeenth century onward, the rapprochement of philosophy and history increased almost from generation to generation at an ever accelerated pace. Toward the end of the seventeenth century it became customary to speak of "the spirit of a time." In the middle of the eighteenth century the term "philosophy of history" was coined. In the nineteenth century, the history of philosophy came to be generally considered a philosophical discipline. The teaching of the outstanding philosopher of the nineteenth century, Hegel, was meant to be a "synthesis" of philosophy and history. The "historical school" of the nineteenth century brought about the substitution of historical jurisprudence, historical political science, historical economic science for a jurisprudence, a political science, an economic science that were evidently "unhistorical" or at least a-historical.

The specific historicism of the first half of the nineteenth century was violently attacked because it seemed to lose itself in the contemplation of the past. Its victorious opponents did not, however, replace it by a non-historical philosophy, but by a more "advanced," and in some cases a more "sophisticated" form of historicism. The typical historicism of the twentieth century demands that each generation reinterpret the past on the basis of its own experience and with a view to its own future. It is no longer contemplative, but activistic; and it attaches to that study of the past which is guided by the anticipated future, or which starts from and returns to the analysis of the present, a crucial philosophic significance: it expects from it the ultimate guidance for political life. The result is visible in practically every curriculum and textbook of our time. One has the impression that the question of the nature of political things has been superseded by the question of the characteristic "trends" of the social life of the present and of their historical origins, and that the question of the best, or the just, political order has been superseded by the question of the probable or desirable future. The questions of the modern state, of modern government, of the ideals of Western civilization, and so forth, occupy a place that was formerly occupied by the questions of *the* state and of *the* right way of life. Philosophic questions have been transformed into historical questions—or more precisely into historical questions of a "futuristic" character.

This orientation characteristic of our time can be rendered legitimate only by historicism. Historicism appears in the most varied guises and on the most different levels. Tenets and arguments that are the boast of one type of historicism, provoke the smile of the adherents of others. The most common form of historicism expresses itself in the demand that the questions of the nature of political things, of the state, of the nature of man, and so forth, be replaced by the questions of the modern state, of modern government, of the present political situation, of modern man, of our society, our culture, our civilization, and so forth. Since it is hard to see, however, how one can speak adequately of the modern state, of our civilization, of modern man, etc., without knowing first what a state is, what a civilization is, what man's nature is, the more thoughtful forms of historicism admit that the universal questions of traditional philosophy cannot be abandoned. Yet they assert that any answer to these questions, any attempt at clarifying or discussing them, and indeed any precise formulation

of them, is bound to be "historically conditioned," *i.e.*, to remain
dependent on the specific situation in which it is suggested. No
answer to, no treatment or precise formulation of, the universal
questions can claim to be of universal validity, of validity for all
times. Other historicists go to the end of the road by declaring
that while the universal questions of traditional philosophy cannot
be abandoned without abandoning philosophy itself, philosophy
itself and its universal questions themselves are "historically conditioned," *i.e.*, essentially related to a specific "historic" type, *e.g.*,
to Western man or to the Greeks and their intellectual heirs.

To indicate the range of historicism, we may refer to two assumptions characteristic of historicism and today generally accepted. "History" designated originally a particular kind of
knowledge or inquiry. Historicism assumes that the object of historical knowledge, which it calls "History," is a "field," a "world"
of its own fundamentally different from, although of course related to, that other "field," "Nature." This assumption distinguishes historicism most clearly from the pre-historicist view, for
which "History" as an object of knowledge did not exist, and
which therefore did not even dream of a "philosophy of history"
as an analysis of, or a speculation about, a specific "dimension of
reality." The gravity of the assumption in question appears only
after one has started wondering what the Bible or Plato, *e.g.*, would
have called that X which we are in the habit of calling "History."
Equally characteristic of historicism is the assumption that restora-
tions of earlier teachings are impossible, or that every intended
restoration necessarily leads to an essential modification of the
restored teaching. This assumption can most easily be understood
as a necessary consequence of the view that every teaching is essentially related to an unrepeatable "historical" situation.

An adequate discussion of historicism would be identical with
a critical analysis of modern philosophy in general. We cannot
dare to try to do more than indicate some considerations which
should prevent one from taking historicism for granted.

To begin with, we must dispose of a popular misunderstanding
which is apt to blur the issue. It goes back to the attacks of early
historicism on the political philosophy which had paved the way
for the French Revolution. The representatives of the "historical
school" assumed that certain influential philosophers of the eight-

eenth century had conceived of the right political order, or of the rational political order, as an order which should or could be established at any time and in any place, without any regard to the particular conditions of time and place. Over against this opinion they asserted that the only legitimate approach to political matters is the "historical" approach, *i.e.*, the understanding of the institutions of a given country as a product of its past. Legitimate political action must be based on such historical understanding, as distinguished from, and opposed to, the "abstract principles" of 1789 or any other "abstract principles." Whatever the deficiencies of eighteenth-century political philosophy may be, they certainly do not justify the suggestion that the non-historical philosophic approach must be replaced by a historical approach. Most political philosophers of the past, in spite or rather because of the non-historical character of their thought, distinguished as a matter of course between the philosophic question of the best political order, and the practical question as to whether that order could or should be established in a given country at a given time. They naturally knew that all political action, as distinguished from political philosophy, is concerned with individual situations, and must therefore be based on a clear grasp of the situation concerned, and therefore often on an understanding of the antecedents of that situation. They took it for granted that political action guided by the belief that what is most desirable in itself must be put into practice in all circumstances, regardless of the circumstances, befits harmless doves, ignorant of the wisdom of the serpent, but not sensible and good men. In short, the truism that all political action is concerned with, and therefore presupposes appropriate knowledge of, individual situations, individual commonwealths, individual institutions, and so on, is wholly irrelevant to the question raised by historicism.

For a large number, that question is decided by the fact that historicism comes later in time than the non-historical political philosophy: "history" itself seems to have decided in favor of historicism. If, however, we do not worship "success" as such, we cannot maintain that the victorious cause is necessarily the cause of truth. For even if we grant that truth will prevail in the end, we cannot be certain that the end has already come. Those who prefer historicism to non-historical political philosophy because of the temporal relation of the two, interpret then that relation in a specific manner: they believe that the position which historically comes later can be presumed, other things being equal, to be more mature than the positions preceding it. Historicism, they would say, is based on an experience which required many centuries to mature—on the experience of many centuries which teaches us that non-historical political philosophy is a failure or a delusion. The political philosophers of the past attempted to answer the question of the best political order once and for all. But the result of all their efforts has been that there are almost as many answers, as many political philosophies as there have been political philosophers. The mere spectacle of "the anarchy of systems," of "the disgraceful variety" of philosophies seems to refute the claim of each philosophy. The history of political philosophy, it is asserted, refutes non-historical political philosophy as such, since the many irreconcilable political philosophies refute each other.

Actually, however, that history does not teach us that the political philosophies of the past refute each other. It teaches us merely that they contradict each other. It confronts us then with the philosophic question as to which of two given contradictory theses concerning political fundamentals is true. In studying the history of political philosophy, we observe, *e.g.*, that some political philosophers distinguish between State and Society, whereas others explicitly or implicitly reject that distinction. This observation compels us to raise the philosophic question whether and how far the distinction is adequate. Even if history could teach us that the political philosophy of the past has failed, it would not teach us more than that non-historical political philosophy has hitherto failed. But what else would this mean except that we do not truly know the nature of political things and the best, or just, political order? This is so far from being a new insight due to historicism that it is implied in the very name "philosophy." If the "anarchy of systems" exhibited by the history of philosophy proves anything, it proves our ignorance concerning the most important subjects (of which ignorance we can be aware without historicism), and therewith it proves the necessity of philosophy. It may be added that the "anarchy" of the historical political philosophies of our time, or of present-day interpretations of the past, is not conspicuously smaller than that of the non-historical political philosophies of the past.

Yet it is not the mere variety of political philosophies which allegedly shows the futility of non-historical political philosophy. Most historicists consider decisive the fact, which can be established by historical studies, that a close relation exists between each political philosophy and the historical situation in which it emerged. The variety of political philosophies, they hold, is above all a function of the variety of historical situations. The history of political philosophy does not teach merely that the political philosophy of Plato, *e.g.*, is irreconcilable with the political philosophy, say, of Locke. It also teaches that Plato's political philosophy is essentially related to the Greek city of the fourth century B.C., just as Locke's political philosophy is essentially related to the English revolution of 1688. It thus shows that no political philosophy can reasonably claim to be valid beyond the historical situation to which it is essentially related.

Yet, not to repeat what has been indicated before, the historical evidence invoked in favor of historicism has a much more limited bearing than seems to be assumed. In the first place, historicists do not make sufficient allowance for the deliberate adaptation, on the part of the political philosophers of the past, of their views to the prejudices of their contemporaries. Superficial readers are apt to think that a political philosopher was under the spell of the historical situation in which he thought, when he was merely adapting the expression of his thought to that situation in order to be listened to at all. Many political philosophers of the past presented their teachings, not in scientific treatises proper, but in what we may call treatise-tracts. They did not limit themselves to expounding what they considered the political truth. They combined with that exposition an exposition of what they considered desirable or feasible in the circumstances, or intelligible on the basis of the generally received opinions; they communicated their views in a manner which was not purely "philosophical," but at the same time "civil."[1] Accordingly, by proving

---

1. Compare Locke, *Of Civil Government*, I, Sect. 109, and II, Sect. 52, with his *Essay Concerning Human Understanding*, III, ch. 9, Sects. 3 and 22.

that their political teaching as a whole is "historically conditioned," we do not at all prove that their political philosophy proper is "historically conditioned."

Above all, it is gratuitously assumed that the relation between doctrines and their "times" is wholly unambiguous. The obvious possibility is overlooked that the situation to which one particular doctrine is related, is particularly favorable to the discovery of *the* truth, whereas all other situations may be more or less unfavorable. More generally expressed, in understanding the genesis of a doctrine we are not necessarily driven to the conclusion that the doctrine in question cannot simply be true. By proving, *e.g.*, that certain propositions of modern natural law "go back" to positive Roman law, we have not yet proven that the propositions in question are not *de jure naturali* but merely *de jure positivo*. For it is perfectly possible that the Roman jurists mistook certain principles of natural law for those of positive law, or that they merely "divined," and did not truly know, important elements of natural law. We cannot then stop at ascertaining the relations between a doctrine and its historical origins. We have to interpret these relations; and such interpretation presupposes the philosophic study of the doctrine in itself with a view to its truth or falsehood. At any rate, the fact (if it is a fact) that each doctrine is "related" to a particular historical setting does not prove at all that no doctrine can simply be true.

The old-fashioned, not familiar with the ravages wrought by historicism, may ridicule us for drawing a conclusion which amounts to the truism that we cannot reasonably reject a serious doctrine before we have examined it adequately. In the circumstances we are compelled to state explicitly that prior to careful investigation we cannot exclude the possibility that a political philosophy which emerged many centuries ago is *the* true political philosophy, as true today as it was when it was first expounded. In other words, a political philosophy does not become obsolete merely because the historical situation, and in particular the political situation to which it was related has ceased to exist. For every political situation contains elements which are essential to all political situations: how else could one intelligibly call all these different political situations "political situations"?

Let us consider very briefly, and in a most preliminary fashion, the most important example. Classical political philosophy is not refuted, as some seem to believe, by the mere fact that the city, apparently the central subject of classical political philosophy, has been superseded by the modern state. Most classical philosophers considered the city the most perfect form of political organization, not because they were ignorant of any other form, nor because they followed blindly the lead given by their ancestors or contemporaries, but because they realized, at least as clearly as we realize it today, that the city is essentially superior to the other forms of political association known to classical antiquity, the tribe and the Eastern monarchy. The tribe, we may say tentatively, is characterized by freedom (public spirit) and lack of civilization (high development of the arts and sciences), and the Eastern monarchy is characterized by civilization and lack of freedom. Classical political philosophers consciously and reasonably preferred the city to other forms of political association, in the light of the standards of freedom and civilization. And this preference was not a peculiarity bound up with their particular historical situation. Up to and including the eighteenth century, some of the most outstanding political philosophers quite justifiably preferred the city to the modern state which had emerged since the sixteenth century, precisely because they measured the modern state of their time by the standards of freedom and civilization. Only in the nineteenth century did classical political philosophy in a sense become obsolete. The reason was that the state of the nineteenth century, as distinguished from the Macedonian and Roman empires, the feudal monarchy, and the absolute monarchy of the modern period, could plausibly claim to be at least as much in accordance with the standards of freedom and civilization as the Greek city had been. Even then classical political philosophy did not become completely obsolete, since it was classical political philosophy which had expounded in a "classic" manner the standards of freedom and civilization. This is not to deny that the emergence of modern democracy in particular has elicited, if it has not been the outcome of, such a reinterpretation of both "freedom" and "civilization" as could not have been foreseen by classical political philosophy. Yet that reinterpretation is of fundamental significance, not because modern democracy has superseded earlier forms of political association, or because it has been victorious—it has not always

been victorious, and not everywhere—but because there are definite
reasons for considering that reinterpretation intrinsically superior
to the original version. Naturally, there are some who doubt the
standards mentioned. But that doubt is as little restricted to
specific historical situations as the standards themselves. There
were classical political philosophers who decided in favor of the
Eastern monarchy.

Before we can make an intelligent use of the historically ascertained relations between philosophic teachings and their "times,"
we must have subjected the doctrines concerned to a philosophic
critique concerned exclusively with their truth or falsehood. A
philosophic critique in its turn presupposes an adequate understanding of the doctrine subjected to the critique. An adequate
interpretation is such an interpretation as understands the thought
of a philosopher exactly as he understood it himself. All historical
evidence adduced in support of historicism presupposes as a matter of course that adequate understanding of the philosophy of
the past is possible on the basis of historicism. This presupposition
is open to grave doubts. To see this we must consider historicism in
the light of the standards of historical exactness which, according
to common belief, historicism was the first to perceive, to elaborate,
or at least to divine.

Historicism discovered these standards while fighting the doctrine which preceded it and paved the way for it. That doctrine
was the belief in progress: the conviction of the superiority, say,
of the late eighteenth century to all earlier ages, and the expectation of still further progress in the future. The belief in progress
stands midway between the non-historical view of the philosophic
tradition and historicism. It agrees with the philosophic tradition
in so far as both admit that there are universally valid standards
which do not require, or which are not susceptible of, historical
proof. It deviates from the philosophic tradition in so far as it
is essentially a view concerning "the historical process"; it asserts
that there is such a thing as "the historical process" and that that
process is, generally speaking, a "progress": a progress of thought
and institutions toward an order which fully agrees with certain
presupposed universal standards of human excellence.

In consequence, the belief in progress, as distinguished from the views of the philosophic tradition, can be legitimately criticized on purely historical grounds. This was done by early historicism, which showed in a number of cases—the most famous example is the interpretation of the Middle Ages—that the "progressivist" view of the past was based on an utterly insufficient understanding of the past. It is evident that our understanding of the past will tend to be the more adequate, the more we are interested in the past. But we cannot be passionately interested, seriously interested in the past if we know beforehand that the present is in the most important respect superior to the past. Historians who started from this assumption felt no necessity to understand the past in itself; they understood it only as a preparation for the present. In studying a doctrine of the past, they did not ask primarily, what was the conscious and deliberate intention of its originator? They preferred to ask, what is the contribution of the doctrine to our beliefs? What is the meaning, unknown to the originator, of the doctrine from the point of view of the present? What is its meaning in the light of later discoveries or inventions? They took it for granted then that it is possible and even necessary to understand the thinkers of the past better than those thinkers understood themselves.

Against this approach, the "historical consciousness" rightly protested in the interest of historical truth, of historical exactness. The task of the historian of thought is to understand the thinkers of the past exactly as they understood themselves, or to revitalize their thought according to their own interpretation. If we abandon this goal, we abandon the only practicable criterion of "objectivity" in the history of thought. For, as is well-known, the same historical phenomenon appears in different lights in different historical situations; new experience seems to shed new light on old texts. Observations of this kind seem to suggest that the claim of any one interpretation to be *the* true interpretation is untenable. Yet the observations in question do not justify this suggestion. For the seemingly infinite variety of ways in which a given teaching can be understood does not do away with the fact that the originator of the doctrine understood it in one way only, provided he was not confused. The indefinitely large variety of equally legitimate interpretations of a doctrine of the past is due to conscious or unconscious attempts to understand its author better than he understood himself. But there is only one way of understanding him as he understood himself.

Now, historicism is constitutionally unable to live up to the standards of historical exactness which it might be said to have discovered. For historicism is the belief that the historicist approach is superior to the non-historical approach, but practically the whole thought of the past was radically "unhistorical." Historicism is therefore compelled, by its principle, to attempt to understand the philosophy of the past better than it understood itself. The philosophy of the past understood itself in a non-historical manner, but historicism must understand it "historically." The philosophers of the past claimed to have found *the* truth, and not merely the truth for their times. The historicist, on the other hand, believes that they were mistaken in making that claim, and he cannot help making that belief the basis of his interpretation. Historicism then merely repeats, if sometimes in a more subtle form, the sin for which it upbraided so severely the "progressivist" historiography. For, to repeat, our understanding of the thought of the past is liable to be the more adequate, the less the historian is convinced of the superiority of his own point of view, or the more he is prepared to admit the possibility that he may have to learn something, not merely about the thinkers of the past, but from them. To understand a serious teaching, we must be seriously interested in it, we must take it seriously, *i.e.*, we must be willing to consider the possibility that it is simply true. The historicist as such denies that possibility as regards any philosophy of the past. Historicism naturally attaches a much greater importance to the history of philosophy than any earlier philosophy has done. But unlike most earlier philosophies, it endangers by its principle, if contrary to its original intention, any adequate understanding of the philosophies of the past.

It would be a mistake to think that historicism could be the outcome of an unbiased study of the history of philosophy, and in particular of the history of political philosophy. The historian may have ascertained that all political philosophies are related to specific historical settings, or that only such men as live in a specific historical situation have a natural aptitude for accepting a given political philosophy. He cannot thus rule out the possibility that the historical setting of one particular political philosophy is the ideal condition for the discovery of *the* political truth. Historicism cannot then be established by historical evidence. Its basis is a philosophic analysis of thought, knowledge, truth, philosophy, political things, political ideals, and so on, a philosophic analysis allegedly leading to the result that thought, knowledge, truth, philosophy, political things, political ideals, and so on, are essentially and radically "historical." The philosophic analysis in question presents itself as the authentic interpretation of the experience of many centuries with political philosophy. The political philosophers of the past attempted to answer the question of the best political order once and for all. Each of them held explicitly or implicitly that all others had failed. It is only after a long period of trial and error that political philosophers started questioning the possibility of answering the fundamental questions once and for all. The ultimate result of that reflection is historicism.

Let us consider how far that result would affect political philosophy. Historicism cannot reasonably claim that the fundamental questions of political philosophy must be replaced by questions of a historical character. The question of the best political order, *e.g.*, cannot be replaced by a discussion "of the operative ideals which maintain a particular type of state," modern democracy, *e.g.*; for "any thorough discussion" of those ideals "is bound to give some consideration to the absolute worth of such ideals."[2] Nor can the question of the best political order be replaced by the question of the future order. For even if we could know with certainty that the future order is to be, say, a communist world society, we should not know more than that the communist world society is the only alternative to the destruction of modern civilization, and we should still have to wonder which alternative is preferable. Under no circumstances can we avoid the question as to whether the probable future order is desirable, indifferent or abominable. In fact, our answer to that question may influence the prospects of the probable future order becoming actually the order of the future. What we consider desirable in the circumstances depends ulti-

---

2. A. D. Lindsay *The Modern Democratic State* (Oxford, 1943), I, 45.

mately on universal principles of preference, on principles whose
political implications, if duly elaborated, would present our answer
to the question of the best political order.

What historicism could reasonably say, if the philosophic
analysis on which it is based is correct, is that all answers to the
universal philosophic questions are necessarily "historically conditioned," or that no answer to the universal questions will in fact
be universally valid. Now, every answer to a universal question
necessarily intends to be universally valid. The historicist thesis
amounts then to this, that there is an inevitable contradiction between the intention of philosophy and its fate, between the non-
historical intention of the philosophic answers and their fate always to remain "historically conditioned." The contradiction is
inevitable because, on the one hand, evident reasons compel us to
raise the universal questions and to attempt to arrive at adequate
answers, *i.e.*, universal answers; and, on the other hand, all human
thought is enthralled by opinions and convictions which differ from
historical situation to historical situation. The historical limitation of a given answer necessarily escapes him who gives the
answer. The historical conditions which prevent any answer from
being universally valid have the character of invisible walls. For
if a man knew that his answer would be determined, not by his free
insight into the truth, but by his historical situation, he could no
longer identify himself with or wholeheartedly believe in, his answer. We should then know with certainty that no answer which
suggests itself to us can be simply true, but we could not know the
precise reason why this is the case. The precise reason would be
the problematic validity of the deepest prejudice, necessarily hidden from us, of our time. If this view is correct, political philosophy would still have to raise the fundamental and universal
questions which no thinking man can help raising once he has
become aware of them, and to try to answer them. But the philosopher would have to accompany his philosophic effort by a coherent reflection on his historical situation in order to emancipate
himself as far as possible from the prejudices of his age. That
historical reflection would be in the service of the philosophic effort
proper, but would by no means be identical with it.

On the basis of historicism, philosophic efforts would then be
enlightened from the outset as to the fact that the answers to which

they may lead will necessarily be "historically conditioned." They would be accompanied by coherent reflections on the historical situation in which they were undertaken. We might think that such philosophic efforts could justly claim to have risen to a higher level of reflection, or to be more philosophic, than the "naive" non-historical philosophy of the past. We might think for a moment that historical political philosophy is less apt to degenerate into dogmatism than was its predecessor. But a moment's reflection suffices to dispel that delusion. Whereas for the genuine philosopher of the past all the answers of which he could possibly think were, prior to his examination of them, open possibilities, the historicist philosopher excludes, prior to his examining them, all the answers suggested in former ages. He is no less dogmatic, he is much more dogmatic, than the average philosopher of the past. In particular, the coherent reflection of the philosopher on his historical situation is not necessarily a sign that, other things being equal, his philosophic reflection is on a higher level than that of philosophers who were not greatly concerned with their historical situation. For it is quite possible that the modern philosopher is in much greater need of reflection on his situation because, having abandoned the resolve to look at things *sub specie aeternitatis*, he is much more exposed to, and enthralled by, the convictions and "trends" dominating his age. Reflection on one's historical situation may very well be no more than a remedy for a deficiency which has been caused by historicism, or rather by the deeper motives which express themselves in historicism, and which did not hamper the philosophic efforts of former ages.

It seems as if historicism were animated by the certainty that the future will bring about the realization of possibilities of which no one has ever dreamt, or can ever dream, whereas non-historical political philosophy lived not in such an open horizon, but in a horizon closed by the possibilities known at the time. Yet the possibilities of the future are not unlimited as long as the differences between men and angels and between men and brutes have not been abolished, or as long as there are political things. The possibilities of the future are not wholly unknown, since their limits are known. It is true that no one can possibly foresee what sensible or mad possibilities, whose realization is within the limits of human nature, will be discovered in the future. But it is also true that it is hard to say anything at present about possibilities which are at present not even imagined. Therefore, we cannot help following the precedent set by the attitude of earlier political philosophy toward the possibilities which have been discovered, or even realized since. We must leave it to the political philosophers of the future to discuss the possibilities which will be known only in the future. Even the absolute certainty that the future will witness such fundamental and at the same time sensible changes of outlook as can not even be imagined now, could not possibly influence the questions and the procedure of political philosophy.

It would likewise be wrong to say that whereas non-historical political philosophy believed in the possibility of answering fundamental questions once and for all, historicism implies the insight that final answers to fundamental questions are impossible. Every philosophic position implies such answers to fundamental questions as claim to be final, to be true once and for all. Those who believe in "the primary significance of the unique and morally ultimate character of the concrete situation," and therefore reject the quest for "general answers supposed to have a universal meaning that covers and dominates all particulars," do not hesitate to offer what claim to be final and universal answers to the questions as to what "a moral situation" is and as to what "*the* distinctively moral traits," or "*the* virtues" are.[3] Those who believe in progress toward a goal which itself is essentially progressive, and therefore reject the question of the best political order as "too static," are convinced that their insight into the actuality of such a progress "has come to stay." Similarly, historicism merely replaced one kind of finality by another kind of finality, by the final conviction that all human answers are essentially and radically "historical." Only under one condition could historicism claim to have done away with all pretence to finality, if it presented the historicist thesis not as simply true, but as true for the time being only. In fact, if the historicist thesis is correct, we cannot escape the consequence that that thesis itself is "historical" or valid, because meaningful, for a specific historical situation only. Historicism is not a cab which one can stop at his convenience: his-

3. John Dewey *Reconstruction in Philosophy* (New York, 1920), 189 and 163 f.

toricism must be applied to itself. It will thus reveal itself as relative to modern man; and this will imply that it will be replaced, in due time, by a position which is no longer historicist. Some historicists would consider such a development a manifest decline. But in so doing they would ascribe to the historical situation favorable to historicism an absoluteness which, as a matter of principle, they refuse to ascribe to any historical situation.

Precisely the historicist approach would compel us then to raise the question of the essential relation of historicism to modern man, or, more exactly, the question as to what specific need, characteristic of modern man, as distinguished from pre-modern man, underlies his passionate turn to history. To elucidate this question, as far as possible in the present context, we shall consider the argument in favor of the fusion of philosophic and historical studies which appears to be most convincing.

Political philosophy is the attempt to replace our opinions about political fundamentals by knowledge about them. Its first task consists therefore in making fully explicit our political ideas, so that they can be subjected to critical analysis. "Our ideas" are only partly our ideas. Most of our ideas are abbreviations or residues of the thought of other people, of our teachers (in the broadest sense of the term) and of our teachers' teachers; they are abbreviations and residues of the thought of the past. These thoughts were once explicit and in the center of consideration and discussion. It may even be presumed that they were once perfectly lucid. By being transmitted to later generations they have possibly been transformed, and there is no certainty that the transformation was effected consciously and with full clarity. At any rate, what were once certainly explicit ideas passionately discussed, although not necessarily lucid ideas, have now degenerated into mere implications and tacit presuppositions. Therefore, if we want to clarify the political ideas we have inherited, we must actualize their implications, which were explicit in the past, and this can be done only by means of the history of political ideas. This means that the clarification of our political ideas insensibly changes into and becomes indistinguishable from the history of political ideas. To this extent the philosophic effort and the historical effort have become completely fused.

Now, the more we are impressed by the necessity of engaging in historical studies in order to clarify our political ideas, the more we must be struck by the observation that the political philosophers of former ages did not feel such a necessity at all. A glance at Aristotle's *Politics, e.g.*, suffices to convince us that Aristotle succeeded perfectly in clarifying the political ideas obtaining in his age, although he never bothered about the history of those ideas. The most natural, and the most cautious, explanation of this paradoxical fact would be, that perhaps our political ideas have a character fundamentally different from that of the political ideas of former ages. Our political ideas have the particular character that they cannot be clarified fully except by means of historical studies, whereas the political ideas of the past could be clarified perfectly without any recourse to their history.

To express this suggestion somewhat differently, we shall make a rather free use of the convenient terminology of Hume. According to Hume, our ideas are derived from "impressions"—from what we may call first-hand experience. To clarify our ideas and to distinguish between their genuine and their spurious elements (or between those elements which are in accordance with first-hand experience and those which are not), we must trace each of our ideas to the impressions from which it is derived. Now it is doubtful whether all ideas are related to impressions in fundamentally the same way. The idea of the city, *e.g.*, can be said to be derived from the impressions of cities in fundamentally the same way as the idea of the dog is derived from the impressions of dogs. The idea of the state, on the other hand, is not derived simply from the impression of states. It emerged partly owing to the transformation, or reinterpretation, of more elementary ideas, of the idea of the city in particular. Ideas which are derived directly from impressions can be clarified without any recourse to history; but ideas which have emerged owing to a specific transformation of more elementary ideas cannot be clarified but by means of the history of ideas.

We have illustrated the difference between our political ideas and earlier political ideas by the examples of the ideas of the state and of the city. The choice of these examples was not accidental; for the difference with which we are concerned is the specific difference between the character of modern philosophy on the one hand, and that of pre-modern philosophy on the other. This fundamental difference was described by Hegel in the following terms: "The manner of study in ancient times is distinct from that of modern times, in that the former consisted in the veritable training and perfecting of the natural consciousness. Trying its powers at each part of its life severally, and philosophizing about everything it came across, the natural consciousness transformed itself into a universality of abstract understanding which was active in every matter and in every respect. In modern times, however, the individual finds the abstract form ready made."[4] Classical philosophy originally acquired the fundamental concepts of political philosophy by starting from political phenomena as they present themselves to "the natural consciousness," which is a pre-philosophic consciousness. These concepts can therefore be understood, and their validity can be checked, by direct reference to phenomena as they are accessible to "the natural consciousness." The fundamental concepts which were the final result of the philosophic efforts of classical antiquity, and which remained the basis of the philosophic efforts of the Middle Ages, were the starting point of the philosophic efforts of the modern period. They were partly taken for granted and partly modified by the founders of modern political philosophy. In a still more modified form they underlie the political philosophy or political science of our time. In so far as modern political philosophy emerges, not simply from "the natural consciousness," but by way of a modification of, and even in opposition to, an earlier political philosophy, a tradition of political philosophy, its fundamental concepts cannot be fully understood until we have understood the earlier political philosophy from which, and in opposition to which, they were acquired, and the specific modification by virtue of which they were acquired.

It is not the mere "dependence" of modern philosophy on classi-

---

4. *The Phenomenology of the Mind*, tr. J. B. Baillie, 2nd edition (London, New York, 1931), 94. I have changed Baillie's translation a little in order to bring out somewhat more clearly the intention of Hegel's remark. For a more precise analysis, see Jacob Klein, "Die griechische Logistik und die Entstehung der modernen Algebra," *Quellen und Studien zur Geschichte der Mathematik, Astronomie und Physik*, vol. 3, Heft 1 (Berlin, 1934), 64-66, and Heft 2 (Berlin, 1936), 122 ff. See also the same author's "Phenomenology and Science," *Philosophical Essays in Memory of Edmund Husserl* (Harvard University Press, 1940), 143-163.

cal philosophy, but the specific character of that "dependence," which accounts for the fact that the former needs to be supplemented by an intrinsically philosophic history of philosophy. For medieval philosophy too was "dependent" on classical philosophy, and yet it was not in need of the history of philosophy as an integral part of its philosophic efforts. When a medieval philosopher studied Aristotle's *Politics, e.g.,* he did not engage in a historical study. The *Politics* was for him an authoritative text. Aristotle was *the* philosopher, and hence the teaching of the *Politics* was, in principle, *the* true philosophic teaching. However he might deviate from Aristotle in details, or as regards the application of the true teaching to circumstances which Aristotle could not have foreseen, the basis of the medieval philosopher's thought remained the Aristotelian teaching. That basis was always present to him; it was contemporaneous with him. His philosophic study was identical with the adequate understanding of the Aristotelian teaching. It was for this reason that he did not need historical studies in order to understand the basis of his own thought. It is precisely that contemporaneity of philosophic thought with its basis which no longer exists in modern philosophy, and whose absence explains the eventual transformation of modern philosophy into an intrinsically historical philosophy. Modern thought is in all its forms, directly or indirectly, determined by the idea of progress. This idea implies that the most elementary questions can be settled once and for all so that future generations can dispense with their further discussion, but can erect on the foundations once laid an ever-growing structure. In this way, the foundations are covered up. The only proof necessary to guarantee their solidity seems to be that the structure stands and grows. Since philosophy demands, however, not merely solidity so understood, but lucidity and truth, a special kind of inquiry becomes necessary whose purpose it is to keep alive the recollection, and the problem, of the foundations hidden by progress. This philosophic inquiry is the history of philosophy or of science.

We must distinguish between inherited knowledge and independently acquired knowledge. By inherited knowledge we understand the philosophic or scientific knowledge a man takes over from former generations, or, more generally expressed, from others; by independently acquired knowledge we understand the philosophic or scientific knowledge a mature scholar acquires in his unbiased intercourse, as fully enlightened as possible as to its horizon and its presuppositions, with his subject matter. On the basis of the belief in progress, this difference tends to lose its crucial significance. When speaking of a "body of knowledge" or of "the results of research," *e.g.*, we tacitly assign the same cognitive status to inherited knowledge and to independently acquired knowledge. To counteract this tendency a special effort is required to transform inherited knowledge into genuine knowledge by revitalizing its original discovery, and to discriminate between the genuine and the spurious elements of what claims to be inherited knowledge. This truly philosophic function is fulfilled by the history of philosophy or of science.

If, as we must, we apply historicism to itself, we must explain historicism in terms of the specific character of modern thought, or, more precisely, of modern philosophy. In doing so, we observe that modern political philosophy or science, as distinguished from pre-modern political philosophy or science, is in need of the history of political philosophy or science as an integral part of its own efforts, since, as modern political philosophy or science itself admits or even emphasizes, it consists to a considerable extent of inherited knowledge whose basis is no longer contemporaneous or immediately accessible. The recognition of this necessity cannot be mistaken for historicism. For historicism asserts that the fusion of philosophic and historical questions marks in itself a progress beyond "naive" non-historical philosophy, whereas we limit ourselves to asserting that that fusion is, within the limits indicated, inevitable on the basis of modern philosophy, as distinguished from pre-modern philosophy or "the philosophy of the future."

III

ON CLASSICAL
POLITICAL
PHILOSOPHY

The purpose of the following remarks is to discuss especially those characteristic features of classical political philosophy which are in particular danger of being overlooked or insufficiently stressed by the schools that are most influential in our time. These remarks are not intended to sketch the outlines of an adequate interpretation of classical political philosophy. They will have fulfilled their purpose if they point to the way which, as it seems to me, is the only one whereby such an interpretation can eventually be reached by us.

Classical political philosophy is characterized by the fact that it was related to political life directly. It was only after the classical philosophers had done their work that political philosophy became definitely "established" and thus acquired a certain remoteness from political life. Since that time the relationship of political philosophers to political life, and their grasp of it, have been determined by the existence of an inherited political philosophy: since then political philosophy has been related to political life through the medium of a tradition of political philosophy. The tradition of political philosophy, being a tradition, took for granted the necessity and possibility of political philosophy. The tradition that originated in classical Greece was rejected in the sixteenth and seventeenth centuries in favor of a new political philosophy. But this "revolution" did not restore the direct relation to political life that had existed in the beginning: the new political philosophy was related to political life through the medium of the inherited general notion of political philosophy or political science, and through the medium of a new concept of science. The modern political philosophers tried to replace both the teaching and the method of traditional political philosophy by what they considered as the true teaching and the right method; they took it for granted that political philosophy as such is necessary and possible. Today, political science may believe that by rejecting or by emancipating itself from political philosophy, it stands in the most direct relation to political life; actually it is related to political life through the medium of modern natural science, or of the reaction to modern natural science, and through a number of basic concepts inherited from the philosophic tradition, however despised or ignored.

It was its direct relation to political life which determined the orientation and scope of classical political philosophy. Accordingly, the tradition which was based on that philosophy, and which preserved its orientation and scope, preserved that direct relation to a certain extent. The fundamental change in this respect begins with the new political philosophy of the early modern period and reaches its climax in present-day political science. The most striking difference between classical political philosophy and present-day political science is that the latter is no longer concerned at all with what was the guiding question for the former: the question of the best political order. On the other hand, modern political science is greatly preoccupied with a type of question that was of much less importance to classical political philosophy: questions concerning method. Both differences must be traced to the same reason: to the different degree of directness in which classical political philosophy, on the one hand, and present-day political science, on the other, are related to political life.

Classical political philosophy attempted to reach its goal by accepting the basic distinctions made in political life exactly in the sense and with the orientation in which they are made in political life, and by thinking them through, by understanding them as

perfectly as possible. It did not start from such basic distinctions
as those between "the state of nature" and "the civil state,"
between "facts" and "values," between "reality" and "ideologies,"
between "the world" and "the worlds" of different societies, or
between "the I, Me, Thou and We," distinctions which are alien,
and even unknown, to political life as such and which originate
only in philosophic or scientific reflection. Nor did it try to bring
order into that chaos of political "facts" which exists only for
those who approach political life from a point of view outside of
political life, that is to say, from the point of view of a science
that is not itself essentially an element of political life. Instead,
it followed carefully and even scrupulously the articulation which
is inherent in, and natural to, political life and its objectives.

The primary questions of classical political philosophy, and
the terms in which it stated them, were not specifically philosophic
or scientific; they were questions that are raised in assemblies,
councils, clubs and cabinets, and they were stated in terms intelligible and familiar, at least to all sane adults, from everyday
experience and everyday usage. These questions have a natural
hierarchy which supplies political life, and hence political philosophy, with its fundamental orientation. No one can help distinguishing among questions of smaller, of greater, and of paramount importance, and between questions of the moment and
questions that are always present in political communities; and
intelligent men apply these distinctions intelligently.

Similarly it can be said that the method, too, of classical political philosophy was presented by political life itself. Political life
is characterized by conflicts between men asserting opposed claims.
Those who raise a claim usually believe that what they claim
is good for them. In many cases they believe, and in most cases
they say, that what they claim is good for the community at
large. In practically all cases claims are raised, sometimes sincerely
and sometimes insincerely, in the name of justice. The opposed
claims are based, then, on opinions of what is good or just. To
justify their claims, the opposed parties advance arguments. The
conflict calls for arbitration, for an intelligent decision that will give
each party what it truly deserves. Some of the material required
for making such a decision is offered by the opposed parties themselves, and the very insufficiency of this partial material—an in-

sufficiency obviously due to its partisan origin—points the way
to its completion by the umpire. The umpire par excellence is the
political philosopher.[1] He tries to settle those political controversies
that are both of paramount and of permanent importance.

This view of the function of the political philosopher—that he
must not be a "radical" partisan who prefers victory in civil war to
arbitration—is also of political origin: it is the duty of the good
citizen to make civil strife cease and to create, by persuasion,
agreement among the citizens.[2] The political philosopher first comes
into sight as a good citizen who can perform this function of the
good citizen in the best way and on the highest level. In order
to perform his function he has to raise ulterior questions, questions that are never raised in the political arena; but in doing so
he does not abandon his fundamental orientation, which is the
orientation inherent in political life. Only if that orientation were
abandoned, if the basic distinctions made by political life were
considered merely "subjective" or "unscientific" and therefore
disregarded, would the question of how to approach political things
in order to understand them, that is to say, the question of method,
become a fundamental question, and, indeed, *the* fundamental
question.

It is true that political life is concerned primarily with the
individual community to which the people happen to belong, and
mostly even with individual situations, whereas political philosophy
is concerned primarily with what is essential to all political communities. Yet there is a straight and almost continuous way leading
from the pre-philosophic to the philosophic approach. Political
life requires various kinds of skills, and in particular that apparently highest skill which enables a man to manage well the
affairs of his political community as a whole. That skill—the art,
the prudence, the practical wisdom, the specific understanding pos-

1. Note the procedure of Aristotle in *Politics*, 1280a7-1284b34 and 1297a6-7;
also Plato, *Eighth Letter*, 354a1-5 and 352c8 ff., and *Laws*, 627d11-628a4.

2. See Xenophon, *Memorabilia*, IV 6, 14-15 and context; also Aristotle,
Athenian Constitution, 28, 5; also the remark by Hume (in his essay "Of the
Original Contract"): "But philosophers, who have embraced a party (if that
be not a contradiction in terms) . . ." The difference between the classical
political philosopher and the present day political scientist is illustrated by
Macaulay's remark on Sir William Temple: "Temple was not a mediator. He
was merely a neutral." Cf. de Tocqueville, *De la démocratie en Amérique*:
"J'ai entrepris de voir, non pas autrement, mais plus loin que les partis."

sessed by the excellent statesman or politician—and not "a body of
true propositions" concerning political matters which is transmitted
by teachers to pupils, is what was originally meant by "political
science." A man who possesses "political science" is not merely able
to deal properly with a large variety of situations in his own community; he can, in principle, manage well even the affairs of any
other political community, be it "Greek" or "barbarian." While
all political life is essentially the life of this or that political community, "political science," which essentially belongs to political
life, is essentially "transferable" from one community to any other.
A man like Themistocles was admired and listened to not only in
Athens, but, after he had to flee from Athens, among the barbarians
as well; such a man is admired because he is capable of giving sound
political advice wherever he goes.[3]

"Political science" designated originally the skill by virtue of
which a man could manage well the affairs of political communities by deed and by speech. The skill of speaking takes precedence
over the skill of doing since all sensible action proceeds from deliberation, and the element of deliberation is speech. Accordingly,
that part of political skill which first became the object of instruction was the skill of public speaking. "Political science" in a more
precise sense, that is, as a skill that is essentially teachable, appeared
first as rhetoric, or as a part of it. The teacher of rhetoric was not
necessarily a politician or statesman; he was, however, a teacher of
politicians or statesmen. Since his pupils belonged to the most different political communities, the content of his teaching could not
possibly be bound up with the particular features of any individual political community. "Political science," on the level which it
reached as a result of the exertions of the rhetoricians, is more
"universal," is to an even higher degree "transferable," than is
"political science" as the skill of the excellent statesman or politician: whereas strangers as statesmen or political advisers were an
exception, strangers as teachers of rhetoric were the rule.[4]

3. Xenophon, *Memorabilia*, III 6, 2; Thucydides, I 138. See also Plato, *Lysis*,
209d5-210b2, and *Republic*, 494c7-d1. One of the purposes of the *Menexenus*
is to illustrate the "transferable" character of political science: a sufficiently
gifted foreign woman is as capable as Pericles, or more capable than he, to
compose a most solemn speech to be delivered on behalf of the city of Athens.

4. Plato, *Protagoras*, 319a1-2, and *Timaeus*, 19e; also Aristotle, *Nicomachean
Ethics*, 1181a12 ff. as well as *Politics*, 1264b33-34 and 1299a1-2; Isocrates,
Nicocles 9; Cicero, *De oratore*, III, 57.

Classical political philosophy rejected the identification of political science with rhetoric; it held that rhetoric, at its best, was only an instrument of political science. It did not, however, descend from the level of generality that had been reached by the rhetoricians. On the contrary, after that part of political skill which is the skill of speaking had been raised to the level of a distinct discipline, the classical philosophers could meet that challenge only by raising the whole of "political science," as far as possible or necessary, to the rank of a distinct discipline. By doing this they became the founders of political science in the precise and final sense of the term. And the way in which they did it was determined by the articulation natural to the political sphere.

"Political science" as the skill of the excellent politician or statesman consists in the right handling of individual situations; its immediate "products" are commands or decrees or advices effectively expressed, which are intended to cope with an individual case. Political life knows, however, a still higher kind of political understanding, which is concerned not with individual cases but, as regards each relevant subject, with all cases, and whose immediate "products"—laws and institutions—are meant to be permanent. The true legislators—"the fathers of the Constitution," as modern men would say—establish, as it were, the permanent framework within which the right handling of changing situations by excellent politicians or statesmen can take place. While it is true that the excellent statesman can act successfully within the most different frameworks of laws and institutions, the value of his achievement depends ultimately on the value of the cause in whose service he acts; and that cause is not his work but the work of him or those who made the laws and institutions of his community. The legislative skill is, therefore, the most "architectonic" political skill[5] that is known to political life.

Every legislator is primarily concerned with the individual community for which he legislates, but he has to raise certain questions which regard all legislation. These most fundamental

5. Aristotle, *Nicomachean Ethics*, 1141b24-29 (compare 1137b13); also Plato, *Gorgias*, 464b7-8, and *Minos*, 320c1-5; Cicero, *Offices*, I, 75-76. The classical view was expressed as follows by Rousseau, who still shared it, or rather restored it: "s'il est vrai qu'un grand prince est un homme rare, que sera-ce d'un grand législateur? Le premier n'a qu'à suivre le modèle que l'autre doit proposer" (*Contrat social*, II, 7).

and most universal political questions are naturally fit to be made the subject of the most "architectonic," the truly "architectonic" political knowledge: of that political science which is the goal of the political philosopher. This political science is the knowledge which would enable a man to teach legislators. The political philosopher who has reached his goal is the teacher of legislators.[6] The knowledge of the political philosopher is "transferable" in the highest degree. Plato demonstrated this *ad oculos* in his dialogue on legislation, by presenting in the guise of a stranger the philosopher who is a teacher of legislators.[7] He illustrated it less ambiguously by the comparison, which frequently occurs in his writings, of political science with medicine.

It is by being the teacher of legislators that the political philosopher is the umpire par excellence. All political conflicts that arise within the community are at least related to, if they do not proceed from, the most fundamental political controversy: the controversy as to what type of men should rule the community. And the right settlement of that controversy appears to be the basis of excellent legislation.

Classical political philosophy was related to political life directly, because its guiding subject was a subject of actual political controversy carried on in pre-philosophic political life. Since all political controversies presuppose the existence of the political community, the classics are not primarily concerned with the question of whether and why there is, or should be, a political community; hence the question of the nature and purpose of the political community is not the guiding question for classical political philosophy. Similarly, to question the desirability or necessity of the survival and independence of one's political community normally means to commit the crime of treason; in other words, the ultimate aim of foreign policy is not essentially controversial. Hence classical political philosophy is not guided by questions concerning the external relations of the political community. It is concerned primarily with

---

6. Consider Plato, *Laws*, 630b8-c4 and 631d-632d, and Aristotle, *Nicomachean Ethics*, 1180a33 ff. and 1109b34 ff. as well as *Politics*, 1297b37-38; cf. Isocrates, *To Nicocles* 6 and Montesquieu, *Esprit des Lois*, beginning of the 29th book. On the difference between political science proper and political skill see Thomas Aquinas' commentary on Aristotle's *Ethics*, VI, lectio 7, and also Fārābī's *Enumeration of the Sciences*, Chapter 5.

7. Not to mention the fact that the authors of the *Politics* and the *Cyropaedia* were "strangers" when they wrote those books. Cf. *Politics*, 1273b27-32.

the inner structure of the political community, because that inner structure is essentially the subject of such political controversy as essentially involves the danger of civil war.[8]

The actual conflict of groups struggling for political power within the community naturally gives rise to the question what group should rule, or what compromise would be the best solution—that is to say, what political order would be the best order. Either the opposed groups are merely factions made up of the same type of men (such as parties of noblemen or adherents of opposed dynasties), or each of the opposed groups represents a specific type. Only in the latter case does the political struggle go to the roots of political life; then it becomes apparent to everyone, from everyday political life, that the question as to what type of men should have the decisive say is the subject of the most fundamental political controversy.

The immediate concern of that controversy is the best political order for the given political community, but every answer to that immediate question implies an answer to the universal question of the best political order as such. It does not require the exertions of philosophers to lay bare this implication, for the political controversy has a natural tendency to express itself in universal terms. A man who rejects kingship for Israel cannot help using arguments against kingship as such; a man who defends democracy in Athens cannot help using arguments in favor of democracy as such. When they are confronted with the fact that monarchy is the best political order, say, for Babylon, the natural reaction of such men will be that this fact shows the inferiority of Babylon and not that the question of the best political order does not make sense.

The groups, or types, whose claims to rule were considered by the classical philosophers were "the good" (men of merit), the rich, the noble, and the multitude, or the poor citizens; in the foreground of the political scene in the Greek cities, as well as in other places, was the struggle between the rich and the poor. The claim to rule which is based on merit, on human excellence, on "virtue," appeared to be least controversial: courageous and skilful generals, incorruptible and equitable judges, wise and unselfish magistrates, are generally preferred. Thus "aristocracy" (rule of

8. Aristotle, *Politics*, 1300b36-39; Rousseau, *Contrat social*, ii, 9.

the best) presented itself as the natural answer of all good men
to the natural question of the best political order. As Thomas
Jefferson put it, "That form of government is the best, which
provides the most effectually for a pure selection of [the] natural
aristoi into offices of the government."[9]

What is to be understood by "good men" was known also from
political life: good men are those who are willing, and able, to
prefer the common interest to their private interest and to the
objects of their passions, or those who, being able to discern in
each situation what is the noble or right thing to do, do it because
it is noble and right and for no ulterior reason. It was also generally recognized that this answer gives rise to further questions
of almost overwhelming political significance: that results which
are generally considered desirable can be achieved by men of
dubious character or by the use of unfair means; that "just" and
"useful" are not simply identical; that virtue may lead to ruin.[10]

Thus the question guiding classical political philosophy, the
typical answer that it gave, and the insight into the bearing of
the formidable objections to it, belong to pre-philosophic political
life, or precede political philosophy. Political philosophy goes
beyond pre-philosophic political knowledge by trying to understand fully the implications of these pre-philosophic insights, and
especially by defending the second of them against the more or
less "sophisticated" attacks made by bad or perplexed men.

When the pre-philosophic answer is accepted, the most urgent
question concerns the "materials" and institutions which would
be most favorable to "the rule of the best." It is primarily by
answering this question, by thus elaborating a "blueprint" of the
best polity, that the political philosopher becomes the teacher of
legislators. The legislator is strictly limited in his choice of institutions and laws by the character of the people for whom he legislates, by their traditions, by the nature of their territory, by their
economic conditions, and so on. His choosing this or that law is
normally a compromise between what he would wish and what
circumstances permit. To effect that compromise intelligently, he
must first know what he wishes, or, rather, what would be most

---

9. Letter to John Adams, October 28, 1813.

10. See Aristotle, *Nicomachean Ethics*, 1094b18 ff.; Xenophon, *Memorabilia*,
IV 2, 32 ff.

desirable in itself. The political philosopher can answer that question because he is not limited in his reflections by any particular set of circumstances, but is free to choose the most favorable conditions that are possible—ethnic, climatic, economic and other—and thus to determine what laws and institutions would be preferable under those conditions.[11] After that, he tries to bridge the gulf between what is most desirable in itself and what is possible in given circumstances, by discussing what polity, and what laws, would be best under various types of more or less unfavorable conditions, and even what kinds of laws and measures are appropriate for preserving any kind of polity, however defective. By thus erecting on the "normative" foundation of political science a "realistic" structure, or, to speak somewhat more adequately, by thus supplementing political physiology with political pathology and therapeutics, he does not retract or even qualify, he rather confirms, his view that the question of the best polity is necessarily the guiding question.[12]

By the best political order the classical philosopher understood that political order which is best always and everywhere.[13] This does not mean that he conceived of that order as necessarily good for every community, as "a perfect solution for all times and for every place": a given community may be so rude or so depraved that only a very inferior type of order can "keep it going." But it does mean that the goodness of the political order realized anywhere and at any time can be judged only in terms of that political order which is best absolutely. "The best political order" is, then, not intrinsically Greek: it is no more intrinsically Greek than health, as is shown by the parallelism of political science and medicine. But just as it may happen that the members of one nation are more likely to be healthy and strong than those of others, it may also happen that one nation has a greater natural fitness for political excellence than others.

When Aristotle asserted that the Greeks had a greater natural fitness for political excellence than the nations of the north and those of Asia, he did not assert, of course, that political excellence

---

11. See Aristotle, *Politics*, 1265a17 ff. and 1325b33-40; Plato, *Laws*, 857e8-858c3; Cicero, *Republic*, I, 33.

12. See Plato, *Laws*, 739b8 ff., and the beginning of the fourth book of Aristotle's *Politics*.

13. Aristotle, *Nicomachean Ethics*, 1135a4-5.

was identical with the quality of being Greek or derivative from it; otherwise he could not have praised the institutions of Carthage as highly as the institutions of the most renowned Greek cities. When Socrates asked Glaucon in the *Republic* whether the city that Glaucon was founding would be a Greek city, and Glaucon answered emphatically in the affirmative, neither of them said any more than that a city founded by Greeks would necessarily be a Greek city. The purpose of this truism, or rather of Socrates' question, was to induce the warlike Glaucon to submit to a certain moderation of warfare: since a general prohibition of wars was not feasible, at least warfare among Greeks should keep within certain limits. The fact that a perfect city founded by Glaucon would be a Greek city does not imply that any perfect city was necessarily Greek: Socrates considered it possible that the perfect city, which certainly did not exist at that time anywhere in Greece, existed at that time "in some barbarian place."[14] Xenophon went so far as to describe the Persian Cyrus as *the* perfect ruler, and to imply that the education Cyrus received in Persia was superior even to Spartan education; and he did not consider it impossible that a man of the rank of Socrates would emerge among the Armenians.[15]

Because of its direct relation to political life classical political philosophy was essentially "practical"; on the other hand, it is no accident that modern political philosophy frequently calls itself political "theory."[16] The primary concern of the former was not the description, or understanding, of political life, but its right guidance. Hegel's demand that political philosophy refrain from construing a state as it ought to be, or from teaching the state how it should be, and that it try to understand the present and actual state as something essentially rational, amounts to a rejection of the *raison d'être* of classical political philosophy. In contrast with present-day political science, or with well-known interpretations of present-day political science, classical political

---

14. Plato, *Republic*, 427c2-3, 470e4 ff. and 499c7-9; see also *Laws*, 739c3 (compare *Republic*, 373e, with *Phaedo*, 66c5-7); also *Theaetetus*, 175a1-5, *Politicus*, 262c8-263a1, *Cratylus*, 390a, *Phaedo*, 78a3-5, and *Laws*, 656d-657b and 799a ff.; also *Minos*, 316d.

15. *Cyropaedia*, I 1 and 2, III 1, 38-40; compare II 2, 26.

16. Hegel, *Vorlesungen ueber die Geschichte der Philosophie*, ed. Michelet-Glockner, I, 291: "Wir werden ueberhaupt die praktische Philosophie nicht spekulativ werden sehen, bis auf die neuesten Zeiten." Cf. Schelling, *Studium Generale*, ed. Glockner, 94-95.

philosophy pursued practical aims and was guided by, and cul-
minated in, "value judgments." The attempt to replace the quest
for the best political order by a purely descriptive or analytical
political science which refrains from "value judgments" is, from
the point of view of the classics, as absurd as the attempt to replace
the art of making shoes, that is, good and well-fitting shoes, by
a museum of shoes made by apprentices, or as the idea of a medicine
which refuses to distinguish between health and sickness.

Since political controversies are concerned with "good things"
and "just things," classical political philosophy was naturally guided
by considerations of "goodness" and "justice." It started from the
moral distinctions as they are made in everyday life, although it
knew better than the dogmatic skeptic of our time the formidable
theoretical objections to which they are exposed. Such distinctions
as those between courage and cowardice, justice and injustice,
human kindness and selfishness, gentleness and cruelty, urbanity
and rudeness, are intelligible and clear for all practical purposes,
that is, in most cases, and they are of decisive importance in guiding
our lives: this is a sufficient reason for considering the fundamental
political questions in their light.

In the sense in which these distinctions are politically relevant,
they cannot be "demonstrated," they are far from being perfectly
lucid, and they are exposed to grave theoretical doubts. Accordingly, classical political philosophy limited itself to addressing
men who, because of their natural inclinations as well as their
upbringing, took those distinctions for granted. It knew that one
can perhaps silence but not truly convince such people as have
no "taste" for the moral distinctions and their significance: not
even Socrates himself could convert, though he could silence, such
men as Meletus and Callicles, and he admitted the limits set to
demonstrations in this sphere by taking recourse to "myths."

The political teaching of the classical philosophers, as distinguished from their theoretical teaching, was primarily addressed
not to all intelligent men, but to all decent men.[17] A political teaching which addressed itself equally to decent and indecent men
would have appeared to them from the outset as unpolitical, that
is, as politically, or socially, irresponsible; for if it is true that

17. See Aristotle, *Nicomachean Ethics*, 1095b4-6 and 1140b13-18; Cicero,
Laws, I, 37-39.

the well-being of the political community requires that its members be guided by considerations of decency or morality, the political community cannot tolerate a political science which is morally "neutral" and which therefore tends to loosen the hold of moral principles on the minds of those who are exposed to it. To express the same view somewhat differently, even if it were true that when men are talking of right they are thinking only of their interests, it would be equally true that that reserve is of the essence of political man, and that by emancipating oneself from it one would cease to be a political man or to speak his language.

Thus the attitude of classical political philosophy toward political things was always akin to that of the enlightened statesman; it was not the attitude of the detached observer who looks at political things in the way in which a zoologist looks at the big fishes swallowing the small ones, or that of the social "engineer" who thinks in terms of manipulating or conditioning rather than in terms of education or liberation, or that of the prophet who believes that he knows the future.

In brief, the root of classical political philosophy was the fact that political life is characterized by controversies between groups struggling for power within the political community. Its purpose was to settle those political controversies which are of a fundamental and typical character in the spirit not of the partisan but of the good citizen, and with a view to such an order as would be most in accordance with the requirements of human excellence. Its guiding subject was the most fundamental politically controversial subject, understood in the way, and in the terms, in which it was understood in pre-philosophic political life.

In order to perform his function the philosopher had to raise an ulterior question which is never raised in the political arena. That question is so simple, elementary and unobtrusive that it is, at first, not even intelligible, as is shown by a number of occurrences described in the Platonic dialogues. This distinctly philosophic question is "What is virtue?" What is that virtue whose possession—as everyone admits spontaneously or is reduced to silence by unanswerable arguments—gives a man the highest right to rule? In the light of this question the common opinions about virtue appear at the outset as unconscious attempts to answer an unconscious question. On closer examination their radical insufficiency is more specifically revealed by the fact that some of them are contradicted by other opinions which are equally common. To reach consistency the philosopher is compelled to maintain one part of common opinion and to give up the other part which contradicts it; he is thus driven to adopt a view that is no longer generally held, a truly paradoxical view, one that is generally considered "absurd" or "ridiculous."

Nor is that all. He is ultimately compelled to transcend not merely the dimension of common opinion, of political opinion, but the dimension of political life as such; for he is led to realize that the ultimate aim of political life cannot be reached by political life, but only by a life devoted to contemplation, to philosophy. This finding is of crucial importance for political philosophy, since it determines the limits set to political life, to all political action and all political planning. Moreover, it implies that the highest subject of political philosophy is the philosophic life: philosophy—not as a teaching or as a body of knowledge, but as a way of life—offers, as it were, the solution to the problem that keeps political life in motion. Ultimately, political philosophy transforms itself into a discipline that is no longer concerned with political things in the ordinary sense of the term: Socrates called his inquiries a quest for "the *true* political skill," and Aristotle called his discussion of virtue and related subjects "a *kind* of political science."[18]

No difference between classical political philosophy and modern political philosophy is more telling than this: the philosophic life, or the life of "the wise," which was the highest subject of classical political philosophy, has in modern times almost completely ceased to be a subject of political philosophy. Yet even this ultimate step of classical political philosophy, however absurd it seemed to the common opinion, was nevertheless "divined" by pre-philosophic political life: men wholly devoted to the political life were sometimes popularly considered "busybodies," and their unresting habits were contrasted with the greater freedom and the higher dignity of the more retired life of men who were "minding their own business."[19]

---

18. Plato, *Gorgias*, 521d7; Aristotle, *Nicomachean Ethics*, 1094b11 and 1130b26-29 (*Rhetoric*, 1356a25 f.).
19. Aristotle, *Nicomachean Ethics*, 1142a1-2 (compare 1177a25 ff.), and *Metaphysics*, 982b25-28; Plato, *Republic*, 620c4-7 and 549c2 ff., and *Theaetetus*, 172c8 ff. and 173c8 ff. See also Xenophon, *Memorabilia*, I 2, 47 ff. and II 9, 1.

The direct relation of classical political philosophy to pre-philo-sophic political life was due not to the undeveloped character of classical philosophy or science, but to mature reflection. This reflection is summed up in Aristotle's description of political philos-ophy as "the philosophy concerning the human things." This description reminds us of the almost overwhelming difficulty which had to be overcome before philosophers could devote any serious attention to political things, to human things. The "human things" were distinguished from the "divine things" or the "natural things," and the latter were considered absolutely superior in dignity to the former.[20] Philosophy, therefore, was at first exclusively concerned with the natural things. Thus, in the beginning, philosophic effort was concerned only negatively, only accidentally, with political things. Socrates himself, the founder of political philosophy, was famous as a philosopher before he ever turned to political philos-ophy. Left to themselves, the philosophers would not descend again to the "cave" of political life, but would remain outside in what they considered "the island of the blessed"—contemplation of the truth.[21]

But philosophy, being an attempt to rise from opinion to science, is necessarily related to the sphere of opinion as its essential starting point, and hence to the political sphere. Therefore the political sphere is bound to advance into the focus of philosophic interest as soon as philosophy starts to reflect on its own doings. To under-stand fully its own purpose and nature, philosophy has to under-stand its essential starting-point, and hence the nature of political things.

The philosophers, as well as other men who have become aware of the possibility of philosophy, are sooner or later driven to wonder "Why philosophy?" Why does human life need philos-ophy, why is it good, why is it right, that opinions about the nature of the whole should be replaced by genuine knowledge of the nature of the whole? Since human life is living together or, more

<hr>

20. Aristotle, *Nicomachean Ethics*, 1181b15, 1141a20-b9, 1155b2 ff., and 1177b30 ff. Compare the typical disagreement between the philosopher and the legislator in Plato's *Laws*, 804b5-c1, with his *Meno*, 94e3-4, and *Apologia Socratis*, 23a6-7 (also *Republic*, 517d4-5, *Theaetetus*, 175c5, and *Politicus*, 267e9 ff.). Compare also Xenophon, *Memorabilia*, I 1, 11-16, and Seneca, *Naturales Quaestiones*, I, beginning.
21. Plato, *Republic*, 519b7-d7; compare *ibid.*, 521b7-10.

exactly, is political life, the question "Why philosophy?" means "Why does political life need philosophy?" This question calls philosophy before the tribunal of the political community: it makes philosophy politically responsible. Like Plato's perfect city itself, which, once established, does not permit the philosophers to devote themselves any longer exclusively to contemplation, this question, once raised, forbids the philosophers any longer to disregard political life altogether. Plato's *Republic* as a whole, as well as other political works of the classical philosophers, can best be described as an attempt to supply a political justification for philosophy by showing that the well-being of the political community depends decisively on the study of philosophy. Such a justification was all the more urgent since the meaning of philosophy was by no means generally understood, and hence philosophy was distrusted and hated by many well-meaning citizens.[22] Socrates himself fell victim to the popular prejudice against philosophy.

To justify philosophy before the tribunal of the political community means to justify philosophy in terms of the political community, that is to say, by means of a kind of argument which appeals not to philosophers as such, but to citizens as such. To prove to citizens that philosophy is permissible, desirable or even necessary, the philosopher has to follow the example of Odysseus and start from premises that are generally agreed upon, or from generally accepted opinions:[23] he has to argue *ad hominem* or "dialectically." From this point of view the adjective "political" in the expression "political philosophy" designates not so much a subject matter as a manner of treatment;[24] from this point of view, I say, "political philosophy" means primarily not the philosophic treatment of politics, but the political, or popular, treatment of philosophy, or the political introduction to philosophy—the attempt

---

22. Plato, *Republic,* 520b2-3 and 494a4-10, *Phaedo,* 64b, and *Apologia Socratis,* 23d1-7. Compare Cicero, *Tusculanae disputationes,* II 1, 4, and *De officiis,* II 1, 2, and Plutarch, *Nicias,* 23.

23. Xenophon, *Memorabilia,* IV 6, 15.

24. Aristotle, *Politics,* 1275b25 (compare J. F. Gronovius' note to Grotius, *De jure belli,* Prolegomena, § 44) and *Nicomachean Ethics,* 1171a15-20; Polybius, v 33.5; see also Locke, *Essay Concerning Human Understanding,* III, 9, §§ 3 and 22. Note especially the derogatory meaning of "political" in the term "political virtue": Plato, *Phaedo,* 82a10 ff., and *Republic,* 430c3-5, and Aristotle, *Nicomachean Ethics,* 1116a17 ff.

to lead the qualified citizens, or rather their qualified sons, from the political life to the philosophic life. This deeper meaning of "political philosophy" tallies well with its ordinary meaning, for in both cases "political philosophy" culminates in praise of the philosophic life. At any rate, it is ultimately because he means to justify philosophy before the tribunal of the political community, and hence on the level of political discussion, that the philosopher has to understand the political things exactly as they are understood in political life.

In his political philosophy the philosopher starts, then, from that understanding of political things which is natural to pre-philosophic political life. At the beginning the fact that a certain habitual attitude or a certain way of acting is generally praised, is a sufficient reason for considering that attitude, or that way of acting, a virtue. But the philosopher is soon compelled, or able, to transcend the dimension of pre-philosophic understanding by raising the crucial question "What is virtue?" The attempt to answer this question leads to a critical distinction between the generally praised attitudes which are rightly praised, and those which are not; and it leads to the recognition of a certain hierarchy, unknown in pre-philosophic life, of the different virtues. Such a philosophic critique of the generally accepted views is at the bottom of the fact that Aristotle, for example, omitted piety and sense of shame from his list of virtues,[25] and that his list starts with courage and moderation (the least intellectual virtues) and, proceeding via liberality, magnanimity and the virtues of private relations, to justice, culminates in the dianoetic virtues.[26] Moreover, insight into the limits of the moral-political sphere as a whole can be expounded fully only by answering the question of the nature of political things. This question marks the limit of political philosophy as a practical discipline: while essentially practical in itself, the question functions as an entering wedge for others whose purpose is no longer to guide action but simply to understand things as they are.[27]

25. *Eudemian Ethics*, 1221a1.
26. *Nicomachean Ethics*, 1117b23 ff., and *Rhetoric*, I 5, 6. See also Plato, *Laws*, 630c ff. and 963e, and *Phaedrus*, 247d5-7; Xenophon, *Memorabilia*, IV 8, 11 (compare his *Apologia Socratis*, 14-16); Thomas Aquinas, *Summa theologica*, 2, 2, qu. 129 art. 2 and qu. 58 art. 12.
27. See, for example, Aristotle, *Politics*, 1258b8 ff., 1279b11 ff., and 1299a28 ff.

IV

RESTATEMENT
ON XENOPHON'S
HIERO

A social science that cannot speak of tyranny with the same confidence with which medicine speaks, for example, of cancer, cannot understand social phenomena as what they are. It is therefore not scientific. Present day social science finds itself in this condition. If it is true that present day social science is the inevitable result of modern social science and of modern philosophy, one is forced to think of the restoration of classical social science. Once we have learned again from the classics what tyranny is, we shall be enabled and compelled to diagnose as tyrannies a number of contemporary regimes which appear in the guise of dictatorships. This diagnosis can only be the first step toward an exact analysis of present day tyranny, for present day tyranny is fundamentally different from the tyranny analyzed by the classics.

But is this not tantamount to admitting that the classics were wholly unfamiliar with tyranny in its contemporary form? Must one not therefore conclude that the classical concept of tyranny is too narrow and hence that the classical frame of reference must be radically modified, i.e., abandoned? In other words, is the

attempt to restore classical social science not utopian since it
implies that the classical orientation has not been made obsolete
by the triumph of the biblical orientation?

This seems to be the chief objection to which my study of
Xenophon's *Hiero* is exposed. At any rate, this is the gist of the
only criticisms of my study from which one could learn anything.
Those criticisms were written in complete independence of each
other and their authors, Professor Eric Voegelin and M. Alexandre
Kojève, have, so to speak, nothing in common. Before discussing
their arguments, I must restate my contention.

The fact that there is a fundamental difference between classical tyranny and present day tyranny, or that the classics did not
even dream of present day tyranny, is not a good or sufficient reason for abandoning the classical frame of reference. For that fact
is perfectly compatible with the possibility that present day tyranny
finds its place within the classical framework, i.e., that it cannot
be understood adequately except within the classical framework.
The difference between present day tyranny and classical tyranny
has its root in the difference between the modern notion of philosophy or science and the classical notion of philosophy or science.
Present day tyranny, in contradistinction to classical tyranny, is
based on the unlimited progress in the "conquest of nature" which
is made possible by modern science, as well as on the popularization
or diffusion of philosophic or scientific knowledge. Both possibilities—the possibility of a science that issues in the conquest of
nature and the possibility of the popularization of philosophy or
science—were known to the classics. (Compare Xenophon, *Memorabilia* I 1.15 with Empedocles, fr. 111; Plato, *Theaetetus* 180c7-d5.)
But the classics rejected them as "unnatural," i.e., as destructive
of humanity. They did not dream of present day tyranny because
they regarded its basic presuppositions as so preposterous that they
turned their imagination in entirely different directions.

Voegelin, one of the leading contemporary historians of political thought, seems to contend (*The Review of Politics*, 1949, pp.
241-244) that the classical concept of tyranny is too narrow because it does not cover the phenomenon known as Caesarism: when
calling a given regime tyrannical, we imply that "constitutional"
government is a viable alternative to it; but Caesarism emerges only
after "the final breakdown of the republican constitutional order";

hence, Caesarism or "post-constitutional" rule cannot be understood as a subdivision of tyranny in the classical sense of tyranny. There is no reason to quarrel with the view that genuine Caesarism is not tyranny, but this does not justify the conclusion that Caesarism is incomprehensible on the basis of classical political philosophy: Caesarism is still a sub-division of absolute monarchy as the classics understood it. If in a given situation "the republican constitutional order" has completely broken down, and there is no reasonable prospect of its restoration within all the foreseeable future, the establishment of permanent absolute rule cannot, as such, be justly blamed; therefore, it is fundamentally different from the establishment of tyranny. Just blame could attach only to the manner in which that permanent absolute rule that is truly necessary is established and exercised; as Voegelin emphasizes, there are tyrannical as well as royal Caesars. One has only to read Coluccio Salutati's defense of Caesar against the charge that he was a tyrant—a defense which in all essential points is conceived in the spirit of the classics— in order to see that the distinction between Caesarism and tyranny fits perfectly into the classical framework.

But the phenomenon of Caesarism is one thing, the current concept of Caesarism is another. The current concept of Caesarism is certainly incompatible with classical principles. The question thus arises whether the current concept or the classical concept is more nearly adequate. More particularly, the question concerns the validity of the two implications of the current concept which Voegelin seems to regard as indispensable, and which originated in 19th century historicism. In the first place, he seems to believe that the difference between "the constitutional situation" and "the post-constitutional situation" is more fundamental than the difference between the good king or the good Caesar on the one hand, and the bad king or the bad Caesar on the other. But is not the difference between good and bad the most fundamental of all practical or political distinctions? Secondly, Voegelin seems to believe that "post-constitutional" rule is not per se inferior to "constitutional" rule. But is not "post-constitutional" rule justified by necessity or, as Voegelin says, by "historical necessity"? And is not the necessary essentially inferior to the noble or to what is choiceworthy for its own sake? Necessity excuses: what is justified by necessity is in need of excuse. The Caesar, as Voegelin conceives of him, is "the

avenger of the misdeeds of a corrupt people." Caesarism is then
essentially related to a corrupt people, to a low level of political
life, to a decline of society. It presupposes the decline, if not the
extinction, of civic virtue or of public spirit, and it necessarily per-
petuates that condition. Caesarism belongs to a degraded society, and
it thrives on its degradation. Caesarism is just, whereas tyranny is
unjust. But Caesarism is just in the way in which deserved punishment is just. It is as little choiceworthy for its own sake as is deserved
punishment. Cato refused to see what his time demanded because he
saw too clearly the degraded and degrading character of what his
time demanded. It is much more important to realize the low level of
Caesarism (for, to repeat, Caesarism cannot be divorced from the
society which deserves Caesarism) than to realize that under certain
conditions Caesarism is necessary and hence legitimate.

While the classics were perfectly capable of doing justice to
the merits of Caesarism, they were not particularly concerned with
elaborating a doctrine of Caesarism. Since they were primarily concerned with the best regime, they paid less attention to "post-constitutional" rule, or to late kingship, than to "pre-constitutional"
rule, or to early kingship: rustic simplicity is a better soil for the
good life than is sophisticated rottenness. But there was another
reason which induced the classics to be almost silent about "post-
constitutional" rule. To stress the fact that it is just to replace
constitutional rule by absolute rule, if the common good requires
that change, means to cast a doubt on the absolute sanctity of the
established constitutional order. It means encouraging dangerous
men to confuse the issue by bringing about a state of affairs in
which the common good requires the establishment of their absolute rule. The true doctrine of the legitimacy of Caesarism is a
dangerous doctrine. The true distinction between Caesarism and
tyranny is too subtle for ordinary political use. It is better for the
people to remain ignorant of that distinction and to regard the
potential Caesar as a potential tyrant. No harm can come from this
theoretical error which becomes a practical truth if the people have
the mettle to act upon it. No harm can come from the political
identification of Caesarism and tyranny: Caesars can take care of
themselves.

The classics could easily have elaborated a doctrine of Caesarism
or of late kingship if they had wanted, but they did not want to do

it. Voegelin however contends that they were forced by their historical situation to grope for a doctrine of Caesarism, and that they failed to discover it. He tries to substantiate his contention by referring to Xenophon and to Plato. As for Plato, Voegelin was forced by considerations of space to limit himself to a summary reference to the royal ruler in the *Statesman*. As for Xenophon, he rightly asserts that it is not sufficient to oppose "the *Cyropaedia* as a mirror of the perfect king to the *Hiero* as a mirror of the tyrant," since the perfect king Cyrus and the improved tyrant who is described by Simonides "look much more opposed to each other than they really are." He explains this fact by suggesting that "both works fundamentally face the same historical problem of the new [*sc.* post-constitutional] rulership," and that one cannot solve this problem except by obliterating at the first stage, the distinction between king and tyrant. To justify this explanation he contends that "the very motivation of the *Cyropaedia* is the search for a stable rule that will make an end to the dreary overturning of democracies and tyrannies in the Hellenic polis." This contention is not supported by what Xenophon says or indicates in regard to the intention of the *Cyropaedia*. Its explicit intention is to make intelligible Cyrus' astonishing success in solving the problem of ruling human beings. Xenophon conceives of this problem as one that is coeval with man. Like Plato in the *Statesman*, he does not make the slightest reference to the particular "historical" problem of stable rule in "the post-constitutional situation." In particular, he does not refer to "the dreary over-turning of democracies and tyrannies in the Hellenic polis": he speaks of the frequent overturning of democracies, monarchies and oligarchies and of the essential instability of all tyrannies. As for the implicit intention of the *Cyropaedia*, it is partly revealed by the remark, towards the end of the work, that "after Cyrus died, his sons immediately quarrelled, cities and nations immediately revolted, and all things turned to the worse." If Xenophon was not a fool, he did not intend to present Cyrus' regime as a model. He knew too well that the good order of society requires stability and continuity. (Compare the opening of the *Cyropaedia* with the parallel in the *Agesilaus*, 1. 4.) He rather used Cyrus' meteoric success and the way in which it was brought about as an example for making intelligible the nature of political things. The work which describes Cyrus' whole life is

entitled *The Education of Cyrus*: the education of Cyrus is the
clue to his whole life, to his astonishing success, and hence to Xenophon's intention. A very rough sketch must here suffice. Xenophon's Cyrus was the son of the king of Persia, and until he was
about twelve years old he was educated according to the laws of the
Persians. The laws and the polity of Xenophon's Persians, however,
are an improved version of the laws and polity of the Spartans. The
Persia in which Cyrus was raised was an aristocracy superior to
Sparta. The political activity of Cyrus—his extraordinary success—
consisted in transforming a stable and healthy aristocracy into an
unstable "Oriental despotism" whose rottenness showed itself at
the latest immediately after his death. The first step in this transformation was a speech which Cyrus addressed to the Persian nobles and
in which he convinced them that they ought to deviate from the
habit of their ancestors by practicing virtue no longer for its own
sake, but for the sake of its rewards. The destruction of aristocracy
begins, as one would expect, with the corruption of its principle.
(*Cyropaedia* I 5.5-14; compare Aristotle, *Eudemian Ethics* 1248b
38 ff., where the view of virtue which Xenophon's Cyrus instills
into the minds of the Persian gentlemen is described as the Spartan
view.) The quick success of Cyrus' first action forces the reader
to wonder whether the Persian aristocracy was a genuine aristocracy; or more precisely, whether the gentleman in the political or
social sense is a true gentleman. This question is identical with the
question which Plato answers explicitly in the negative in his story
of Er. Socrates says outright that a man who has lived in his former life in a well-ordered regime, participating in virtue by habit
and without philosophy, will choose for his next life "the greatest
tyranny," for "mostly people make their choice according to the
habits of their former life" (*Republic* 619b6-620a3). There is no
adequate solution to the problem of virtue or happiness on the
political or social plane. Still, while aristocracy is always on the
verge of declining into oligarchy or something worse, it is the best
possible political solution of the human problem. It must here suffice
to note that Cyrus' second step is the democratization of the army,
and that the end of the process is a regime that might seem barely
distinguishable from the least intolerable form of tyranny. But one
must not overlook the essential difference between Cyrus' rule and
tyranny, a distinction that is never obliterated. Cyrus is and re-

mains a legitimate ruler. He is born as the legitimate heir to the reigning king, a scion of an old royal house. He becomes the king of other nations through inheritance or marriage and through just conquest, for he enlarges the boundaries of Persia in the Roman manner: by defending the allies of Persia. The difference between Cyrus and a Hiero educated by Simonides is comparable to the difference between William III and Oliver Cromwell. A cursory comparison of the history of England with the history of certain other European nations suffices to show that this difference is not unimportant to the well-being of peoples. Xenophon did not even attempt to obliterate the distinction between the best tyrant and the king because he appreciated too well the charms, nay, the blessings of legitimacy. He expressed this appreciation by subscribing to the maxim (which must be reasonably understood and applied) that the just is identical with the legal.

Voegelin might reply that what is decisive is not Xenophon's conscious intention, stated or implied, but the historical meaning of his work, the historical meaning of a work being determined by the historical situation as distinguished from the conscious intention of the author. Yet opposing the historical meaning of Xenophon's work to his conscious intention, implies that we are better judges of the situation in which Xenophon thought than Xenophon himself was. But we cannot be better judges of that situation if we do not have a clearer grasp than he had of the principles in whose light historical situations reveal their meaning. After the experience of our generation, the burden of proof would seem to rest on those who assert rather than on those who deny that we have progressed beyond the classics. And even if it were true that we could understand the classics better than they understood themselves, we would become certain of our superiority only after understanding them exactly as they understood themselves. Otherwise we might mistake our superiority to our notion of the classics for superiority to the classics.

According to Voegelin, it was Machiavelli, as distinguished from the classics, who "achieved the theoretical creation of a concept of rulership in the post-constitutional situation," and this achievement was due to the influence on Machiavelli of the Biblical tradition. He refers especially to Machiavelli's remark about the "armed prophets" (*Prince* VI). The difficulty to which Voegelin's contention is exposed is indicated by these two facts: he speaks on the one hand of "the apocalyptic [hence thoroughly non-classical] aspects of the 'armed prophet' in the *Prince*," whereas on the other hand he says that Machiavelli claimed "for [the] paternity" of the "armed prophet" "besides Romulus, Moses and Theseus, precisely the Xenophontic Cyrus." This amounts to an admission that certainly Machiavelli himself was not aware of any non-classical implication of his notion of "armed prophets." There is nothing unclassical about Romulus, Theseus, and Xenophon's Cyrus. It is true that Machiavelli adds Moses; but, after having made his bow to the Biblical interpretation of Moses, he speaks of Moses in exactly the same manner in which every classical political philosopher would have spoken of him; Moses was one of the greatest legislators or founders (*fondatori*: *Discorsi* I 9) who ever lived. When reading Voegelin's statement on this subject, one receives the impression that in speaking of armed prophets, Machiavelli put the emphasis on "prophets" as distinguished from non-prophetic rulers like Cyrus, for example. But Machiavelli puts the emphasis not on "prophets," but on "armed." He opposes the armed prophets, among whom he counts Cyrus, Romulus and Theseus as well as Moses, to unarmed prophets like Savonarola. He states the lesson which he intends to convey with remarkable candor: "all armed prophets succeed and the unarmed ones come to ruin." It is difficult to believe that in writing this sentence Machiavelli should have been completely oblivious of the most famous of all unarmed prophets. One certainly cannot understand Machiavelli's remark on the "unarmed prophets" without taking into consideration what he says about the "unarmed heaven" and "the effeminacy of the world" which, according to him, are due to Christianity. (*Discorsi* II 2 and III 1.) The tradition which Machiavelli continues, while radically modifying it, is not, as Voegelin suggests, that represented by Joachim of Floris, for example, but the one which we still call, with pardonable ignorance, the Averroistic tradition. Machiavelli declares that Savonarola, that unarmed prophet, was right in saying that the ruin of Italy was caused by "our sins," "but our sins were not what he believed they were," namely, religious sins, "but those which I have narrated," namely, political or military sins (*Prince* XII). In the same vein Maimonides declares that the ruin of the Jewish kingdom was caused by the "sins of our fathers," namely, by their idolatry; but idolatry worked its effect in a perfectly natural manner: it led to astrology and thus induced the Jewish people to devote themselves to astrology instead of to the practice of the arts of war and the conquest of countries. But apart from all this, Voegelin does not give any indication of what the armed prophets have to do with "the post-constitutional situation." Certainly Romulus, Theseus and Moses were "pre-constitutional" rulers. Voegelin also refers to "Machiavelli's complete drawing of the savior prince in the *Vita di Castruccio Castracani*" which, he says, "is hardly thinkable without the standardized model of the *Life of Timur.*" Apart from the fact that Voegelin has failed to show any connection between the *Castruccio* and the *Life of Timur* and between the *Life of Timur* and the Biblical tradition, the *Castruccio* is perhaps the most impressive document of Machiavelli's longing for classical *virtù* as distinguished from, and opposed to, Biblical righteousness. Castruccio, that idealized condottiere who preferred in so single-minded a manner the life of the soldier to the life of the priest, is compared by Machiavelli himself to Philip of Macedon and to Scipio of Rome.

Machiavelli's longing for classical *virtù* is only the reverse side of his rejection of classical political philosophy. He rejects classical political philosophy because of its orientation by the perfection of the nature of man. The abandonment of the contemplative ideal leads to a radical change in the character of wisdom: Machiavellian wisdom has no necessary connection with moderation. Machiavelli separates wisdom from moderation. The ultimate reason why the *Hiero* comes so close to the *Prince* is that in the *Hiero* Xenophon experiments with a type of wisdom which comes relatively close to a wisdom divorced from moderation: Simonides seems to have an inordinate desire for the pleasures of the table. It is impossible to say how far the epoch-making change that was effected by Machiavelli is due to the indirect influence of the Biblical tradition, before that change has been fully understood in itself.

The peculiar character of the *Hiero* does not disclose itself to cursory reading. It will not disclose itself to the tenth reading, however painstaking, if the reading is not productive of a change of orientation. This change was much easier to achieve for the 18th century reader than for the reader in our century who has been brought up on the brutal and sentimental literature of the last five generations. We are in need of a second education in order to accustom our eyes to the noble reserve and the quiet grandeur of the classics. Xenophon, as it were, limited himself to cultivating exclusively that character of classical writing which is wholly foreign to the modern reader. No wonder that he is today despised or ignored. An unknown ancient critic, who must have been a man of uncommon discernment, called him most bashful. Those modern readers who are so fortunate as to have a natural preference for Jane Austen rather than for Dostoievski, in particular, have an easier access to Xenophon than others might have; to understand Xenophon, they have only to combine the love of philosophy with their natural preference. In the words of Xenophon, "it is both noble and just, and pious and more pleasant to remember the good things rather than the bad ones." In the *Hiero*, Xenophon experimented with the pleasure that comes from remembering bad things, with a pleasure that admittedly is of doubtful morality and piety.

For someone who is trying to form his taste or his mind by studying Xenophon, it is almost shocking to be suddenly confronted by the more than Machiavellian bluntness with which Kojève speaks of such terrible things as atheism and tyranny and takes them for granted. At least on one occasion he goes so far as to call "unpopular" certain measures which the very tyrant Hiero had declared to be criminal. He does not hesitate to proclaim that present day dictators are tyrants without regarding this in the least as an objection to their rule. As for reverence for legitimacy, he has none. But the nascent shock is absorbed by the realization, or rather the knowledge of long standing, that Kojève belongs to the very few who know how to think and who love to think. He does not belong to the many who today are unabashed atheists and more than Byzantine flatterers of tyrants for the same reason for which they would have been addicted to the grossest superstitions, both religious and legal, had they lived in an earlier age. In a word, Kojève is a philosopher and not an intellectual.

Since he is a philosopher, he knows that the philosopher is, in principle, more capable of ruling than other men and hence will be regarded by a tyrant like Hiero as a most dangerous competitor for tyrannical rule. It would not occur to him for a moment to compare the relationship between Hiero and Simonides with the relationship, say, between Stefan George or Thomas Mann and

Hitler. For, to say nothing of considerations too obvious to be mentioned, he could not overlook the obvious fact that the *hypothesis* of the *Hiero* demanded a tyrant of whom it was at least imaginable that he could be taught. In particular, he knows without having to be reminded of the *Seventh Letter* that the difference between a philosopher who is a subject of the tyrant and a philosopher who merely visits the tyrant is immaterial as far as the tyrant's fear of philosophers is concerned. His understanding does not permit him to rest satisfied with the vulgar separation of theory from practice. He knows too well that there never was and there never will be reasonable security for sound practice except after theory has overcome the powerful obstacles to sound practice which originate in theoretical misconceptions of a certain kind. Finally, he brushes aside in sovereign contempt the implicit claim of current, i.e., running or heedless thought to have solved the problems that were raised by the classics—a claim that is only implicit because current thought is unaware of the existence of those problems.

Yet while admitting and even stressing the absolute superiority of classical thought to current thought, Kojève rejects the classical solution of the basic problems. He regards unlimited technological progress and universal enlightenment as essential for the genuine satisfaction of what is human in man. He denies that present day social science is the inevitable outcome of modern philosophy. According to him, present day social science is merely the inevitable product of the inevitable decay of that modern philosophy which has refused to learn the decisive lesson from Hegel. He regards Hegel's teaching as the genuine synthesis of Socratic and Machiavellian (or Hobbian) politics, which, as such, is superior to its component elements. In fact, he regards Hegel's teaching as, in principle, the final teaching.

Kojève directs his criticism in the first place against the classical notion of tyranny. Xenophon reveals an important part of that notion by making Hiero answer with silence to Simonides' description of the good tyrant. As Kojève rightly judges, Hiero's silence signifies that he will not attempt to put into practice Simonides' proposals. Kojève suggests, at least provisionally, that this is the fault of Simonides, who did not tell Hiero what the first step is which the tyrant must take in order to transform bad tyranny into good tyranny. But would it not have been up to Hiero if he seriously desired to become a good tyrant, to ask Simonides about the first step? How does Kojève know that Simonides was not waiting in vain for this very question? Or perhaps Simonides has answered it already implicitly. Yet this defense of Simonides is insufficient. The question returns, for, as Kojève again rightly observes, the attempt to realize Simonides' vision of a good tyrant is confronted with an almost insurmountable difficulty. The only question which Hiero raises while Simonides discusses the improvement of tyranny, concerns the mercenaries. Hiero's imperfect tyranny rests on the support of his mercenaries. The improvement of tyranny would require a shift of part of the power from the mercenaries to the citizens. By attempting such a shift, the tyrant would antagonize the mercenaries without being at all certain that he could regain by that concession, or by any concession, the confidence of the citizens. He would end by sitting between two chairs. Simonides seems to disregard this state of things and thus to reveal a poor understanding of Hiero's situation or a lack of wisdom. To save Simonides' reputation, one seems compelled to suggest that the poet himself did not believe in the viability of his improved tyranny, that he regarded the good tyranny as a utopia, or that he rejected tyranny as a hopelessly bad regime. But, Kojève continues, does this suggestion not imply that Simonides' attempt to educate Hiero is futile? And a wise man does not attempt futile things.

This criticism may be said to be based on an insufficient appreciation of the value of utopias. The utopia in the strict sense describes the simply good social order. As such it merely makes explicit what is implied in every attempt at social improvement. There is no difficulty in enlarging the strict meaning of utopia in such a manner that one can speak of the utopia of the best tyranny. As Kojève emphasizes, under certain conditions the abolition of tyranny may be out of the question. The best one could hope for is that the tyranny be improved, i.e., that the tyrannical rule be exercised as little inhumanely or irrationally as possible. Every specific reform or improvement of which a sensible man could think, if reduced to its principle, forms part of the complete picture of the maximum improvement that is still compatible with the continued existence of tyranny, it being understood that the maximum improvement is possible only under the most favorable conditions. The maximum improvement of tyranny would require, above all, the shift of part of the power from the mercenaries to the citizens. Such a shift is not absolutely impossible, but its actualization is safe only in circumstances which man cannot create or which no sensible man would create (e.g., an extreme danger threatening equally the mercenaries and the citizens, like the danger of Syracuse being conquered, and all its inhabitants being put to the sword, by barbarians). A sensible man like Simonides would think that he had deserved well of his fellow men if he could induce the tyrant to act humanely or rationally within a small area, or perhaps even in a single instance, where, without his advice, the tyrant would have continued an inhuman or irrational practice. Xenophon indicates an example: Hiero's participating at the Olympian and Pythian games. If Hiero followed Simonides' advice to abandon this practice, he would improve his standing with his subjects and in the world at large, and he would indirectly benefit his subjects. Xenophon leaves it to the intelligence of his reader to replace that particular example by another one which the reader, on the basis of his particular experience, might consider to be more apt. The general lesson is to the effect that the wise man who happens to have a chance to influence a tyrant should use his influence for benefiting his fellow men. One may say that the lesson is trivial. It would be more accurate to say that it was trivial in former ages, for today such little actions like that of Simonides are not taken seriously because we are in the habit of expecting too much. What is not trivial is what we learn from Xenophon about how the wise man has to proceed in his undertaking, which is beset with great difficulties and even with dangers.

Kojève denies our contention that the good tyranny is a utopia. To substantiate his denial, he mentions one example by name: the rule of Salazar. I have never been to Portugal, but from all that I have heard about that country, I am inclined to believe that Kojève is right, except that I am not quite certain whether Salazar's rule should not be called "post-constitutional" rather than tyrannical. Yet one swallow does not make a summer, and we never denied that good tyranny is possible under very favorable circumstances. But Kojève contends that Salazar is not an exception. He thinks that circumstances favorable to good tyranny are easily available today. He contends that all present day tyrants are good tyrants in Xenophon's sense. He alludes to Stalin. He notes in particular that the tyranny improved according to Simonides' suggestions is characterized by Stakhanovistic emulation. But Stalin's rule would live up to Simonides' standards only if the introduction of Stakhanovistic emulation had been accompanied by a considerable decline in the use of the NKVD or of "labor" camps. Would Kojève go so far as to say that Stalin could travel outside of the Iron Curtain wherever he liked in order to see sights without having anything to fear? (*Hiero* 11.10 and 1.12.) Would Kojève go so far as to say that everyone living behind the Iron Curtain is an ally of Stalin, or that Stalin regards all citizens of Soviet Russia and the other "people's democracies" as his comrades? (*Hiero* 11.11 and 11.14.)

However this may be, Kojève contends that present day tyranny, and perhaps even classical tyranny, cannot be understood on the basis of Xenophon's principles, and that the classical frame of reference must be modified radically by the introduction of an element of Biblical origin. He argues as follows. Simonides maintains that honor is the supreme or sole goal of the tyrant in particular and of the highest type of human being (the Master) in general. This shows that the poet sees only half of the truth. The other half is supplied by the Biblical morality of Slaves or Workers. The actions of men, and hence also the actions of tyrants, can be, and frequently are prompted by desire for the pleasure deriving from the successful execution of their work, their projects, or their ideals. There is such a thing as devotion to one's work, or to a cause, "conscientious" work, into which no thought of honor or glory enters. But this fact must not induce us to minimize hypocritically the essential contribution of the desire for honor or prestige to the completion of man. The desire for prestige, recognition or authority is the primary motive of all political struggles, and in particular of the struggle that leads a man to tyrannical power. It is perfectly unobjectionable for an aspiring statesman or a potential tyrant to try for no other reason than for the sake of his preferment to oust the incumbent ruler or rulers although he knows that he is in no way better equipped for the job than they are. There is no reason to find fault with such a course of action, for the desire for recognition necessarily transforms itself, in all cases which are of any consequence, into devotion to the work to be done or to a cause. The synthesis of the morality of Masters with the morality of Slaves is superior to its component elements.

Simonides is very far from accepting the morality of Masters or from maintaining that honor is the supreme goal of the highest human type. In translating one of the crucial passages (the last sentence of *Hiero* 7.4.), Kojève omits the qualifying *dokei* ("no human pleasure *seems* to come closer to what is divine than the joy concerning honors"). Nor does he pay attention to the implication of the fact that Simonides declares the desire for honor to be the dominating passion of *andres* (whom Kojève calls Masters) as distinguished from *anthropoi* (whom he calls Slaves). For, according to Xenophon, and hence according to his Simonides, the *anēr* is by no means the highest human type. The highest human type is the wise man. An Hegelian will have no difficulty in admitting that, since the wise man is distinguished from the Master, he will have something important in common with the Slave. This was certainly Xenophon's view. In the statement of the Master's principle, which he entrusted to Simonides, the poet cannot help admitting implicitly the unity of the human species which his statement explicitly denies. And the unity of the human species is thought to be more easily seen by the Slave than by the Master. One does not characterize Socrates adequately by calling him a Master. Xenophon contrasts him with Ischomachus, who is the prototype of the *kalos te kagathos anēr*. Since the work and the knowledge which is best for the type represented by Ischomachus is agriculture and Socrates was not an agriculturist, Socrates was not a *kalos te kagathos anēr*. As Lycon explicitly says, Socrates was a *kalos te kagathos anthropos* (*Symposium* 9.1; *Oeconomicus* 6.8, 12). In this context we may note that in the passage of the *Hiero* which deals with gentlemen living under a tyrant (10.3), Simonides characteristically omits *andres: kaloi te kagathoi andres* could not live happily under a tyrant however good (compare *Hiero* 9.6 and 5.1-2). Xenophon indicates his view most succinctly by failing to mention manliness in his two lists of Socrates' virtues. He sees in Socrates' military activity a sign not of his manliness, but of his justice (*Memorabilia* IV 4.1).

Since Xenophon or his Simonides did not believe that honor is the highest good, or since they did not accept the morality of Masters, there is no apparent need for supplementing their teaching by an element taken from the morality of Slaves or Workers. According to the classics, the highest good is a life devoted to wisdom or to virtue, honor being no more than a very pleasant, but secondary and dispensable reward. What Kojève calls the pleasure deriving from doing one's work well or from realizing one's projects or one's ideals, was called by the classics the pleasure deriving from virtuous or noble activity. The classical interpretation would seem to be truer to the facts. Kojève refers to the pleasure which a solitary child or a solitary painter may derive from executing his projects well. But one can easily imagine a solitary safe-cracker deriving pleasure from executing his project well, and without a thought of the external rewards (wealth or admiration of his competence) which he reaps. There are artists in all walks of life. It does make a difference what kind of a "job" is the source of disinterested pleasure: whether the job is criminal or innocent, whether it is mere play or serious, and so on. By thinking through this observation one arrives at the view that the highest kind of job, or the only job that is truly human, is noble or virtuous activity, or noble or virtuous work. If one is fond of this manner of looking at things, one may say that noble work is the synthesis effected by the classics between the morality of workless nobility and the morality of ignoble work (cf. Plato, *Meno* 81d3 ff.).

Simonides is therefore justified in saying that the desire for honor is the supreme motive of men who aspire to tyrannical power. Kojève seems to think that a man may aspire to tyrannical power chiefly because he is attracted by "objective" tasks of the highest order, by tasks whose performance requires tyrannical power, and that this motive will radically transform his desire for honor or recognition. The classics denied that this is possible. They were struck by the similarity between Kojève's tyrant and the man who is more attracted to safecracking by its exciting problems than by its rewards. One cannot become a tyrant and remain a tyrant without stooping to do base things; hence, a self-respecting man will not aspire to tyrannical power. But, Kojève might object, this still does not prove that the tyrant is motivated chiefly or exclusively by a desire for honor or prestige. He may be motivated, e.g., by a misguided desire to benefit his fellow men. This defense would hold good if error in such matters were difficult to avoid. But it is easy to know that tyranny is base; we all learn as children that one must not give others bad examples and that one must not do base things for the sake of the good that may come out of them. The potential or actual tyrant does not know what every reasonably well-bred child knows, because he is blinded by passion. By what passion? The most charitable answer is that he is blinded by desire for honor or prestige.

Syntheses effect miracles. Kojève's or Hegel's synthesis of classical and Biblical morality effects the miracle of producing an amazingly lax morality out of two moralities both of which made very strict demands on self-restraint. Neither Biblical nor classical morality encourages us to try, solely for the sake of our preferment or our glory, to oust from their positions men who do the required work as well as we could. (Consider Aristotle, *Politics* 1271a10-19.) Neither Biblical nor classical morality encourages all statesmen to try to extend their authority over all men in order to achieve universal recognition. It does not seem to be sound that Kojève encourages others by his speech to a course of action to which he himself would never stoop in deed. If he did not suppress his better knowledge, it would be given him to see that there is no need for having recourse to a miracle in order to understand Hegel's moral and political teaching. Hegel continued, and in a certain respect radicalized, the modern tradition that emancipated the passions and hence "competition." That tradition was originated by Machiavelli and perfected by such men as Hobbes and Adam Smith. It came into being through a conscious break with the strict moral demands made by both the Bible and classical philosophy; those demands were explicitly rejected as too strict. Hegel's moral or political teaching is indeed a synthesis: it is a synthesis of Socratic and Machiavellian or Hobbian politics. Kojève knows as well as anyone living that Hegel's fundamental teaching regarding Master and Slave is based on Hobbes's doctrine of the state of nature. If Hobbes's doctrine of the state of nature is abandoned *en pleine connaissance de cause* (as indeed it should be abandoned), Hegel's fundamental teaching will lose the evidence which it apparently still possesses for Kojève. Hegel's teaching is much more sophisticated than Hobbes's, but it is as much a construction as the latter. Both doctrines construct human society by starting from the untrue assumption that man as man is thinkable as a being that lacks awareness of sacred restraints or as a being that is guided by nothing but a desire for recognition.

But Kojève is likely to become somewhat impatient with what,

as I fear, he might call our Victorian or pre-Victorian *niaiseries*.
He probably will maintain that the whole previous discussion is
irrelevant because it is based on a dogmatic assumption. We assume
indeed that the classical concept of tyranny is derived from an
adequate analysis of the fundamental social phenomena. The classics
understand tyranny as the opposite of the best regime, and they
hold that the best regime is the rule of the best or aristocracy. But,
Kojève argues, aristocracy is the rule of a minority over the majority
of citizens or of adult residents of a given territory, a rule that rests,
in the last resort, on force or terror. Would it then not be more
proper to admit that aristocracy is a form of tyranny? Yet Kojève
apparently thinks that force or terror are indispensable in every
regime, while he does not think that all regimes are equally good
or bad and hence equally tyrannical. If I understand him correctly,
he is satisfied that "the universal and homogeneous state" is the
simply best social order. Lest we get entangled in a merely verbal
difficulty, I shall state his view as follows: the universal and homogeneous state is the only one which is essentially just; the aristocracy
of the classics in particular is essentially unjust.

To see the classical view in the proper light, let us make the
assumption that the wise do not desire to rule. The unwise are very
unlikely to force the wise to rule over them. For the wise cannot
rule as wise if they do not have absolute power or if they are
in any way responsible to the unwise. No broil in which the
unwise may find themselves could be great enough to induce them
to surrender absolute control to the wise, whose first measure would
probably be to expel everyone above the age of ten from the city
(Plato, *Republic* 540d-541a). Hence, what pretends to be absolute
rule of the wise will in fact be absolute rule of unwise men. But
if this is the case, the universal state would seem to be impossible.
For the universal state requires universal agreement regarding the
fundamentals, and such agreement is possible only on the basis of
genuine knowledge or of wisdom. Agreement based on opinion can
never become universal agreement. Every faith that lays claim to
universality, i.e., to be universally accepted, of necessity provokes
a counter-faith which raises the same claim. The diffusion among
the unwise of genuine knowledge that was acquired by the wise
would be of no help, for through its diffusion or dilution, knowledge
inevitably transforms itself into opinion, prejudice or mere belief.

The utmost in the direction of universality that one could expect is, then, an absolute rule of unwise men who control about half of the globe, the other half being ruled by other unwise men. It is not obvious that the extinction of all independent states but two will be a blessing. But it is obvious that absolute rule of the unwise is less desirable than their limited rule: the unwise ought to rule under law. In addition, it is more probable that in a situation that is favorable to radical change, the citizen body will for once follow the advice of a wise man or a founding father by adopting a code of laws which he has elaborated, than that they will ever submit to perpetual and absolute rule of a succession of wise men. Yet laws must be applied or are in need of interpretation. The full authority under law should therefore be given to men who, thanks to their good upbringing, are capable of "completing" the laws (*Memorabilia* IV 6.12) or of interpreting them equitably. "Constitutional" authority ought to be given to the equitable men (*epieikeis*), i.e., to gentlemen—preferably an urban patriciate which derives its income from the cultivation of its landed estates. It is true that it is at least partly a matter of accident—of the accident of birth—whether a given individual does or does not belong to the class of gentlemen and has thereby had an opportunity of being brought up in the proper manner. But in the absence of absolute rule of the wise on the one hand, and on the other hand of a degree of abundance which is possible only on the basis of unlimited technological progress with all its terrible hazards, the apparently just alternative to aristocracy open or disguised will be permanent revolution, i.e., permanent chaos in which life will be not only poor and short but brutish as well. It would not be difficult to show that the classical argument cannot be disposed of as easily as is now generally thought, and that liberal or constitutional democracy comes closer to what the classics demanded than any alternative that is viable in our age. In the last analysis, however, the classical argument derives its strength from the assumption that the wise do not desire to rule.

In discussing the fundamental issue which concerns the relation of wisdom to rule or to tyranny, Kojève starts from the observation that at least up to now there have been no wise men but at best men who strove for wisdom, i.e., philosophers. Since the philosopher is the man who devotes his whole life to the quest for wisdom, he has no time for political activity of any kind: the philosopher cannot possibly desire to rule. His only demand on the political men is that they leave him alone. He justifies his demand by honestly declaring that his pursuit is purely theoretical and does not interfere in any way with the business of the political men. This simple solution presents itself at first glance as the strict consequence from the definition of the philosopher. Yet a short reflection shows already that it suffers from a fatal weakness. The philosopher cannot lead an absolutely solitary life because legitimate "subjective certainty" and the "subjective certainty" of the lunatic are indistinguishable. Genuine certainty must be "inter-subjective." The classics were fully aware of the essential weakness of the mind of the individual. Hence their teaching about the philosophic life is a teaching about friendship: the philosopher is as philosopher in need of friends. To be of service to the philosopher in his philosophizing, the friends must be competent men: they must themselves be actual or potential philosophers, i.e., members of the natural "elite." Friendship presupposes a measure of conscious agreement. The things regarding which the philosophic friends must agree cannot be known or evident truths. For philosophy is not wisdom but quest for wisdom. The things regarding which the philosophic friends agree will then be opinions or prejudices. But there is necessarily a variety of opinions or prejudices. Hence there will be a variety of groups of philosophic friends: philosophy, as distinguished from wisdom, necessarily appears in the form of philosophic schools or of sects. Friendship as the classics understood it offers then no solution to the problem of "subjective certainty." Friendship is bound to lead to, or to consist in, the cultivation and perpetuation of common prejudices by a closely knit group of kindred spirits. It is therefore incompatible with the idea of philosophy. The philosopher must leave the closed and charmed circle of the "initiated" if he intends to remain a philosopher. He must go out to the market place; the conflict with the political men cannot be avoided. And this conflict by itself, to say nothing of its cause or its effect, is a political action.

The whole history of philosophy testifies that the danger eloquently described by Kojève is inevitable. He is equally right in saying that that danger cannot be avoided by abandoning the sect in favor of what he regards as its modern substitute, the Republic of Letters. The Republic of Letters indeed lacks the narrowness of the sect: it embraces men of all philosophic persuasions. But precisely for this reason, the first article of the constitution of the Republic of Letters stipulates that no philosophic persuasion must be taken too seriously or that every philosophic persuasion must be treated with as much respect as any other. The Republic of Letters is relativistic. Or if it tries to avoid this pitfall, it becomes eclectic. A certain vague middle line, which is perhaps barely tolerable for the most easy-going members of the different persuasions if they are in their drowsiest mood, is set up as The Truth or as Common Sense; the substantive and irrepressible conflicts are dismissed as merely "semantic." Whereas the sect is narrow because it is passionately concerned with the true issues, the Republic of Letters is comprehensive because it is indifferent to the true issues: it prefers agreement to truth or to the quest for truth. If we have to choose between the sect and the Republic of Letters, we must choose the sect. Nor will it do that we abandon the sect in favor of the party or more precisely—since a party which is not a mass party is still something like a sect—of the mass party. For the mass party is nothing but a sect with a disproportionately long tail. The "subjective certainty" of the members of the sect, and especially of the weaker brethren, may be increased if the tenets of the sect are repeated by millions of parrots instead of by a few dozens of human beings, but this obviously has no effect on the claim of the tenets in question to "objective truth." Much as we loathe the snobbish silence or whispering of the sect, we loathe even more the savage noise of the loudspeakers of the mass party. The problem stated by Kojève is not then solved by dropping the distinction between those who are able and willing to think and those who are not. If we must choose between the sect and the party, we must choose the sect.

But must we choose the sect? The decisive premise of Kojève's argument is that philosophy "implies necessarily 'subjective certainties' which are not 'objective truths' or, in other words, which are prejudices." But philosophy in the original meaning of the term is nothing but knowledge of one's ignorance. The "subjective certainty" that one does not know coincides with the "objective truth" of that certainty. But one cannot know that one does not know without knowing what one does not know. What Pascal said with antiphilosophic intent about the impotence of both dogmatism and scepticism, is the only possible justification of philosophy which as such is neither dogmatic nor sceptic, and still less "decisionist," but zetetic (or skeptic in the original sense of the term). Philosophy as such is nothing but genuine awareness of the problems, i.e., of the fundamental and comprehensive problems. It is impossible to think about these problems without becoming inclined toward a solution, toward one or the other of the very few typical solutions. Yet as long as there is no wisdom but only quest for wisdom, the evidence of all solutions is necessarily smaller than the evidence of the problems. Therefore the philosopher ceases to be a philosopher at the moment at which the "subjective certainty" of a solution becomes stronger than his awareness of the problematic character of that solution. At that moment the sectarian is born. The danger of succumbing to the attraction of solutions is essential to philosophy which, without incurring this danger, would degenerate into playing with the problems. But the philosopher does not necessarily succumb to this danger, as is shown by Socrates, who never belonged to a sect and never founded one. And even if the philosophic friends are compelled to be members of a sect or to found one, they are not necessarily members of one and the same sect: *Amicus Plato*.

At this point we seem to get involved in a self-contradiction. For, if Socrates is the representative *par excellence* of the philosophic life, the philosopher cannot possibly be satisfied with a group of philosophic friends but has to go out to the market place where, as everyone knows, Socrates spent much or most of his time. However, the same Socrates suggested that there is no essential difference between the city and the family, and the thesis of Friedrich Mentz, *Socrates nec officiosus maritus nec laudandus paterfamilias* (Leipzig 1716), is defensible: Xenophon goes so far as not to count the husband of Xanthippe among the married men (*Symposium in fine*).

The difficulty cannot be discussed here except within the context of a limited exegetic problem. Xenophon indicates in the *Hiero* that the motivation of the philosophic life is the desire for being honored or admired by a small minority, and ultimately the desire for "self-admiration," whereas the motivation of the political life is the desire for love, i.e., for being loved by human beings irrespective of their qualities. Kojève rejects this view altogether. He is of the opinion that the philosopher and the ruler or tyrant are equally motivated by the desire for satisfaction, i.e., for recognition (honor) and ultimately for universal recognition, and that neither of the two is motivated by a desire for love. A human being is loved because he is and regardless of what he does. Hence love is at home within the family rather than in the public spheres of politics and of philosophy. Kojève regards it as particularly unfortunate that Xenophon tries to establish a connection between the "tyrannical" desire and sexual desire. He is equally averse to the suggestion that whereas the tyrant is guided by the desire for recognition by others, the philosopher is concerned exclusively with "self-admiration"; the self-satisfied philosopher is as such not distinguishable from the self-satisfied lunatic. The philosopher is then necessarily concerned with approval or admiration by others and he cannot help being pleased with it when he gets it. It is practically impossible to say whether the primary motive of the philosopher is the desire for admiration or the desire for the pleasures deriving from understanding. The very distinction has no practical meaning unless we gratuitously assume that there is an omniscient God who demands from men a pure heart.

What Xenophon indicated in the *Hiero* about the motivations of the two ways of life is admittedly incomplete. How can any man in his senses ever have overlooked the role played by ambition in political life? How can a friend of Socrates ever have overlooked the role played by love in the philosophic life? Simonides' speech on honor alone, to say nothing of Xenophon's other writings, proves abundantly that what Xenophon indicates in the *Hiero* about the motivations of the two ways of life is deliberately incomplete. It is incomplete because it proceeds from a complete disregard of everything but what one may call the most fundamental difference between the philosopher and the ruler. To understand this difference, one must start from the desire which the philosopher and the ruler have in common with each other and indeed with all men. All men desire "satisfaction." But satisfaction cannot be identified with recognition and even universal recognition. The classics identified satisfaction with happiness. The difference between the philosopher and the political man will then be a difference with respect to happiness. The philosopher's dominating passion is the desire for truth, i.e., for knowledge of the eternal order, or the eternal cause or causes of the whole. As he looks up in search for the eternal

order, all human things and all human concerns reveal themselves
to him in all clarity as paltry and ephemeral, and no one can find
solid happiness in what he knows to be paltry and ephemeral. He
has then the same experience regarding all human things, nay, regarding man himself, which the man of high ambition has regarding
the low and narrow goals, or the cheap happiness, of the general
run of men. The philosopher, being the man of the largest views,
is the only man who can be properly described as possessing *mega-
loprepreia* (which is commonly rendered by "magnificence") (Plato,
Republic 486a). Or, as Xenophon indicates, the philosopher is the
only man who is truly ambitious. Chiefly concerned with eternal
beings, or the "ideas," and hence also with the "idea" of man, he
is as unconcerned as possible with individual and perishable human
beings and hence also with his own "individuality," or his body, as
well as with the sum total of all individual human beings and their
"historical" procession. He knows as little as possible about the way
to the market place, to say nothing of the market place itself, and
he almost as little knows whether his very neighbor is a human
being or some other animal (Plato, *Theaetetus* 173c8-d1, 174b1-6).
The political man must reject this way altogether. He cannot tolerate this radical depreciation of man and of all human things (Plato,
Laws 804b5-c1). He could not devote himself to his work with all
his heart or without reservation if he did not attach absolute importance to man and to human things. He must "care" for human beings
as such. He is essentially attached to human beings. This attachment
is at the bottom of his desire to rule human beings, or of his ambition. But to rule human beings means to serve them. Certainly an
attachment to beings which prompts one to serve them may well
be called love of them. Attachment to human beings is not peculiar
to the ruler; it is characteristic of all men as mere men. The difference
between the political man and the private man is that in the case
of the former, the attachment enervates all private concerns; the
political man is consumed by erotic desire, not for this or that human
being, or for a few, but for the large multitude, for the *demos*
(Plato, *Gorgias* 481d1-5, 513d7-8; *Republic* 573e6-7, 574e2, 575a1-2),
and in principle, for all human beings. But erotic desire craves reci-
procity: the political man desires to be loved by all his subjects.
The political man is characterized by the concern with being loved
by all human beings regardless of their quality.

Kojève will have no difficulty in granting that the family man can be characterized by "love" and the ruler by "honor." But if, as we have seen, the philosopher is related to the ruler in a way comparable to that in which the ruler is related to the family man, there can be no difficulty in characterizing the ruler, in contradistinction to the philosopher, by "love" and the philosopher by "honor." Furthermore, prior to the coming of the universal state, the ruler is concerned with, and cares for, his own subjects as distinguished from the subjects of other rulers, just as the mother is concerned with, and cares for, her own children as distinguished from the children of other mothers; and the concern with, or care for, what is one's own is what is frequently meant by "love." The philosopher on the other hand is concerned with what can never become private or exclusive property. We cannot then accept Kojève's doctrine regarding love. According to him, we love someone "because he *is* and independently of what he *does*." He refers to the mother who loves her son in spite of all his faults. But, to repeat, the mother loves her son, not because he is, but because he is her own, or because he has the quality of being her own. (Compare Plato, *Republic* 330c3-6.)

But if the philosopher is radically detached from human beings as human beings, why does he communicate his knowledge, or his questionings, to others? Why was the same Socrates, who said that the philosopher does not even know the way to the market place, almost constantly in the market place? Why was the same Socrates, who said that the philosopher barely knows whether his neighbor is a human being, so well informed about so many trivial details regarding his neighbors? The philosopher's radical detachment from human beings must then be compatible with an attachment to human beings. While trying to transcend humanity (for wisdom is divine) or while trying to make it his sole business to die and to be dead to all human things, the philosopher cannot help living as a human being who as such cannot be dead to human concerns, although his soul will not be in these concerns. The philosopher cannot devote his life to his own work if other people do not take care of the needs of his body. Philosophy is possible only in a society in which there is "division of labor." The philosopher needs the services of other human beings and has to pay for them with services of his own if he does not want to be reproved as a thief or fraud.

But man's need for other men's services is founded on the fact that man is by nature a social animal or that the human individual is not self-sufficient. There is therefore a natural attachment of man to man which is prior to any calculation of mutual benefit. This natural attachment to human beings is weakened in the case of the philosopher by his attachment to the eternal beings. On the other hand, the philosopher is immune to the most common and the most powerful dissolvent of man's natural attachment to man, the desire to have more than one has already and in particular to have more than others have; for he has the greatest self-sufficiency which is humanly possible. Hence the philosopher will not hurt anyone. While he cannot help being more attached to his family and his city than to strangers, he is free from the delusions bred by collective egoisms; his benevolence or humanity extends to all human beings with whom he comes into contact. (*Memorabilia* I 2.60-61; 6.10; IV 8.11.) Since he fully realises the limits set to all human action and all human planning (for what has come into being must perish again), he does not expect salvation or satisfaction from the establishment of the simply best social order. He will therefore not engage in revolutionary or subversive activity. But he will try to help his fellow man by mitigating, as far as in him lies, the evils which are inseparable from the human condition. (Plato, *Theaetetus* 176a5-b1; *Seventh Letter* 331c7-d5; Aristotle, *Politics* 1301a39-b2.) In particular, he will give advice to his city or to other rulers. Since all advice of this kind presupposes comprehensive reflections which as such are the business of the philosopher, he must first have become a political philosopher. After this preparation he will act as Simonides did when he talked to Hiero, or as Socrates did when he talked to Alcibiades, Critias, Charmides, Critobulus, the younger Pericles and others.

The attachment to human beings as human beings is not peculiar to the philosopher. As philosopher, he is attached to a particular type of human being, namely to actual or potential philosophers or to his friends. His attachment to his friends is deeper than his attachment to other human beings, even to his nearest and dearest, as Plato shows with almost shocking clarity in the *Phaedo*. The philosopher's attachment to his friends is based in the first place on the need which arises from the deficiency of "subjective certainty." Yet we see Socrates frequently engaged in conversations from which he cannot have benefited in any way. We shall try to explain what this means in a popular and hence unorthodox manner. The philosopher's attempt to grasp the eternal order is necessarily an ascent from the perishable things which as such reflect the eternal order. Of all perishable things known to us, those which reflect that order most, or which are most akin to that order, are the souls of men. But the souls of men reflect the eternal order in different degrees. A soul that is in good order or healthy reflects it to a higher degree than a soul that is chaotic or diseased. The philosopher who as such has had a glimpse of the eternal order is therefore particularly sensitive to the difference among human souls. In the first place, he alone knows what a healthy or well-ordered soul is. And secondly, precisely because he has had a glimpse of the eternal order, he cannot help being intensely pleased by the aspect of a healthy or well-ordered soul, and he cannot help being intensely pained by the aspect of a diseased or chaotic soul, without any regard to his own needs or benefits. Hence he cannot help being attached to men of well-ordered souls: he desires "to be together" with such men all the time. He admires such men not on account of any services which they may render to him but simply because they are what they are. On the other hand, he cannot help being repelled by ill-ordered souls. He avoids men of ill-ordered souls as much as he can, while trying of course not to offend them. Last but not least, he is highly sensitive to the promise of good or ill order, or of happiness or misery, which is held out by the souls of the young. Hence he cannot help desiring, without any regard to his own needs or benefits, that those among the young whose souls are by nature fitted for it, acquire good order of their souls. But the good order of the soul is philosophizing. The philosopher therefore has the urge to educate potential philosophers simply because he cannot help loving well-ordered souls.

But did we not surreptitiously substitute the wise man for the philosopher? Does the philosopher of whom we have spoken not possess knowledge of many most important things? Philosophy, being knowledge of our ignorance regarding the most important things, is impossible without some knowledge regarding the most important things. By realizing that we are ignorant of the most important things, we realize at the same time that the most important thing for us, or the one thing needful, is quest for knowledge of the most important things, or philosophy. In other words, we realize that only by philosophizing can man's soul become well-ordered. We know how ugly or deformed a boaster's soul is; but everyone who thinks that he knows, while in truth he does not, is a boaster. Still, observations of this kind do not prove the assumption, for example, that the well-ordered soul is more akin to the eternal order, or to the eternal cause or causes of the whole, than is the chaotic soul. And one does not have to make that assumption in order to be a philosopher, as is shown by Democritus and other pre-Socratics, to say nothing of the moderns. If one does not make the assumption mentioned, one will be forced, it seems, to explain the philosopher's desire to communicate his thoughts by his need for remedying the deficiency of "subjective certainty" or by his desire for recognition or by his human kindness. We must leave it open whether one can thus explain, without being forced to use *ad hoc* hypotheses, the immediate pleasure which the philosopher experiences when he sees a well-ordered soul or the immediate pleasure which we experience when we observe signs of human nobility.

We may have explained why the philosopher is urged, not in spite of but because of his radical detachment from human beings as such, to educate human beings of a certain kind. But cannot exactly the same be said of the tyrant or ruler? May a ruler not likewise be penetrated by a sense of the ultimate futility of all human causes? It is undeniable that detachment from human beings, or what is popularly known as the philosophic attitude toward all things which are exposed to the power of chance, is not a preserve of the philosopher. But a detachment from human concerns which is not constantly nourished by genuine attachment to eternal things, i.e., by philosophizing, is bound to wither or to degenerate into lifeless narrowness. The ruler too tries to educate human beings and he too is prompted by love of some kind. Xenophon indicates his view of the ruler's love in the *Education of Cyrus*, which is, at any rate at first glance, his description of the greatest ruler. Xenophon's Cyrus is a cold or unerotic nature. That is to say, the ruler is not motivated by true or Socratic *eros* because he does not know what a well-ordered soul is. The ruler knows political virtue, and nothing prevents his being attracted by it; but political virtue, or the virtue of the non-philosopher, is a mutilated thing; therefore it cannot elicit more than a shadow or an imitation of true love. The ruler is in fact dominated by love based on need in the common meaning of need, or by mercenary love; for "all men by nature believe they love those things by which they believe they are benefited" (*Oeconomicus* 20.28). In the language of Kojève, the ruler is concerned with human beings because he is concerned with being recognized by them. This explains incidentally why the indications of the *Hiero* about love are so strikingly incomplete; the purpose of the work required the disregard of non-mercenary love just as it required that wisdom be kept in its ordinary ambiguity.

We cannot agree then with Kojève's contention that the educative tendency of the ruler has the same character or scope as that of the philosopher. The ruler is essentially the ruler of all his subjects; his educative effort must therefore be directed toward all his subjects. If every educative effort is a kind of conversation, the ruler is forced by his position to converse with every subject. Socrates, however, is not compelled to converse with anyone except those with whom he likes to converse. If the ruler is concerned with universal recognition, he must be concerned with enlarging universally the class of competent judges of his merits. But Kojève does not seem to believe that all men are capable of becoming competent judges in political matters. He limits himself to contending that the number of men of philosophic competence is not smaller than the number of men of political competence. Yet contrary to what he seems to say in the text of his essay as distinguished from his note number five, many more men are capable of judging competently of the greatness of a ruler than of the greatness of a philosopher. This is the case not merely because a much greater intellectual effort is required for competent judgment of a philosophic achievement than for competent judgment of a political achievement. Rather is it true because philosophy requires liberation from the most potent natural charm whose undiminished power in no way obstructs political competence as the ruler understands political competence: from that charm that consists in unqualified attachment to human things as such. If the philosopher addresses himself, therefore, to a small minority, he is not acting on the basis of an *a priori* judgment. He is following the constant experience of all times and countries and, no doubt, the experience of Kojève himself. For try as one may to expel nature with a hayfork, it will always come back. The philosopher will certainly not be compelled, either by the need to remedy the deficiency of "subjective certainty" or by ambition, to strive for universal recognition. His friends alone suffice to remedy that deficiency, and no shortcomings in his friends can be remedied by having recourse to utterly incompetent people. And as for ambition, as a philosopher, he is free from it.

According to Kojève, one makes a gratuitous assumption in saying that the philosopher as such is free from ambition or from the desire for recognition. Yet the philosopher as such is concerned with nothing but the quest for wisdom and kindling or nourishing the love of wisdom in those who are by nature capable of it. We do not have to pry into the heart of any one in order to know that, insofar as the philosopher, owing to the weakness of the flesh, becomes concerned with being recognized by others, he ceases to be a philosopher. According to the strict view of the classics he turns into a sophist. The concern with being recognized by others is perfectly compatible with, and in fact required by, the concern essential to the ruler who is the ruler of others. But concern with being recognized by others has no necessary connection with the quest for the eternal order. Therefore, concern with recognition necessarily detracts from the singleness of purpose which is characteristic of the philosopher. It blurs his vision. This fact is not at variance with the other fact that high ambition is frequently a sign by which one can recognize the potential philosopher. But to the extent to which high ambition is not transformed into full devotion to the quest for wisdom, and to the pleasures which accompany that quest, he will not become an actual philosopher. One of the pleasures accompanying the quest for truth comes from the awareness of progress in that quest. Xenophon goes so far as to speak of the self-admiration of the philosopher. This self-admiration or self-satisfaction does not have to be confirmed by the admiration of others in order to be reasonable. If the philosopher, trying to remedy the deficiency of "subjective certainty," engages in conversation with others and observes again and again that his interlocutors, as they themselves are forced to admit, involve themselves in self-contradictions or are unable to give any account of their questionable contentions, he will be reasonably confirmed in his estimate of himself without necessarily finding a single soul who admires him. (Consider Plato, *Apology of Socrates* 21d1-3.) The self-admiration of the philosopher is in this respect akin to "the good conscience" which as such does not require confirmation by others.

The quest for wisdom is inseparable from specific pleasures just as the quest for these pleasures is inseparable from the quest for wisdom. Thus it might seem possible to understand the quest for wisdom in terms of the quest for pleasure. That this is in fact possible is asserted by all hedonists. In the *Hiero*, Xenophon (or his Simonides) is forced to argue on the basis of the hedonistic thesis. Hence the argument of the *Hiero* implies the question whether the philosophic life can be understood in hedonistic terms. It implies the answer that it cannot be so understood because the rank of the various kinds of pleasure ultimately depends upon the rank of the activities to which the pleasures are related. Neither the quantity nor the purity of the pleasures determines in the last resort the rank of human activities. The pleasures are essentially secondary; they cannot be understood but with reference to the activities. The question as to whether the activities or the pleasures are in themselves primary has nothing to do with the question as to whether someone who engages in an activity is prompted to do so primarily by the intrinsic value of the activity or by the pleasure which he expects to enjoy as a consequence of the activity. Kojève may be perfectly right in saying that the latter question does not permit a responsible answer and is unimportant from the point of view of philosophy. But the consideration is irrelevant to Xenophon's argument, which is concerned exclusively with the former question.

While I must disagree with a considerable part of Kojève's reasoning, I agree with his conclusion that the philosopher has to go to the market place, or in other words, that the conflict between the philosopher and the city is inevitable. The philosopher must go to the market place in order to fish there for potential philosophers. His attempts to convert young men to the philosophic life will necessarily be regarded by the city as an attempt to corrupt the young. The philosopher is therefore forced to defend the cause of philosophy. He must therefore act upon the city or upon the ruler. Up to this point Kojève is in perfect agreement with the classics.

But does the final consequence mean, as he maintains, that the philosopher must desire to determine or codetermine the politics of the city or of the rulers? Must the philosopher desire "to participate, in one way or another, in the total direction of public affairs, so that the State be organized and governed in such a manner that the philosopher's philosophic pedagogy be possible and effectual"? Or must we conceive of philosophic politics, i.e., of the philosopher's action on behalf of philosophy, in entirely different terms?

Contrary to what Kojève apparently implies, it seems to us that there is no necessary connection between the philosopher's indispensable philosophic politics and the efforts which he might or might not make to contribute toward the establishment of the best regime. For philosophy and philosophic education are possible in all kinds of more or less imperfect regimes. One may illustrate this by an example taken from the eighth book of Plato's *Republic*. There Plato contends that the Spartan regime is superior to the Athenian, although he knows that the Athenian is more favorable than the Spartan regime to the possibility and the survival of philosophic education (consider 557c6 and d4). It is true that it was in Athens that Socrates was compelled to drink the hemlock. But he was permitted to live and engage in philosophic education until he was seventy: in Sparta he would have been exposed as an infant. Plato could not have decided, however provisionally, in favor of the Spartan regime, if the philosopher's concern with a good political order were absolutely inseparable from the concern guiding his philosophic politics. In what then does philosophic politics consist? In satisfying the city that the philosophers are not atheists, that they do not desecrate everything sacred to the city, that they reverence what the city reverences, that they are not subversives, in short, that they are not irresponsible adventurers but good citizens and even the best of citizens. This is the defense of philosophy which was required always and everywhere, whatever the regime might have been. For, as the philosopher Montesquieu says, "dans tous les pays du monde, on veut de la morale" and "les hommes, fripons en détail, sont en gros de très honnêtes gens; ils aiment la morale." This defense of philosophy before the tribunal of the city was achieved by Plato with a resounding success (Plutarch, *Nicias* ch. 23). The effects have lasted down to the present throughout all ages except the darkest ones. What Plato did in the Greek city and for it was done in and for Rome by Cicero, whose political action on behalf of philosophy has nothing in common with his actions against Catiline and for Pompey, for example. It was done in and for the Islamic world by Fārābī and in and for Judaism by Maimonides. Contrary to what Kojève seems to suggest, the political action of the philosophers on behalf of philosophy has achieved full success. One sometimes wonders whether it has not been too successful.

Kojève, I said, fails to distinguish between philosophic politics and that political action which the philosopher might undertake with a view to establishing the best regime or to the improvement of the actual order. He thus arrives at the conclusion that on the one hand the philosopher does not desire to rule, and on the other hand he must desire to rule, and that this contradiction involves a tragic conflict. The classics did not regard the conflict between philosophy and the city as tragic. Xenophon at any rate seems to have viewed that conflict in the light of Socrates' relation to Xanthippe. At least in this point there appears then something like an agreement between Xenophon and Pascal. For the classics, the conflict between philosophy and the city is as little tragic as the death of Socrates.

Kojève's argument continues as follows: Since the philosopher does not desire to rule because he has no time for ruling, but on the other hand is forced to rule, he has been satisfied with a compromise solution; with devoting a little time to giving advice to tyrants or rulers. Reading the chronicles, one receives the impression that this action of the philosophers has been wholly ineffectual—as ineffectual as Simonides' action that consisted in his conversation with Hiero. This conclusion does not entitle one, however, to infer that the philosopher should abstain from mingling in politics, for the strong reason for mingling in politics remains in force. The problem of what the philosopher should do in regard to the city remains, therefore, an open question, the subject of an unfinishable discussion. But the problem which cannot be solved by the dialectics of discussion may well be solved by the higher dialectics of History. The philosophic study of our past shows that philosophy, far from being politically ineffectual, has radically revolutionized the character of political life. One is even entitled to say that philosophic ideas alone have had significant political effect. For what else is the whole political history of the world except a movement toward the universal and homogeneous state? The decisive stages in the movement were actions of tyrants or rulers (Alexander the Great and Napoleon, e.g.). But these tyrants or rulers were and are pupils of philosophers. Classical philosophy created the idea of the universal state. Modern philosophy, which is the secularized form of Christianity, created the idea of the universal and homogeneous state. On the other hand, the progress of philosophy and its eventual transmutation into wisdom requires the "active negation" of the previous political states, i.e., requires the action of the tyrant: only when "all possible active (political) negations" have been effected and thus the final stage of the political development has been reached, can and will the quest for wisdom give way to wisdom.

I need not examine Kojève's sketch of the history of the Western world. That sketch would seem to presuppose the truth of the thesis which it is meant to prove. Certainly the value of the conclusion which he draws from his sketch depends entirely on the truth of the assumption that the universal and homogeneous state is the simply best social order. The simply best social order, as he conceives of it, is the state in which every human being finds his full satisfaction. A human being finds his full satisfaction if his human dignity is universally recognized and if he enjoys "equality of opportunity," i.e., the opportunity, corresponding to his capacities, of deserving well of the state or of the whole. Now if it were true that in the universal and homogeneous state, no one has any good reason for being dissatisfied with that state, or for negating it, it would not yet follow that everyone will in fact be satisfied with it and never think of actively negating it, for men do not always act reasonably. Does Kojève not underestimate the power of the passions? Does he not have an unfounded belief in the eventually rational effect of the movements instigated by the passions? In addition, men will have very good reasons for being dissatisfied with the universal and homogeneous state. To show this, I must have recourse to Kojève's more extensive exposition in his *Introduction à la lecture de Hegel*. There are degrees of satisfaction. The satisfaction of the humble citizen, whose human dignity is universally recognized and who enjoys all opportunities that correspond to his humble capacities and achievements, is not comparable to the satisfaction of the Chief of State. Only the Chief of State is *"really satisfied."* He alone is "truly free" (p. 146). Did Hegel not say something to the effect that the state in which one man is free is the Oriental despotic state? Is the universal and homogeneous state then merely a planetary Oriental despotism? However this may be, there is no guarantee that the incumbent Chief of State deserves his position to a higher degree than others. Those others then have very good reason for dissatisfaction: a state which treats equal men unequally is not just. A change from the universal-homogeneous monarchy into a universal-homogeneous aristocracy would seem to be reasonable. But we cannot stop here. The universal and homogeneous state, being the synthesis of the Masters and the Slaves, is the state of the working warrior or of the war-waging worker. In fact, all its members are warrior workers (pp. 114, 146). But if the state is universal and homogenous, "wars and revolutions are henceforth impossible" (pp. 145, 561). Besides, work in the strict sense, namely the conquest or domestication of nature, is completed, for otherwise the universal and homogeneous state could not be the basis for wisdom (p. 301). Of course, work of a kind will still go on, but the citizens of the final state will work as little as possible, as Kojève notes with explicit reference to Marx (p. 435). To borrow an expression which someone used recently in the House of Lords on a similar occasion, the citizens of the final state are only so-called workers, workers by courtesy. "There is no longer fight nor work. History has come to its end. There is nothing more to *do*" (pp. 385, 114). This end of History would be most exhilarating but for the fact that, according to Kojève, it is the participation in bloody political struggles as well as in real work or, generally expressed, the negating action, which raises man above the brutes (pp. 490-492, 560, 378n.). The state through which man is said to become reasonably satisfied is, then, the state in which the basis of man's humanity withers away, or in which man loses his humanity. It is the state of Nietzsche's "last man." Kojève in fact confirms the classical view that unlimited technological progress and its accompaniment, which are the indispensable conditions of the universal and homogeneous state, are destructive of humanity. It is perhaps possible to say that the universal and homogeneous state is fated to come. But it is certainly impossible to say that man can reasonably be satisfied with it. If the universal and homogeneous state is the goal of History, History is absolutely "tragic." Its completion will reveal that the human problem, and hence in particular the problem of the relation of philosophy and politics, is insoluble. For centuries and centuries men have unconsciously done nothing but worked their way through infinite labors and struggles and agonies, yet ever again catching hope, toward the universal and homogeneous state, and as soon as they have arrived at the end of their journey, they realize that through arriving at it they have destroyed their humanity and thus returned, as in a cycle, to the pre-human beginnings of History. *Vanitas vanitatum. Recognitio recognitionum.* Yet there is no reason for despair as long as human nature has not been conquered completely, i.e., as long as sun and man still generate man. There will always be men (*andres*) who will revolt against a state which is destructive of humanity or in which there is no longer a possibility of noble action and of great deeds. They may be forced into a mere negation of the universal and homogeneous state, into a negation not enlightened by any positive goal, into a nihilistic negation. While perhaps doomed to failure, that nihilistic revolution may be the only action on behalf of man's humanity, the only great and noble deed that is possible once the universal and homogeneous state has become inevitable. But no one can know whether it will fail or succeed. We still know too little about the workings of the universal and homogeneous state to say anything about where and when its corruption will start. What we do know is only that it will perish sooner or later (see Friedrich Engels' *Ludwig Feuerbach*, ed. by Hans Hajek, p. 6). Someone may object that the successful revolt against the universal and homogeneous state could have no other effect than that the identical historical process which has led from the primitive horde to the final state will be repeated. But would such a repetition of the process—a new lease of life for man's humanity—not be preferable to the indefinite continuation of the inhuman end? Do we not enjoy every spring although we know the cycle of the seasons, although we know that winter will come again? Kojève does seem to leave an outlet for action in the universal and homogeneous state. In that state the risk of violent death is still involved in the struggle for political leadership (p. 146). But this opportunity for action can exist only for a tiny minority. And besides, is this not a hideous prospect: a state in which the last refuge of man's humanity is political assassination in the particularly sordid form of the palace revolution? Warriors and workers of all countries, unite, while there is still time, to prevent the coming of "the realm of freedom." Defend with might and main, if it needs to be defended, "the realm of necessity."

But perhaps it is not war nor work but thinking that constitutes the humanity of man. Perhaps it is not recognition (which for many men may lose in its power to satisfy what it gains in universality) but wisdom that is the end of man. Perhaps the universal and homogeneous state is legitimated by the fact that its coming is the necessary and sufficient condition for the coming of wisdom: in the final state all human beings will be reasonably satisfied, they will be truly happy, because all will have acquired wisdom or are about to acquire it. "There is no longer fight nor work; History is completed; there is nothing more to *do*": man is at last free from all drudgery and for the highest and most divine activity, for the contemplation of the unchangeable truth (Kojève, *op. cit.*, p. 385). But if the final state is to satisfy the deepest longing of the human soul, every human being must be capable of becoming wise. The most relevant difference among human beings must have practically disappeared. We understand now why Kojève is so anxious to refute the classical view according to which only a minority of men are capable of the quest for wisdom. If the classics are right, only a few men will be truly happy in the universal and homogeneous state and hence only a few men will find their satisfaction in and through it. Kojève himself observes that the ordinary citizens of the final state are only "potentially satisfied" (p. 146). The actual satisfaction of all human beings, which allegedly is the goal of History, is impossible. It is for this reason, I suppose, that the final social order, as Kojève conceives of it, is a State and not a stateless society: the State, or coercive government, cannot wither away because it is impossible that all human beings should ever become actually satisfied.

The classics thought that, owing to the weakness or dependence of human nature, universal happiness is impossible, and therefore they did not dream of a fulfillment of History and hence not of a meaning of History. They saw with their mind's eye a society within which that happiness of which human nature is capable would be possible in the highest degree: that society is the best

regime. But because they saw how limited man's power is, they held
that the actualization of the best regime depends on chance. Modern man, dissatisfied with utopias and scorning them, has tried to
find a guarantee for the actualization of the best social order.
In order to succeed, or rather in order to be able to believe that
he could succeed, he had to lower the goal of man. One form in
which this was done was to replace moral virtue by universal
recognition, or to replace happiness by the satisfaction deriving
from universal recognition. The classical solution is utopian in the
sense that its actualization is improbable. The modern solution is
utopian in the sense that its actualization is impossible. The classical
solution supplies a stable standard by which to judge of any actual
order. The modern solution eventually destroys the very idea of a
standard that is independent of actual situations.

It seems reasonable to assume that only a few, if any, citizens
of the universal and homogeneous state will be wise. But neither
the wise men nor the philosophers will desire to rule. For this
reason alone, to say nothing of others, the Chief of the universal
and homogeneous state, or the Universal and Final Tyrant will be
an unwise man, as Kojève seems to take for granted. To retain his
power, he will be forced to suppress every activity which might
lead people into doubt of the essential soundness of the universal
and homogeneous state: he must suppress philosophy as an attempt
to corrupt the young. In particular he must in the interest of the
homogeneity of his universal state forbid every teaching, every
suggestion, that there are politically relevant natural differences
among men which cannot be abolished or neutralized by progressing scientific technology. He must command his biologists to prove
that every human being has, or will acquire, the capacity of becoming a philosopher or a tyrant. The philosophers in their turn will be
forced to defend themselves or the cause of philosophy. They will
be obliged, therefore, to try to act on the Tyrant. Everything
seems to be a re-enactment of the age-old drama. But this time, the
cause of philosophy is lost from the start. For the Final Tyrant
presents himself as a philosopher, as the highest philosophic authority, as the supreme exegete of the only true philosophy, as the
executor and hangman authorized by the only true philosophy. He
claims therefore that he persecutes not philosophy but false philosophies. The experience is not altogether new for philosophers. If

philosophers were confronted with claims of this kind in former ages, philosophy went underground. It accommodated itself in its explicit or exoteric teaching to the unfounded commands of rulers who believed they knew things which they did not know. Yet its very exoteric teaching undermined the commands or dogmas of the rulers in such a way as to guide the potential philosophers toward the eternal und unsolved problems. And since there was no universal state in existence, the philosophers could escape to other countries if life became unbearable in the tyrant's dominions. From the Universal Tyrant, however, there is no escape. Thanks to the conquest of nature and to the completely unabashed substitution of suspicion and terror for law, the Universal and Final Tyrant has at his disposal practically unlimited means for ferreting out, and for extinguishing, the most modest efforts in the direction of thought. Kojève would seem to be right although for the wrong reason: the coming of the universal and homogeneous state will be the end of philosophy on earth.

V

HOW FĀRĀBĪ
READ PLATO'S
LAWS

Fārābī's brief summary of Plato's *Laws* consists of a preface and 9 chapters (or "speeches").[1] Each chapter is devoted to a book of the *Laws*. Fārābī says that he has seen only the first nine books but not the subsequent ones. He asserts that according to some the *Laws* consist of 10 books, while according to others they consist of 14 books (43,5-13). The correct number which Fārābī does not mention is exactly in the middle between ten and fourteen. Regardless of how this accident may have to be understood, Fārābī certainly did not summarize the 10th book of the *Laws*, i.e. Plato's theological statement *par excellence*.

Fārābī's preface consists of 3 parts: a general statement, a story, and the application of the lesson conveyed through both the general statement and the story to the question of how to read Plato's *Laws*. We may summarize the general statement as

1. Figures in parentheses and notes indicate the pages and lines of Gabrieli's edition of Fārābī's *Compendium Legum Platonis* (Alfarabius, *Compendium Legum Platonis*, edidit et latine vertit Franciscus Gabrieli, London, 1952.). The Arabic text (including the app. crit.) consists of 41 pages. I am grateful to Dr. Muhsin Mahdi for kindly checking my translations from the Arabic.

follows. Let us call "men of judgment" such men as have acquired the habit of discerning and attaining what is useful. They acquired that habit through observation and the proper evaluation of their observations. The proper evaluation of observations consists in forming true universal judgments on the basis of a number of observations of particular cases. It is in the nature of all men to form universal judgments on the basis of a number of particular observations. For instance if a man says the truth once or twice or frequently he is naturally judged to be a truthful man and always to say the truth. But judgments of this kind, however natural, are not necessarily true. The men of judgment have observed men's natural inclination to make unwarranted generalizations and they, the men of judgment, evaluate this observation properly. On the basis of this evaluation they act with a view to what is useful: by acting sometimes in a given manner, they induce the public to judge falsely that they will always act in that manner, so much so that it will escape the public if they act differently on occasion; the deviation will be thought to be a repetition (3,1-17).

Fārābī illustrates this general remark by referring to a story. Once upon a time there was a pious ascetic—a man who withdraws and abstains for the sake of mortification and abasement, or who habitually and knowingly prefers the painful to the pleasant (cf. 27,9-10). He was known as a man of probity, propriety, abstinence, and devotion to divine worship. In spite of this, or because of this, he aroused the hostility of the oppressive ruler of his city. Seized with fear of the ruler, he desired to flee. The ruler ordered his arrest and, lest he escape, caused all the gates of the city to be carefully watched. The pious ascetic obtained clothes which would be suitable for his purpose and put them on; how he obtained them is not told in the story. Then taking a cymbal in his hand, pretending to be drunk, and singing to the tune of the cymbal, he approached one of the gates of the city at the beginning of the night. When the guard asked him "who are you?" he replied in a mocking vein, "I am that pious ascetic you are looking for." The guard thought that he was making fun of him and let him go. Thus the pious ascetic escaped safely without having lied in his speech (4,1-9).

Let us consider the story in the light of the general remark and the general remark in the light of the story. The hero of the story is a man of judgment, but a man of judgment of a particular kind:

a man of judgment who happens to be a pious ascetic. Accordingly
he has established his character as a man of the strictest morality
and religion. His action is prompted by the desire to save himself: he acts appropriately with a view to what is useful for himself. To save himself, to escape, he must be unrecognizable: he
does not look and act like a pious ascetic; on this singular occasion
he acts differently than he is known to act. And yet his deviation
from his habitual behavior is thought to be in full accord with
his habitual behavior: the public thinks that the man who acted in
this manner could not possibly be the pious ascetic. And when the
public, which has very severe notions of decency, will find out,
sooner or later, that it was the pious ascetic who escaped by acting
in a manner which is not appropriate to a pious ascetic, it will still
say that he did not deviate from his habitual behavior in the decisive
respect: he did not lie in his speech. It would appear then that
unqualified veracity is essential to a pious ascetic. However this
may be, the public is mistaken in the decisive respect: the pious
ascetic lied in deed. His not lying in speech was part of his lying in
deed. Only because he lied in deed could he afford not to lie in
speech. The public is mistaken as regards the reason why the pious
ascetic's seemingly indecent action is not indecent: that action is
justified by compulsion or persecution (cf. 14,17-15,3). At any
rate the story shows, among other things, that one can safely tell a
very dangerous truth provided one tells it in the proper surroundings, for the public will interpret the absolutely unexpected speech
in terms of the customary and expected meaning of the surroundings rather than it will interpret the surroundings in terms of the
dangerous character of the speech.

The explicit purpose of both the general remark and the story
is to make intelligible the behavior of one particular man of
judgment, Plato. Plato acted rightly in not permitting himself the
seeming generosity of revealing the sciences to all men but rather
presenting the sciences by means of allusive, ambiguous, misleading
and obscure speech lest they lose their character or be misused. It
became a matter of very common, nay, universal knowledge that
Plato was famous for speaking or writing in the manner indicated.
Hence, when he expressed a thought without any concealment, as
he sometimes did, his readers or hearers assumed that in these cases
too his speech was allusive and expressed something different from,

or opposite to, what it explicitly and unambiguously said. "This is one of the secrets of his books" (4,10-16).

Plato, as a man of judgment, acted appropriately with a view to what is useful, although he thought less of what was useful for himself than what is useful for the sciences or their existence in the cities and nations. He established for himself the character of a man who never explicitly and unambiguously says what he thinks about the highest themes. He thus enabled himself sometimes to say explicitly and unambiguously what he thought about the highest themes: his explicit and unambiguous utterances are not taken seriously.

We must understand this in the light of the story of the pious ascetic. Plato was not a pious ascetic. Whereas the pious ascetic almost always says explicitly and unambiguously what he thinks, Plato almost never says explicitly and unambiguously what he thinks. But Plato has something in common with the pious ascetic. Both are sometimes compelled to state truths which are dangerous either to themselves or others. Since they are both men of judgment, they act in such cases in the same way; they state the dangerous truth by surrounding it properly, with the result that they are not believed in what they say. It is in this manner that Plato has written about laws (4,18-19).

Fārābī resolved to bring to light, or to extract, some of the thoughts to which Plato had alluded in his *Laws* or, as he also says, to bring to light, or to extract, some of the thoughts which Plato had intended to explain in his *Laws* (4,19-20; 43,6-9). For to allude to a thought means, not indeed to explain that thought, but to intend to explain it; whether or not the intention is consummated depends decisively, not on the author, but on the reader. Fārābī's resolution must be understood in the light of his unqualified agreement with Plato's principle of secretiveness. Just as Plato before him, Fārābī does not permit himself the seeming generosity of trying to help all men toward knowledge but employs a kind of secretiveness which is mitigated or enhanced by unexpected and unbelievable frankness. Accordingly his resolution is two-fold: his summary of the *Laws* is meant "to be a help to him who desires to know [the *Laws*] and to be sufficient to him who cannot bear the toil of study and of meditation" (4,20-21). Those who desire to know the *Laws* form a different class from those who cannot bear the

toil of study and of meditation; the desire of those who have the
velleity to know the *Laws*, while they cannot bear the toil of
study and meditation, turns necessarily into aversion, since knowledge of the *Laws* cannot be acquired without the toil of study and
meditation. Accordingly, Fārābī's *Summary* is intended to have
a two-fold meaning. One can articulate the two-foldness of works
of this kind by comparing them to men on horseback: to seeming
wholes which consist of a discerning and slow ruler and a fast
and less discerning subject, and which are well fitted for unexpected attack as well as for flight.

Fārābī's *Summary* consists of allusions to those thoughts to
which, as he thinks, Plato has alluded in the *Laws*. Fārābī's allusions
are meant to be helpful for men for whom Plato's allusions are
not equally helpful: allusions which were intelligible to some of
Plato's contemporaries are not equally intelligible to men of the
same type among Fārābī's contemporaries. One cannot grasp
Fārābī's allusions unless one undergoes the toil of studying carefully what he explicitly says. But since he is secretive, the study
of what he explicitly says must include consideration of what he
leaves unsaid. One ought to begin the study of his *Summary* by
wondering which is the most important subject that he fails to mention in that work. Fārābī enables us to answer that question in the
proper manner since he has written a companion work to the
Summary: the treatise which he entitled *The Philosophy of Plato,
its parts and the ranks of its parts, from its beginning to its end.*
According to the *Philosophy of Plato*, the necessary and sufficient
condition of happiness, or man's ultimate perfection, is philosophy
(§§1,16-18). The *Summary* is silent about philosophy; the terms
"philosophy" and "philosopher," or derivations from them, do not
occur in that work.[2] Since, according to the *Philosophy of Plato*,
philosophy is the science of the substances of all beings (§2), the
Summary, which is characterized by silence about philosophy,
avoids the term "beings" altogether and employs the term "substance" only once (32,22).[3] Since "philosopher" is necessarily understood in contradistinction to *jamhūr* (the vulgar), the *Summary*,
which is characterized by silence about philosophy, avoids the

---

2. Plato is referred to as *al-ḥakīm* (4,10; 29,7; 43,7). Cf. also 3,9 and 7,4.
3. Cf. 15, 11 ff.

word *jamhūr*.[4] To understand the silence of the *Summary* on philosophy, one has to consider the corresponding silence of the
Philosophy of Plato on other subjects. The *Philosophy of Plato*
teaches that philosophy is the necessary and sufficient condition of
happiness. According to the *Summary* it would rather seem that
happiness is brought about by obedience to the divine law or to the
gods (cf. 12,17-18 and 16,14-15 with 6,17-19). At any rate the
Summary speaks rather frequently of God, gods, the other life,
the revealed law (*shariʿa*) and divine laws, whereas the *Philosophy
of Plato* is completely silent about those subjects. The relation
between the *Philosophy of Plato* and the *Summary* reflects the
relation between philosophy and the divine law as between two
entirely different worlds.

At the beginning of the last chapter of the *Summary*, Fārābī
says that up to that point, i.e., up to the end of the eighth book of the
Laws, Plato has discussed "the roots" of the laws and those subjects with which the legislator has to be greatly concerned, namely,
"the laws proper and the roots" (40,21-22). It would appear that
the subject matter of Plato, as distinguished from the legislator,
is "the roots" of the laws rather than the laws proper. In describing
Plato's manner of dealing with the roots, Fārābī uses the expression
takallama. On another occasion he explicitly contrasts the way of
speaking employed by the legislator, which is unambiguous com-
manding, with that employed by the *mutakallim* among others,
which is a kind of discussion that is not necessarily free from self-
contradiction (24,3-7; cf. 34,22-35,3). Derivatives from the root
klm occur quite frequently in the *Summary* (twenty-six times, I
believe). On the other hand they are completely absent from the
Philosophy of Plato. As Fārābī elsewhere explains, *kalām*, or discussion of the roots of the laws or religions, is the art of defending the
laws or religions. We shall venture to describe the relation of the
Summary and the *Philosophy of Plato* as follows: the *Philosophy
of Plato* presents Plato's philosophy whereas the *Summary* presents
his art of *kalām*. This conclusion is obviously not contradicted by
the fact that, according to Fārābī, Plato begins in the ninth book of
the *Laws* to explain things which are ancillary to the roots of the
laws (40,22-41,2). Our conclusion is rather confirmed by the fact

4. Cf. 20,5.

that only in the ninth chapter of the *Summary* which is meant to reproduce the content of the ninth book of the *Laws* does Fārābī refer to punishment in the other life (42,20; 43,2). From here we see without great difficulty how Fārābī would have interpreted the tenth book of the *Laws* had he been in a position to do so.[5]

There is another subject which Fārābī fails to mention in the *Philosophy of Plato* although he mentions it quite frequently in the *Summary*. In the *Philosophy of Plato* he never mentions himself. He speaks in that work three times of "us," but he means there by that expression "us human beings" (§§8-9). In the *Summary* however he speaks of himself in the singular five times and in the plural twenty-one times, if I am not mistaken. It is primarily for this reason that the *Summary* may be said to be more "personal" than the *Philosophy of Plato*.

At a first reading, and at any superficial reading, the *Summary* presents itself as a pedantic, pedestrian and wooden writing which abounds in trivial or insipid remarks and which reveals an amazing lack of comprehension of Plato. To say nothing of many Platonic thoughts to which Fārābī hardly alludes, he ascribes to Plato many contentions for which one seeks in vain in the text of the *Laws*. At first glance one receives the impression that Fārābī is trying to the best of his powers to give a mere report of the content of the *Laws*, a simple enumeration of the subjects discussed in the *Laws*: "he explained a; then he explained b; then he explained c. . . ." This apparent character of the *Summary* is surprising since Fārābī assumes, as he gradually discloses, that the *Laws* are accessible to the reader of the *Summary*, not to say at his elbow. In one case he goes so far as to explain a Platonic expression which he had not used in summarizing the passage concerned (12,1-2). The opening of the *Summary* suggests accordingly that the work is meant to consist less of summaries than of explanations, of simple and straightforward explanations—e.g., of the meaning of "cause" in the first sentence of the *Laws* or of "Zeus" (5,2-4). Yet explanations of this kind occur very rarely. Fārābī's chief concern is rather to set forth those purposes of Plato which Plato himself had not set forth, e.g. his purpose in discussing a given subject.[6] In addition, a

5. Cf. *Laws* 887b5-c2, 890d4-6, e6-7, 891a5-7.
6. Cf. especially 40, 17-19 with the earlier parallels, viz. 12, 1-2; 17, 15-16 and 28, 10-11; cf. also 5, 4-5 with 5, 2-4.

second glance at the *Summary* reveals that the work is much less monotonous than it appears to be at first sight. In a considerable number of instances Fārābī voices his assent to Plato's contentions or his approval of other features of the *Laws,* and he does this in a great variety of ways. It is obviously not the same thing to say that Plato was right in holding or uttering a certain view (4,13; 7,20; 9,8; 16,7-9) and to say that Plato demonstrated a certain view (19,5); or to say that Plato mentioned a useful subject (11,5; 21,5; 27,18; 32,3,22) or even a subject of exceeding usefulness (42,20-21), and to say that he mentioned a subject knowledge of which is useful (42,10); or to say that he discussed a subject in a copious speech (26,7-8; 27,7-8; 31,2) and to say that he discussed a subject with impressive terseness (27,22-23; 35,6; 42,21-22). The reader who is able to bear the toil of study and meditation and therefore pays attention to these varieties of expression is compelled to raise questions like these: Did Fārābī agree with those Platonic assertions to which he does not explicitly assent? What did he think of those Platonic assertions of which he does not say that Plato demonstrated them? What are we to understand by subjects which are useful while knowledge of them is perhaps not useful? What did Fārābī think of those Platonic subjects of which he does not say that they are useful or fine (19,12) or subtle (31,23; 36,21) but which he does not describe at all or else qualifies merely as "other subjects" (16,22; 22,3,5)?

Fārābī suggests then by no means that Plato "explained" all subjects on which he touches in the *Laws.* In many cases Plato is merely said to have "said" something or to have "mentioned" a subject or to have "intimated" a thought or to have "alluded" to it or to have "undertaken to explain" it or to have "begun to explain" it or to have "desired to explain" it (cf., e.g., 29,19; 30,5; 31,11,22; cf. especially 26,2-3 with 25,20 and 26,7-8). Thus the chief function of the *Summary* may be said to be to bring to light the difference in character and weight of the various utterances of Plato—utterances which, in the eyes of the undiscerning reader, would seem to possess, all of them, the same character and weight. At the very outset, Fārābī says that Plato intimated that it is correct to examine the laws, that he explained that the laws are "superior to all wisdoms," and that he examined the particulars of that law which was famous in his time. In the fourth chapter he states what Plato said when "he undertook to explain the subject of tyranny," while in the fifth chapter he states what Plato said when "he mentioned another useful subject" which he discussed with impressive terseness; in the first statement, tyranny is declared to be good if used for rule over slaves and wicked people, and to be bad if used for rule over free and virtuous men; in the second statement tyranny is said to be indispensable as a prelude to divine laws for two reasons, the first reason being the need for purging the city of wicked people of a certain kind, and the second reason being the expectation that these wicked people will be a lesson and a warning to the good so that they will accept easily and gladly the laws of those who assimilate themselves to God or gods (22,16-23,3; 27,18-23).[7] At the beginning of the eighth chapter, "mentioning" is referred to 5 times and is contrasted with Plato's "intimating" another aspect of the same subject in the beginning of the book.[8] Since Fārābī frequently claims that he is summarizing what Plato only alluded to or intimated or began to explain, it is unreasonable to expect that one has merely to look up the corresponding passages of the *Laws* in order to find there the thoughts which Fārābī extracted from them: there is bound to be a great divergence between what Plato explicitly says in the *Laws* and what Fārābī explicitly says in the *Summary*.

We note furthermore that "then" does not occur in the *Summary* with deadening regularity. The "then's" are unevenly distributed. There are sections in which every sentence begins with a "Then he . . . ," but there are also comparatively extensive sections in which that uninviting expression does not occur a single time.[9] This observation leads us easily to the more revealing observation that it is sometimes impossible to say where the alleged report of what Plato did ends and Fārābī's independent exposition, which

---

7. Cf. also 18, 3-5 with 12, 18-13, 1 and 18, 10-14; 20, 18-22; 21, 2-3; 21, 11-13.

8. 36, 20-37, 2; cf. 8, 7-10 and 12, 3-15. Cf. the use of "mentioning" in the seventh chapter.

9. See, e.g., 5-6; cf. e.g., 28, 11-15 with 28, 15-29, 17. On an average the expression "then he . . ." occurs once in every six lines; in the second chapter it occurs least frequently (once in every twelve lines), while in the seventh chapter it occurs most frequently (once in every four lines). The second and seventh chapters are the only ones in which expressions of the type "he mentioned a useful (or fine, or subtle) subject (or thought)" do not occur. This is not to deny that Fārābī says in the second chapter that the art of song is truly very useful.

no longer claims simply to reproduce Plato's thought, begins. At
the end of the fourth chapter Fārābī reproduces Plato's thought
that the laws are in need of preludes or *prooemia*. But when he
adds the remark that there are three kinds of such *prooemia*, namely,
accidental, imposed, and natural, and thus incidentally excludes
rational *prooemia*, he does not suggest that this distinction is taken
from Plato.[10] There occur a few examples in the body of the
Summary where Fārābī speaks in the first person (plural) and thus
draws our attention to the difference between his speech and Plato's
speech. When Fārābī speaks of a suspicion "which we have described" (9,20), he draws our attention to the difference between
his description of the suspicion in question and Plato's description.
When speaking of "those whom we have enumerated," one of the
enumerated types being the *mutakallim*, he indicates that Plato had
not spoken of the *mutakallim*, in spite of the fact that Fārābī had
said shortly before that Plato did speak of the *mutakallim* (24,3-7);
he explains in that very passage that self-contradiction is not incompatible with the character of *kalām*. At the end of the eighth chapter Fārābī appears to contrast "all these things which he mentioned"
with "his intention which we mentioned." (cf. also 30,19-20). If I
am not mistaken, Fārābī's expression "he [Plato] said," which occurs
rarely, refers only in one third of the cases to sayings which can
be found in the Platonic text.

To summarize: There is a great divergence between what
Fārābī explicitly says and what Plato explicitly says; it is frequently
impossible to say where Fārābī's alleged report of Plato's views
ends and his own exposition begins; and Fārābī does not often voice
assent to Plato's views. We begin to understand these features of the
Summary when we consider the most startling example of complete
deviation of a statement of Fārābī's from its model. This example
is the seventh chapter which is meant to reproduce the content of
the seventh book of the *Laws* and of the content of which one barely
finds a single trace in the alleged source. In regard to one section of
the seventh chapter the editor says: "In hoc praecepto conscribendo,
quod apud graecum Platonem omnino deest, videtur Alfarabius
Mahometi ipsius rationem de priorum prophetarum legibus ante
oculos habuisse." The editor also notes, although in a different
context, that Fārābī had no delusions about the fundamental dif-

---

10. Cf. also e.g., 7, 4-7; 12, 16-13; 13; 16, 13-19; 37, 9-14.

ference between the Islamic laws and Plato's laws.[11] We begin to
wonder whether the bewildering features of the *Summary* cannot
be partly understood if one takes into consideration Fārābī's awareness of the fundamental difference between Islam and Plato's philosophic politics. Fārābī may have rewritten the *Laws*, as it were,
with a view to the situation that was created by the rise of Islam or
of revealed religion generally. He may have tried to preserve
Plato's purpose by adapting the expression of that purpose to the
new medium. Desiring to act appropriately with a view to what
is useful, he may have desired to ascribe his revised version of
Plato's teaching to the dead Plato in order to protect that version,
or the sciences generally speaking, especially by leaving open the
question as to whether he agreed with everything his Plato taught
and by failing to draw a precise line between his mere report and
his independent exposition.

The *Laws* is not a book of whose content one can merely take
cognizance without undergoing a change, or which one can merely
use for inspiring himself with noble feelings. The *Laws* contains a
teaching which claims to be true, i.e. valid for all times. Every
serious reader of the *Laws* has to face this claim. Every Muslim
reader in the Middle Ages did face it. He could do this in at least
three different ways. He could reject Plato's claim by contending
that Plato lacked completely the guidance supplied by Revelation.
He could use the Platonic standards for judging, or criticizing,
specific Islamic institutions, if not for rejecting Islam altogether. He
could contend that Islam, and Islam alone, lives up to the true
standards set forth by Plato, and on this basis elaborate a purely
rational justification of both the content and the origin of Islam.

Fārābī knew well that there were important differences between
the Greek laws and the Islamic law. Toward the end of the second
chapter he says: "The art of singing was of marvelous importance
with the Greeks; the legislators bestowed on it consummate care;
that art is truly very useful. . . ." In the section immediately following he mentions the fact that the same institution is employed
by one code and rejected by another, and explains the conditions
under which this variety is unobjectionable. At the end of the sixth
chapter he says that taking care of the leaders of the musicians is
necessary in every time, but that the care for this was greater "in

11. Latin translation p. 27 n.; Praefatio, pp. X-XI.

those times." But Fārābī knew equally well that in other respects which are no less important there was no difference between Greek laws and Islamic law. For instance, as he notes toward the end of the last chapter, Plato had discussed the question as to whether a man who knows nothing except the laws and does nothing except what the laws demand is virtuous or not, and as regards this question "there is still grave disagreement among men." At the beginning of the third chapter he says: "He began to explain that the establishment of laws, their destruction, and their restoration is not a novelty belonging to this time, but something that happened in the past and will happen in the future." It would seem that Fārābī means by "this time" his own time, although not merely his own lifetime. Immediately afterward he summarizes Plato's natural explanation of the coming into being as well as of the perishing of "the divine law" (cf. 18,14). The mere possibility that Fārābī applied to his own time a remark which Plato might be thought to have made about his time would force one to wonder whether he contemplated the application to Islam of what Plato had said about the natural beginning and the necessary perishing of every code. It is not a sufficient answer to say that Fārābī did not explicitly assent to Plato's thesis or that he did not describe it as useful or fine, nor to refer to Fārābī's independent discussion of the counsel or ruse to be employed in the establishment of laws in a new political society (30,5-20), nor to allude to the obvious connection between Plato's thesis and the issue "eternity or creation" (17,2 ff.).[12] Finally, we note that the expressions "that city," "those cities," and "their cities" which occur in the seventh chapter as frequently as the expression "the city," are ambiguous, as appears clearly from a passage of the sixth chapter (30,3).

Fārābī agreed with Plato certainly to the extent that he, too, presented what he regarded as the truth by means of ambiguous, allusive, misleading, and obscure speech. The *Summary* is rich in obscure passages. "It is incumbent on the legislator to teach the rulers and authorities how they should guide every individual among the human beings in order that they will walk in that way of his and that they will go in that right road, lest there arise aversion

---

12. The third chapter is the only part of the *Summary* in which the expression "in this chapter" or "in this section" does not occur. The expression "in this chapter" occurs in six chapters at the beginning of the chapter. For other peculiarities of the third chapter, see 17, 9 and 12 as well as 20, 5.

from their bad guidance. He mentioned this subject and illustrated it with examples from the free and the slaves, and from the bees in beehives and men's dealings with them; he meant by this the wicked and the lazy" (39,3-7). The editor is quite certain that "by this" means "by the bees." But we fail to see why he is so certain of this interpretation. We observe that Fārābī mentions three pairs, apart from the pair consisting of the wicked and the lazy: the bees and the beekeepers, the free and the slaves, the way of the legislator and the right road. On the basis of this observation we raise a few questions, starting from these: Do the beekeepers take care of every single bee? Do the beekeepers treat the bees in the way in which one ought to treat freemen or in the way in which one ought to treat slaves? What is the relation of the way of the beekeeper to the way of the legislator? Is there a point of view from which one could regard the free as wicked? No one would claim that mere study of the quoted passage could lead to answers to these questions, although it is not irrelevant to note that in the immediate sequel Fārābī adumbrates the problem inherent in any universal law or more particularly in any code meant to be valid everywhere on earth.[13] We prefer to turn to two other passages which we shall quote in the editor's translation while italicizing those words which do not occur in the text.

Impudens vero sibi ipsi tantum et suae felicitati consulit, ideoque dis invisus est, at *dis* invisus *deorum* non firmatur auxilio; et qui *eorum* auxilio non firmatur, nullum pulchrum et gratum vestigium relinquit. Coepit deinde eum describere (*scil. optimum principem vel legislatorem*) et ea memoravit quae illi curanda sunt; et dixit eum primo curam corporis deinde animi deinde externarum rerum gradatim adhibere; cuius rei exempla attulit et copiose disseruit, cum hoc perutile sit. (23, 16-21.)

We do not see that Fārābī's Plato describes here unambiguously a man who is concerned with things other than his own felicity.

Explicavit deinde alios homines ex aliis rebus voluptatem capere, prout condicione et indole et moribus differunt, et ad hoc explicandum fortium virorum et artificum exempla attulit; quod enim alii artifici gratum est alii ingratum est, et idem ad rectum et pulchrum et justum pertinet. Deinde diffuse disseruit in hoc capite ad explicandum omnia haec pulchra esse turpia, quod ad aliquid referenda sint, non quod ipsa per se pulchra

---

13. As regards the latter problem, cf. also 5, 4-5; 12, 17-13, 7 (cf. 21, 11-13); 13, 14-19; 14, 11-12; 16, 12-15; 18, 16-17.

aut turpia sint; et artifices cum de hoc rogentur procul dubio assensuros esse dixit. (15, 4-10.)

For the interpretation of this passage one would have to dwell on the fact that whereas, according to Fārābī, the relativity of the just and noble things will be granted by the artisans, it does not appear that it will be granted by the heroes. This is not the only place in the *Summary* where Fārābī alludes to the fact that the noble things belong to the realm of opinion, or in other words, where he alludes to the fundamental difference between courage, war, city and kindred things on the one hand, and the arts on the other.[14] He understood in a rare way what Plato thought about the problem inherent in any universal or absolutely valid rule of action, the connection between such rules and warlike heroism, and the light supplied by the contrast between men's agreement in the despised and lowly arts on the one hand and their fanatical disagreement regarding the high and holy on the other.

These examples show how easy it is to put too narrow a construction on Fārābī's secretiveness. He is secretive not only by being completely silent about some subjects but likewise by being silent about other subjects in certain places only. We have noted that he is completely silent about God and gods in his *Philosophy of Plato* whereas in his *Summary* he mentions God and gods frequently, or, to be precise, fourteen times. We must now consider the distribution of his mentions of God and gods in various parts of the *Summary*. In the preface and the first chapter taken together, or, to be somewhat more exact, in the first six pages, God is mentioned three times as often as are gods; God is mentioned three times, gods are mentioned once. Thereafter, there occurs only a single mention of God, and this mention occurs in a genuine quotation from Plato (19,8); Fārābī himself speaks exclusively of gods. I distinctly remember one case in which Fārābī, summarizing a passage in which Plato speaks of God, goes so far as to replace God by gods (cf. 27,3-7 with *Laws* 732c7). There are even some sections in which there is complete silence, not only about God, but about gods as well: chapters 6, 7 and 9. This silence is prepared by a number of steps of which we may note the following ones. We begin with the fourth chapter. Summarizing *Laws* 709b-c where

---

14. Cf. 11, 1-4 and 13-14; 17, 16-18, 4; 22, 3-10; 26, 7-13; 31, 9-10; 37, 5-21. Cf. *Philosophy of Plato* §§ 12 (10, 8-10) and 14 (13, 2).

Plato speaks of the rule of God and Chance over human affairs, Fārābī preserves only the mention of Chance.[15] Summarizing *Laws* 716a, he fails even to allude to Plato's opening remark according to which "God holds the beginning, the end, and the center of all beings" and to Plato's immediately following remark that "God is the measure of all things" (23,14-16). This is perhaps the most striking parallel, within the *Summary*, to his silence about the tenth book. In the immediate sequel, when he summarizes *Laws* 716d-717a, he does refer to the gods as Plato does, but Fārābī's reference is strangely elliptical as we noted when quoting the editor's translation of the passage in the preceding paragraph. Summarizing the end of the fourth book of the *Laws*, Fārābī drops Plato's repeated reference to the gods (723e-724a). We have now reached, in our rapid survey, the very center of the *Summary*. At the beginning of the fifth chapter, which is literally the central chapter, Fārābī does exactly the same thing that he did at the end of the fourth chapter: he drops Plato's repeated and unambiguous reference to the gods (726a1,3; 727a1). The beginning of the fifth chapter reads as follows: "He explained in this chapter that what has to be cared for in the first place is the soul, since the soul is the most noble of things and on the third rank from the rank of the divine; the most worthy thing regarding the soul among the kinds of care is honor, since contempt of the soul is base. He explained that honor is of the class of the divine things and in fact is the most noble of them, and the soul is noble; the soul ought therefore to be honored." Fārābī does not reproduce Plato's statement that one ought to honor one's soul "next after the gods" (726a6-727a2). He seems to say that the soul is inferior to the divine. But he certainly says that the soul is the most noble of things. Could he possibly mean that the soul is superior in nobility or dignity to the divine? He cannot mean that the divine is not noble, for he says that honor is the most noble of the divine things. Nor can he mean that the divine does not belong to the sphere of "things" (*ashyā* or *umūr*), for he speaks of divine "things" in both the *Philosophy of Plato* and the *Summary*. The following divine things are mentioned in the *Summary*: divine virtues, divine pleasures, divine music, divine law, divine government, divine rulers, human occupations of a

---

15. 22, 11-15. Cf. also 32, 5-6 with *Laws* 757e4.

certain kind.[16] In most of these cases "divine" obviously designates
a certain quality of human beings or of human achievements or
of human pursuits, namely, their excellence. If one considers the
fact that the divine laws are the work of a human legislator (8,18-20;
22,19; 29,15-17), there hardly remains a single example in which
"divine" has a meaning different from the one that we have indicated. And the soul is certainly not a quality but has a different
dignity. We note in parenthesis that the usage followed in the
Summary is not altogether at variance with that followed in the
Philosophy of Plato. In the *Philosophy of Plato* "divine" occurs
eight times. It is mentioned seven times in a single paragraph (§ 22)
which consists partly of a report of the opinions of people other
than Plato; when the use of the term is ascribed to Plato, it is
employed in contradistinction to "human" or "bestial." In the repetition of that passage, Fārābī replaces the dichotomy "divine-human"
by the dichotomy "human-bestial" (§ 24). The eighth mention of
"divine" is in a class by itself: Fārābī mentions once in the *Philosophy of Plato* "divine beings." He does this in § 26. And he never
mentions "divine beings" in the *Summary*. Later on in the fifth
chapter of the *Summary* Fārābī mentions gods three times in a
single section. The section concludes with the remark that man loves
to put his hope in the gods with a view to greater happiness of his
existence and greater nobility of his life; "and the noble life is
sometimes noble in the eyes of a people and sometimes it is noble
in the eyes of gods; one must consider this and meditate on it
thoroughly." (27,3-7.) One sees that this section does not dispel
the obscurities of the passage with which the fifth chapter opens.
As for the sixth chapter, it is the only chapter of the *Summary* in
which there does not occur a single mention of any of the following
themes: God, gods, revealed law and the other life. The sixth
chapter represents therefore the closest approximation, within the
Summary, to the *Philosophy of Plato*. It is also the only chapter
of the *Summary* in which the term "substance" occurs. The sixth
chapter goes even beyond the *Philosophy of Plato* since it avoids
the terms "divine" and "religion." While God, religion and divine

---

16. 7, 1, 2, 2, 3, 6, 7; 12, 8, 9, 15; 18, 14; 20, 11; 21, 21; 22, 19; 23, 5, 7;
25, 12, 16; 27, 5, 19, 22; 29, 15. Seven mentions of "divine" as a quality occur
in the fifth chapter. The mention of "divine" in 25, 10 is in a class by itself.

are no longer mentioned in the rest of the *Summary*, the revealed law reappears in the seventh chapter, gods in the eighth chapter, and the other life in the ninth chapter. For regarding the other life, the *Summary* proceeds in fundamentally the same way in which it proceeds regarding the gods. The other life is mentioned in the first chapter and punishments in the other life are mentioned in the last chapter: there is silence in a central section.[17]

These remarks will suffice to give a notion of the kind of difficulties with which the student of the *Summary* has to contend. We would be foolish to claim that we are in a position to explain these difficulties. We imagine that one would have to know much more about the religious situation in Fārābī's age than we know at present, before one could expect a clarification of Fārābī's own position. On the other hand, it cannot be denied that in reflecting for some time on writings like the *Summary*, one acquires a certain understanding of the manner in which such writings need to be read. We believe we have succeeded in following one of the threads of the argument of the first chapter.

Whatever assumptions we may have made regarding the way towards the truth, man's bliss and the law, Plato confronts us abruptly with the question, raised by one of his characters, concerning the efficient cause of legislation, i.e. concerning the legislator, and with the answer, given by another Platonic character, that the legislator was Zeus, a god, as is vouched for by popular accounts. While, as Plato makes clear, the laws are superior to wisdom of every kind, it is right, as he intimates, to examine the laws, i.e., not indeed to examine their origin or efficient cause, but to discover in what way their particular stipulations are agreeable to right reason (5,7-16). Such examination presupposes clarity as to what constitutes the virtuous city. It leads to the result that "those people" to whom the laws of Zeus were given, did not form a virtuous city. It is for this reason that their laws are judged explicitly with reference to standards supplied, not by these laws, but by certain poems (5,16-6,16). These steps make us receptive to the distinction which is not immediately made with full explicitness, between the true legislator and impostors, a distinction which had been completely disregarded in the unqualified praise of laws

---

17. 6, 17-18 (cf. the parallel in 16, 14-15); 42, 20; 43, 2. Cf. also 14, 5-10; 23, 22-24, 1; 25, 18-20 (cf. *Laws* 727d1-5).

at the beginning. The intention of the legislator is that men should
seek the countenance of God, desire reward in the other life, and
acquire the highest virtue which is above the four moral virtues
(6,16-18). Could Zeus have had the intention to make his subjects
seek the countenance, not of Zeus, but of God? Fārābī merely notes
here that Plato warned men against impostors (6,18-22). As for the
true legislator, he is concerned with his subjects acquiring both the
human virtues, which include science, and the divine virtues. The
acquisition of the human virtues must precede that of the divine
virtues. If a man who possesses human virtue uses it according to
the prescription of the law, his human virtue becomes divine virtue
(7,1-7). It would appear that one can acquire human virtue without
obeying the law, that to be religious means to be virtuous according to the prescriptions of the law, i.e., to obey the gods (cf. 16,14-
15), or that the specific objective of the law is the production of
divine virtue. Does the divine virtue which one can only acquire
by obeying the law lead one to seek the countenance of God and
to desire the other life? Fārābī does not answer this question. Nor
does he answer the question of how the law brings about the transformation of human virtue into divine virtue. He merely speaks
about the causes through which the legislators produce the virtues,
without distinguishing any further between human and divine virtues (7,7-12). Both Zeus and Apollo used in their codes or in the
ordinances of their revealed laws all the causes through which
virtue is produced (7,12-14). Only sometime thereafter does Plato
begin to censure certain prescriptions of the laws of Zeus and Apollo
explicitly and contrast those laws unfavorably with some older laws
which were made by gods and which contained precepts of consummate soundness (8,2-10). This justifies the contention that the
laws of the victors are not necessarily superior in goodness to the
laws of the vanquished (8,13-17; cf.12,13-15 and 16,7-9). It certainly casts some doubt on the divinity of Zeus and Apollo. We
learn now that every true legislator is created and formed by God
for the purpose of legislation, just as every leader in any craft is
created and formed by god for his craft (8,18-20) and that the
legislator must obey his own law (9,1 ff.), which cannot be said
without qualification of gods: gods do not pray. Yet in spite of
those doubts of the laws which may have suggested themselves
to us, or may still suggest themselves to us (9,13-20), the law in

itself is noble and virtuous, and superior to everything which is
said for it or against it (9,21-22). Still, in order that we may have
genuine knowledge of the goodness of the law and, as a matter
of fact, genuine knowledge of the truth regarding anything,
we need training in logic, just as the legislator needs training, from
his early youth, in the handling of political affairs (9,23-10,9). If
we think of the connection between human virtue in the comprehensive sense of the term and training in logic, we are not surprised
by Plato's next step. Morality may be said to consist in the proper
resolution of the conflicts which arise between the discerning power
of the soul and the bestial power of the soul: "It is incumbent on
the individual to meditate on the states of his soul in these conflicts
and to follow the discerning power, and on the people of the city
altogether, if they are unable to discern by themselves, to accept
the truth from the legislators and from the followers of the legislators and those who state the truth about them and the good and
virtuous" (10,10-17). It would seem that the reasonable individuals
do not need guidance by the legislator (11,5-17). At the end of the
first chapter we are thus already somewhat prepared for the following remark which occurs unexpectedly in the center of the last
chapter and which still strikes us as unbelievable: "Then he explained that when men are good and most excellent they do not
need the laws and the *nomoi* at all and they are altogether happy;
but the *nomoi* and laws are needed by those whose characters are
not proper or right." (41,21-23)[18] We are much less surprised to
find that shortly afterward, when he mentions the question as to
whether a man is virtuous and praiseworthy who knows nothing
except the laws and does nothing except what the laws demand,
he leaves the question unanswered (42,15-18).

Only by understanding Fārābī's thoughts about the problematic
character of law can one hope to understand the succinct remark
which the *Philosophy of Plato* devotes to Plato's *Laws*: "Then he
presented in the *Laws* the virtuous ways of life which are followed
by the people of this city." By "this city" he means in all probability
the virtuous city described in the *Republic*, for the passage on the
Laws (§27) follows immediately after the summaries of the *Repub-*

18. Cf. 25, 2-6 and 26, 24-27, 2. Cf. also the teaching of the *Summary* regarding punishment: punishment forms part of the training of the body as
distinguished from the training of the soul; cf. 26, 7-13 with 31, 18-21; 33,
19-34, 2; 41, 7-14; 42, 14-43, 4.

lic (§25) and the *Timaeus* (§26). We are surprised by the extreme
brevity of the passage devoted to the *Laws* as well as by the silence
of that passage about the obvious and guiding theme of the *Laws*,
namely, the laws. As a matter of fact, laws are mentioned in the
Philosophy of Plato only in §§29, 30, 32. We find however one
other reference to the *Laws* in the *Philosophy of Plato*. In §28, a
distinction is made between the science and art embodied in the
Laws and the science and art embodied in the *Timaeus;* whereas
the latter science and art is ascribed to Timaeus, the science and
art embodied in the only Platonic dialogue in which Socrates does
not occur is ascribed to Socrates. If we combine the information
supplied by §28 with that supplied by §27, we reach the conclusion
that Socrates was silent about laws; this conclusion is, to say the
least, not at variance with Fārābī's summary of the *Crito* (§23).
Socrates' silence about laws, in its turn, must be understood in the
light of the implicit distinction, made in §30, between the way of
Socrates and the way of Plato. The way of Plato emerges through
a correction of the way of Socrates. The way of Socrates is intransigent: it demands of the philosopher an open break with the
accepted opinions. The way of Plato combines the way of Socrates,
which is appropriate for the philosopher's relations to the elite, with
the way of Thrasymachus, which is appropriate for the philosopher's relations to the vulgar. The way of Plato demands therefore judicious conformity with the accepted opinions. If we consider
the connection, stated in the *Summary*, between the vulgar and
laws, we arrive at the conclusion that the appreciation or legitimation of laws becomes possible by virtue of Plato's correction of the
way of Socrates.[19] It is as if Fārābī had interpreted the absence of
Socrates from the *Laws* to mean that Socrates has nothing to do
with laws, and as if he had tried to express this interpretation by
suggesting that if *per impossibile* the *Laws* were Socratic, they would
not deal with laws.

   The statement about the *Laws* in the *Philosophy of Plato* must
then be understood as part of such a presentation of Plato's philosophy as is guided by a peculiar distinction between the way of
Socrates and the way of Plato. The importance of this distinction
for the *Philosophy of Plato* as a whole does not appear at first

------

   19. The first half of the *Philosophy of Plato* ends with "Socrates"; the
second half ends with "their laws," i.e., the laws of the Athenians.

sight. At first it seems as if Fārābī meant to say that all insights
which he ascribed to Plato were peculiar to Plato. What he actually
says however is that Plato did not find the science which he desired
among the sciences and arts which are known to the vulgar (§§6,12,
16). Only at the beginning of the second half of the work, i.e.,
immediately after the first mention of Socrates, does Fārābī explicitly speak of what Plato in contradistinction to all other men
did: Plato attempted to exhibit or present the desired science (§16).
Only in the eighth and last section (§§30-32) does he explicitly
speak of Plato's "repetitions" and thus bring out the difference
between Plato and Socrates. And only in the central paragraph of
the last section (§31) does he mention an alleged remark of Plato
to the effect that his predecessors had neglected something. The
only originality which Fārābī's Plato claims for himself concerns
the investigation, allegedly made in the *Menexenus*, of the ways in
which the citizens ought to honor the philosophers on the one hand,
and the kings and most excellent men on the other. The investigation apparently led to the result that the philosophers, as distinguished from the legislators, cannot expect to be deified by the
citizens. However this may be, Fārābī introduces Plato's correction
of the Socratic teaching only toward the end of the *Philosophy of
Plato;* those summaries of Platonic writings which constitute the
first seven sections of the *Philosophy of Plato* describe therefore the
Platonic teaching as it was prior to Plato's correction of the Socratic
teaching.[20] Yet, as Fārābī indicates by his remark about the Platonic
writings in his preface to the *Summary*, all Platonic writings presuppose already Plato's correction of the Socratic teaching. It follows therefore that not everything Fārābī says in characterizing the
content of the Platonic dialogues is meant to be borne out by the
text of the Platonic dialogues. This conclusion is confirmed by the
comparison of the remark on the *Laws* in the *Philosophy of Plato*
with the *Summary*, to say nothing further about the *Summary*
taken by itself. We admire the ease with which Fārābī invented
Platonic speeches.

---

20. Cf. § 30 (22, 4) and § 15.

VI

MAIMONIDES'

STATEMENT ON

POLITICAL

SCIENCE

Sed quid ego Graecorum? Nescio quo modo
me magis nostra delectant.
—Cicero, *De divinatione*, I

Maimonides discusses the subject matter as well as the function of political science at the end of the last chapter (ch. 14) of his *Treatise on the Art of Logic* (*Millot ha-higgayon*). Philosophy or science, he says, consists of two parts: theoretical philosophy and practical philosophy, the latter also being called human philosophy, political philosophy, or political science. Theoretical philosophy consists of three parts: mathematics, physics, and theology. Practical philosophy consists of four parts: man's governance of himself, governance of the household, governance of the city, and governance of the great [numerous] nation or of the nations. The first part of political science deals with the virtues and the vices, or with good and bad habits. "There are many books by the philosophers on the habits." Ethics does not deal with "commands," i. e., with that form of guidance by which a man guides other men, whereas the three other parts of practical philosophy do deal with them. Governance of the household supplies knowledge of how its members can help each other, and of what is sufficient for the best possible ordering of their affairs with due regard to time and place. Governance of the city is the science that supplies knowledge of human happiness and of the way toward its acquisition, as well as of the opposites of both those things; "furthermore, it lays down the rules of justice through which human associations are ordered properly; furthermore, the wise men belonging to the perfect [ancient][1] nations, each of them according to his perfection, lay down rules of governance through which their subjects are governed [through which their kings govern their multitude]; they called [call] them [sc. those rules of governance] *nomoi;* the nations were governed by those *nomoi.* On all these subjects, the philosophers have many books which have already been translated into Arabic, but perhaps more which have not been translated. But we have no need in these times for all this, viz. for [the commands], the laws, the *nomoi,* the governance by [of] [these] human beings in divine things [for the laws and the *nomoi;* the governance of human beings is now through divine things]."

The meaning of this statement is not entirely clear. The obscurities are partly due to the facts that the Arabic original of about the second half of the *Logic* is lost, and that the differences between the three Hebrew translations, or even between the various MSS of these translations, are sufficiently great as to make doubtful the reconstruction of the original in every important point. In the preceding paragraph, the bracketed expressions correspond to alternative translations or readings which seem to be as defensible as the preferred versions.

Three difficulties strike us at first sight: Maimonides rejects the books of the philosophers on politics proper as useless for "us" "in

---

1. Could the original have read *al-umam al-mādiyuna?* The expression *al-umam al-mādiyuna* in Fārābī's *Siyāsāt* 51, 6 (Hyderabad, 1346) is rendered by Samuel ibn Tibbon *ha-ummot he'ovrot* (42, 7 Filipowski). The adjective does not necessarily mean "ancient" or "past." It might also mean "piercing" or "penetrating." That Maimonides could have applied a term of praise of this kind to the Greeks, the Persians, and so on, in contradistinction to the Chaldeans, the Egyptians, and so on, appears from *Iggeret Teman* 8, 15 Halkin, the *Letter on Astrology* 351, 17-18 Marx, and *Guide* III 29 (63a Munk).

these times." Also, he divides politics proper in an unusual manner. And finally, while assigning the study of the virtues to ethics, he assigns the understanding of happiness, not to ethics, the first part of practical philosophy, but to politics proper, the last part of practical philosophy.

To begin with the first difficulty, we are naturally inclined to believe that "we" means "we Jews": we Jews do not need the political teaching, nor perhaps the economic teaching, of the philosophers, since we have the Torah which guides us perfectly in every respect, and especially in respect of the divine things.[2] Yet this is not precise enough. In the first place, whereas Maimonides says in regard to politics proper, or a part of it, that we do not need the books of the philosophers on this subject, he says in regard to ethics merely that the philosophers have many books on ethics: he does not say that we do not need the books of the philosophers on ethics.[3] He says nothing whatever in this context about the books of the philosophers on theoretical subjects. There is no need to prove that Maimonides knew of the existence of such books and that he was very far from regarding them as useless for "us": the statement under discussion occurs in a summary of logic which is based upon the philosophers' books on logic and on theoretical philosophy. What he suggests then is that of all genuinely philosophic books, only the books on politics proper (and perhaps on economics) have been rendered superfluous by the Torah. This implies that the function of the Torah is emphatically political. This interpretation is confirmed by the *Guide for the Perplexed*. In that work, Maimonides says that the Torah gives only summary indications concerning theoretical subjects, whereas regarding the governance of the city, everything has been done to make it precise in all its details.[4]

Still, Maimonides adds an important qualification to his statement that we do not need the books of the philosophers on politics proper: he says that we do not need those books "in these times." The Torah antedates philosophy, or Greek wisdom, by centuries. If it were the Torah which rendered superfluous the political books

2. Cf. Comtino and Mendelssohn *ad loc.*
3. Cf. *Eight Chapters*, Introduction.
4. III 27 (59b-60a). Cf. I Introd. (5a [cf. *Treatise on Resurrection* 32 Finkel], 11a); I 33 (37a), 71 (93b-94a), III Introd. (2b), 28 (60b-61a), 54 (132a). Cf. Albo, *Ikkarim* I 3 (63, 13-19 Husik), 11 (100, 18), and 15 (133, 9-134, 1).

of the philosophers, those books would not have been needed by the Jewish people at any time. Hence we would seem to be compelled to understand Maimonides' statement as follows: not the Jews as such, but the Jews in exile, the Jews who lack a political existence, do not need the political books of the philosophers. The Torah is not sufficient for the guidance of a political community.[5] This would imply that the political books of the philosophers will again be needed after the coming of the Messiah, as they were needed prior to the exile.

These strange consequences force us to reconsider the assumption that Maimonides means by "we" "we Jews," or that his *Logic* is a Jewish book, i.e., a book written by a Jew as a Jew for Jews as Jews. The author describes himself as a student of logic, and he describes the immediate addressee as an authority on the sciences based upon divinely revealed law, as well as on Arabic eloquence: he does not describe himself and the addressee as Jews. When using the first person plural in his *Logic*, he normally means "we logicians," although he also speaks of "the logicians" in the third person. Yet on some occasions he speaks of subjects which belong to philosophy proper as distinguished from logic. Therefore, "we" might mean in some cases "we philosophers," although Maimonides normally speaks of "the philosophers" in the third person and even seems to indicate that he does not belong to them.[6] We are tempted to say that the *Logic* is the only philosophic book which Maimonides ever wrote. One would not commit a grievous error if he under-

---

5. Cf. Mendelssohn *ad loc.*—Cf. the reference to the military art (which belongs to politics proper and is certainly not a part of the Torah) in Maimonides' *Letter on Astrology* with H. Melakhim XI 4 and XII 2-5 as well as *Resurrection* 21, 11-23, 12. Cf. also *Eight Chapters* VIII (28, 13-20 Wolff) with *ib.* (28, 2-3 and 27, 19-20).

6. *Logic*, Preface; ch. 9 (43, 11-14 Efros), 10 (46, 16-18), and 14 (61, 12-14). —The first person plural is used with unusual frequency in a section of *Eight Chapters* IV (9, 6-10, 16). There "we" occurs in the following four different meanings: 1) the author (3 times), 2) we human beings (3 times), 3) we physicians (4 times), 4) we physicians of the soul (i. e., we men of science; see *ib.* III [7, 6]) (17 times). It goes without saying that in *Eight Chapters* IV "we" frequently means "we Jews"; it occurs there in the meaning "we Jews," I believe, 14 times; see especially *ib.* (12, 23) where Maimonides says that he is speaking only of "our law" or "the adherents of our law." For the interpretation, consider Guide I 71 (97a).—A kindred subtlety (*nukta*) is the emphatic use of "we" (e. g., *anachnu nirah*), in contradistinction to its nonemphatic use, of which one finds good examples in Albo's *Ikkarim* II 4 (27, 9), 5 (48, 3-6), etc.

stood by "we" "we men of theory," which term is more inclusive than "we philosophers" and almost approaches in comprehensiveness the present-day term "we intellectuals." Accordingly, Maimonides must be understood to say that the men who speculate about principles or roots do not "in these times" need the books of the philosophers which are devoted to politics proper because of the dominance of divinely revealed laws.[7] Since Maimonides' statement as a whole implies that the need for the books of the philosophers on ethics and, especially, on theoretical philosophy has not been affected by the rise to dominance of revealed religions, he in effect suggests that the function of revealed religion is emphatically political. Moreover, he regards as useless "in these times" only the books of the philosophers on "the laws, the *nomoi*, the governance by human beings in divine things." He does not deny the validity of the basic part of the political teaching of the philosophers:[8] the philosophers do distinguish adequately between true and imaginary happiness and the means appropriate to both, and they have an adequate knowledge of the rules of justice. Furthermore, if only the most practical part of the political teaching of the philosophers is superfluous "in these times" because its function is at present fulfilled by revealed religions; if, therefore, the function of revealed religion is emphatically political, political philosophy is as necessary "in these times" as in all other times for the theoretical understanding of revealed religion.

The normal division of politics proper may be said to be that which distinguishes governance of the city, governance of the nation, and governance of many or of all nations (i.e., governance of the political union, as distinguished from a mere alliance, of many or of all nations).[9] At first glance, Maimonides seems to replace "city—nation—many [all] nations" by "city—great nation—the nations." He therefore seems to replace the nation by the great nation, which leaves us wondering why the small nation is not a subject of politics. Yet it seems to be equally possible that he uses "the great nation" as equivalent to "the nations" or "many or all nations," in which case

---

7. Cf. H. A. Wolfson, "Notes on Maimonides' Classification of the Sciences," *JQR*, N. S. XXVI 377 n.

8. Note the transition from the perfect tense to the past tense in Maimonides' statement.

9. Fārābī, *Siyāsāt* (Hyderabad 1346) 39 and 50; *Al-madīna al-fādila* 53, 17-19 and 54, 5-10 Dieterici.

he would have dropped the nation altogether, leaving us to wonder why the nation is not a subject of politics. However this may be, he certainly does not substitute a new tri-partition of politics proper for the normal one, but rather replaces the tri-partition by a bi-partition: he assigns the governance of the city to one branch of political philosophy, and the governance of the great nation or of the nations to another branch. The principle underlying the tri-partition was consideration of the difference of size between political communities (small, medium, and large). It is reasonable to assume that the bi-partition is based upon consideration of another important difference between political communities.

Maimonides' references to the nations are framed partly in the past tense. It is possible that he even spoke explicitly of "the ancient nations." Furthermore, he calls the governance of the nations *nomoi.* Finally, in the same context, he speaks of a governance by human beings in divine things such as belongs to the past. With a view to these facts and to certain parallels in the *Guide,* Professor H. A. Wolfson has suggested that "the nations" stands for the ancient pagan nations, and "the great nation" stands for Israel, and therefore that Maimonides tacitly goes over from the distinction between political communities in regard to size to their distinction in regard to religion: the city stands for the "civil state," and the pagan nations and Israel stand for different forms of the "religious state."[10] This suggestion necessarily implies that the governance, or guidance, of Israel, i.e., the Torah, is a subject of political philosophy. More precisely, Wolfson's suggestion necessarily implies that the governance of the great nation, i.e., the Torah, and the governance of the nations, i.e., the *nomoi,* are the subjects of one and the same branch of political philosophy. This should not be surprising: the same science deals with opposites. Accordingly, the chapters of the *Guide* which deal with the difference between the Torah and the *nomoi* of the pagans would belong to political science. Since one of these chapters (II 40) is the central chapter of the part devoted to prophecy, one would be justified in suggesting that Maimonides' prophetology as a whole is a branch of political science. This suggestion is confirmed by considerations which are in no way based on the teaching of the *Logic.* These inferences are in perfect agree-

10. *Loc. cit.,* 372-376.

ment with Maimonides' concluding remark, which is to the effect that we have no need in these times for the books of the philosophers on the laws, the *nomoi*, the governance by human beings in divine things: the practical use of books meant only for practical use is one thing; an entirely different thing is the use for purely theoretical purposes of books which are at least partly theoretical.

Wolfson's suggestion is partly confirmed by Avicenna's division of political philosophy. Avicenna makes use of a bi-partition which is based upon exactly the same principle that Wolfson discerned in Maimonides' statement. According to Avicenna, one branch of political philosophy deals with kingship; the classic texts on this subject are the books of Plato and Aristotle on government. The other branch deals with prophecy and divine law; the classic texts on this subject are the books of Plato and Aristotle on *nomoi*. This second branch considers the existence of prophecy and the need of the human race for divine law; it considers the characteristics common to all divine codes as well as those which are peculiar to individual divine codes; it deals with the difference between genuine and spurious prophecy.[11]

There is then one point in Wolfson's suggestion which must be changed. There is no reason for identifying the great nation with Israel. If Maimonides had spoken of "the nation" or of "the virtuous nation," one might say that he might have meant Israel. But he speaks of "the great nation." He is fond of quoting Deuteronomy 4:6, where Israel is called "a great nation." As he indicates, the Biblical verse implies that Israel is not the only great nation. It is then impossible in precise speech to call Israel "the great nation" simply. On the contrary, since "great" here means "numerous," the term would apply to Islam (and to Christianity) rather than to Israel. Indeed, it would be more appropriate to call Israel the small nation: Jacob "is small" (Amos 7:5).[12] One might for a moment imagine that Maimonides speaks of the great nation precisely in order to exclude the small nation, i.e., Israel, and hence the Torah, from the

---

11. *Tis' Rasā'il*, Istanbul 1298, 73-74. Cf. Falakera, *Reshit hokma* 58-59 David. See Wolfson, "Additional Notes," *HUCA*, III, 1926, 374.

12. *Iggeret Teman* 4, 8-10: 8, 3-6; 38, 1-2; 40, 4-6 (cf. Ibn Tibbon's translation); 40, 11 ff. Halkin. Cf. *Guide* II 11 *vers. fin.* and III 31. Cf. the use of "the great nations" which as such are distinguished from Israel, in Ibn Aknīn's Commentary on the Song of Songs (Halkin in *Alexander Marx Jubilee Volume*, English section, New York 1950, 421).

scope of political philosophy. But this possibility is contradicted by all the considerations which have been set forth here, and in particular by the fact that the *Logic* is not a Jewish book. We suggest then that Maimonides means by "the nations" the ancient pagan nations, and by "the great nation" any group constituted by a universalistic religion. In speaking of the great nation in the singular, he refers to the universalistic and hence exclusive claim raised by each of the three great monotheistic religions: on the premises of each, there can be only one legitimate religious community. In speaking of the nations in the plural, he refers to the national character of the religions of the pagans: that national character explains the co-existence of many equally legitimate religious communities.[13]

It is true that after having divided politics proper into governance of the city and governance of the great nations at the beginning of his statement on political science, Maimonides does not make explicit use of the bi-partition in the sequel: when discussing the function and the scope of politics proper, he identifies the whole of politics proper with governance of the city. This does not mean however that he drops the original bi-partition as unimportant. On the contrary, it means that that bi-partition is a hint which is addressed to the attentive reader and which may safely be lost on the others. To understand Maimonides' thought means to understand his hints. It is possible to explain a particular hint with utmost explicitness, but the nature of the subject matter compels the interpreter to have recourse, sooner or later, to other hints.

These remarks do not suffice to clarify the obscurities of Maimonides' statement. As a rule, he enumerates at the end of each chapter of the *Logic* the terms which he has explained in the body of the chapter. In the enumeration at the end of Chapter 14, he does not mention the terms designating the four parts of practical or political philosophy, whereas he does mention the terms designating the three parts of theoretical philosophy. Thus he does not even claim to have explained the meaning of "governance of the great nation or of the nations" in particular. We have seen how appropriate this silent declaration is. There are only two terms pertaining to politics proper and to economics which he mentions as having

---

13. Cf. *Guide* I 71 (94b): "the Christian nation embraced these nations." As regards the universalistic intention of the Torah, cf., e.g., H. Teshubah IX 9 and *Resurrection* 32, 4-6.

been explained in the chapter: "commands"[14] and *nomoi*. He did
define "command": command is that guidance by which a man
guides other men. But he did not define *nomos*. Yet the remark at
the end of the chapter shows that the definition of *nomos* is implicitly conveyed through the statement on economics and on politics
proper. It is obvious that *nomos* must be a species of the genus "command." Discussing the governance of the household, he says that
that governance takes due account of time and place. He does not
mention the consideration of time and place when discussing
politics proper. We suggest that *nomos* is that species of command
which is general in the sense that it does not regard time and place,
or that it does not consider the individual in his individuality. The
other species of command is that of particular commands, commands
which change in accordance with changing circumstances, and especially in accordance with differences among the individuals to
be guided.[15]

Does this mean that all political governance, or all sound political
governance, is government by law? According to Fārābī, whom
Maimonides regarded as the philosophic authority second only to
Aristotle, the unchangeable divine law (*sharī'a*) is only a substitute
for the government of a perfect ruler who governs without written
laws and who changes his ordinances in accordance with the change
of times as he sees fit.[16] The rule of living intelligence appears to
be superior to the rule of law. There is then a form of sound political
governance which is akin to the governance of the household, or
to paternal rule, in that it pays due regard to time and place as well
as to what is good for each individual—the form of political governance which Plato and Aristotle had praised most highly. Maimonides mentions the rule of living intelligence in the household
and the rule of law in the city; he does not mention the rule of
living intelligence in the city. He omits the central possibility. One
of our first impressions was that he might have omitted from the

14. Ibn Tibbon: *hahuqqim;* Vives: *hahoq;* Ahitub: *hahanhaga.* Could the
original have read *hukm?*
15. Cf. *Guide* III 34 with II 40 (85b), where Maimonides speaks about the
conventional character of the agreement produced by law between individuals
of different and opposite temperaments. Consider the implications of the distinction between those psychically ill people who, being men of science, can
heal themselves and those who are in need of being treated by others in *Eight
Chapters* III-IV.
16. *Siyāsat* 50-51; *Al-madīna al-fādila* 60, 15 ff.

normal enumeration of the kinds of political governance the governance of the nation, i.e., the central item. We see now that this impression was not entirely wrong: he did omit a central item. But whereas it remained uncertain whether he had omitted the nation or only the small nation, it is quite certain that he omitted the rule of living intelligence in the city or nation.

If *nomos* is essentially a general command in the sense indicated, it is not, as we have previously assumed, essentially a religious order. Perhaps Maimonides even made an explicit distinction between *nomos* and "governance by human beings in divine things" at the end of his statement. However this may be, in his thematic discussion of *nomos* in the *Guide*, he suggests that the *nomos*, in contradistinction to the divinely revealed law, is directed only toward the well-being of the body and is unconcerned with divine things.[17] The *nomos* is, then, to use Wolfson's expression, essentially the order of a "civil state" as distinguished from a "religious state." One might think that the philosophers did not admit the possibility of a "civil state": according to them, divine worship is an essential function, and in a sense the primary function, of civil society. But this objection overlooks the fact that while the *nomos* must indeed be strengthened by myth or by a "governmental religion," that religion is not part of the primary intention of the *nomos* and of the association which is ordered by it.[18]

Whereas the *nomos* entails a religion that is in the service of government, the divinely revealed law which is a subject of the same branch of political philosophy as the *nomos* puts government in the service of religion, of the true religion, of the truth. The divinely revealed law is therefore necessarily free from the relativity of the *nomos*, i.e., it is universal as regards place and perpetual as regards time. It is then a much loftier social order than the *nomos*. Hence it is exposed to dangers which did not threaten the pagan *nomoi*. For instance, the public discussion of "the account of creation," i.e., of physics, did not harm the pagans in the way in which it might harm the adherents of revealed laws. The divinely revealed laws

---

17. Cf. II 39 end with II 40 (86a-b).

18. Cf. Aristotle, *Politics* 1299a 18-19, 1322b 16-22, 1328b 11, and *Metaphysics* 1074b 1 ff. Cf. Yehuda Halevi, *Cuzari* I 13; Maimonides' Commentary on 'Abodah zara IV 7 (27 Wiener).

also create dangers which did not exist among the Greeks: they open up a new source of disagreement among men.[19]

To summarize, Maimonides directs our attention first to the differences between political societies in regard to size. He then directs our attention to their differences in regard to religion. He finally directs our attention to their differences in regard to the presence or absence of laws. He thus forces us to consider the effects produced upon the character of laws by the change from paganism to revealed religion.

Maimonides' unusual division of practical or human philosophy has the result that philosophy or science consists of 7 parts. An uncommon chain of reasoning leads to a common result.[20] We cannot in the present case account for the result by its commonness, precisely because it is arrived at in so uncommon a manner. We must consider the significance of the number 7 in Maimonides' own thought. Considerations of this kind are necessarily somewhat playful. But they are not so playful as to be incompatible with the seriousness of scholarship. The *Logic* itself consists of 14 ($= 7 \times 2$) chapters; the number of terms explained in the work is 175 ($= 7 \times 25$); in Chapter 7, Maimonides discusses the 14 moods of valid syllogism. His *Mishneh Torah* consists of 14 books. In the *Guide*, he divides the Biblical commandments into groups in a manner which differs considerably from the division underlying the *Mishneh Torah*, yet the number of groups of commandments is again 14. In *Guide* III 51 (123b-124a) which happens to be the 175th chapter of that work, he assigns, in the first interpretation of a simile, the same place to law which he assigns, in the second interpretation, to logic: there seems to be a certain correspondence between law and logic. Could there be a connection between the number 14 on the one hand, and logic and law on the other? In the 14th chapter of the *Guide*, he explains the meaning of "man." We suggest this explanation: Man, being the animal which possesses speech, is at the same time the rational animal which is perfected by the art of reasoning, and the political animal which is perfected

19. *Guide* I 17, 31 (34b), III 29 (65b). Cf. the variant reading of II 39 (85a Munk; 269, 27 Jonovitz) and *Eight Chapters* IV (15, 13-20).

20. Cf. H. A. Wolfson, "The Classification of Sciences in Medieval Jewish Philosophy," *Hebrew Union College Jubilee Volume*, Cincinnati 1925, 277-279 and 283-285.

by law. Man is a compound of form and matter; he has a dual nature. The number 7 itself, as distinguished from its double, would then seem to refer to beings of a simple nature, to pure intelligences, i.e., to God and the angels which are the subjects of philosophic theology or of "the account of the chariot." The *Guide*, the highest and central theme of which is precisely "the account of the chariot," consists of 7 sections: 1) the names and attributes of God (I 1-70); 2) demonstration of God's existence etc. on the presupposition of the eternity of the world and discussion of that presupposition (i. e., defence of the belief in creation out of nothing) (I 71-II 31); 3) prophecy (II 32-48); 4) "the account of the chariot" (III 1-7); 5) providence (III 8-24); 6) the Torah (III 25-50); 7) conclusion (III 51-54). The central section of Maimonides' *Heptameres*, the thematic discussion of "the account of the chariot," the secret of secrets, consists of 7 chapters. It would be premature to attempt a discussion of the question why the number 7 is preeminent. We must limit ourselves to noting that the section devoted to "the account of the chariot" is surrounded by two sections of 17 chapters each, and to referring the reader to the 17th chapter of the *Guide*.

It is of the essence of devices of this kind that, while they are helpful up to a certain point, they are never sufficient and are never meant to be sufficient: they are merely hints. But there are no isolated hints: the deficiency of one hint is supplied by other hints. The suggestion stated in the preceding paragraph suffers from an obvious flaw. The same strange division of practical philosophy which leads to the result that philosophy or science consists of 7 parts leads to the further result that ethics occupies the central place in the order of the sciences. And, as Maimonides intimates in his statement on political science, ethics does not deserve the central place.

Ethics is the study of the virtues, which means primarily of the moral virtues; it is not the study of happiness or man's true end; the study of man's end belongs to politics proper. This means in the first place that the moral virtues and their exercise are not man's end. It means furthermore that the moral virtues can only be understood with a view to their political function. This does not mean of course that the true end of man is political or, more radically, the well-being of his body. But it does mean that the true end of

man or man's final perfection can only be understood in contradistinction to his first perfection, the well-being of his body, and
hence in contradistinction to man's political life at its best. In other
words, morality in the common sense of the term belongs to the
realm of generally accepted opinions, of the *endoxa*. The theoretical understanding of morality traces morality in the common
sense to two different roots: to the requirements of society and the
requirements of man's final perfection, i.e., theoretical understanding. Common-sense morality belongs to the realm of generally accepted opinion because the requirements of society and the requirements of theoretical understanding are not completely identical but
are in a certain tension with each other. Common-sense morality is
essentially unaware of its being a mixture of heterogeneous elements
which has no clear or exact principle, and yet it is sufficiently consistent for almost all practical purposes: it is *doxa*. It is the most
impressive expression of man's dual nature.[21]

Let us then look once more at Maimonides' division of the sciences. His division of theoretical philosophy into 3 parts and practical philosophy into 4 parts is not final. There is a further subdivision
of two of the parts of theoretical philosophy: of mathematics into
4 parts (arithmetic, geometry, astronomy, music) and theology
into 2 parts (speech about God and the angels, metaphysics). This
might appear strange at first sight, but there is no mention of any
subdivision of physics. We are justified in regarding the subdivisions
of practical philosophy as no more important than the subdivisions
of mathematics: neither of them is mentioned at the end of the
chapter in the enumeration of the terms explained in the body of
the chapter. We arrive then at a division of philosophy or science
into 11 parts (arithmetic, geometry, astronomy, music, physics,
speech about God and the angels, metaphysics, ethics, economics,
governance of the city, governance of the great nation or of the
nations). The central part in this second division, which is slightly
less noticeable than the first, is occupied by speech about God and
the angels, i.e., by a science which obviously deserves the central

21. *Logic*, ch. 8; *Eight Chapters* IV (12, 19-21), VI; *Guide* I 2, II 33 (75a),
36 (79a-b), 40 (86b), III 22 (45b), 27, 28 (61b), 46 (106a). Cf. the distinction
between justice and the virtues in Fārābī's *Plato* sect. 30 Rosenthal-Walser
with the enumeration of the virtues in *Eight Chapters* II on the one hand, and
with their enumeration in *ib.* IV on the other: justice is replaced by wit,
liberality, and sense of shame. Cf. *Guide* III 23 (47b) and I 34 (39b).

place.[22] Yet the very plausibility of this consequence of the second division renders questionable the first division and therewith the significance of the number 7 and the implications thereof.[23] We are therefore forced to wonder whether "the account of the chariot" is identical with the science of God and the angels. By merely raising this question, we recognize the error of those who hold that Maimonides' allusive treatment of "the account of the chariot" is unreasonable because the secret toward which that treatment points is familiar to the scholars of all religions.[24] And to recognize that a scholarly criticism of Maimonides is unreasonable is equivalent to progressing in the understanding of his thought. The section of the *Guide* which is devoted to "the account of the chariot" is most reasonably the most mysterious section of the book.

The study of Maimonides' statement on practical philosophy or political science thus leads directly into the center of the fundamental problem. This is no accident. The recovery of what we are in the habit of calling classical political philosophy and of what Maimonides called simply political science or practical philosophy is, to say the least, an indispensable condition for understanding his thought. Only those, he says, are able to answer the question of whether the Talmudic Sages were men of science or not, who have trained themselves in the sciences to the point of knowing how to address the multitude on the one hand and the elite on the other

22. In *HUCA* III, 1926, 373, Wolfson reports a division of science into 7 parts which is composed in Arabic, and also its Hebrew translation which, while deviating from the original in regard to the sciences mentioned, preserves the division of science into 7 parts: in both the original and the translation the central place is occupied by metaphysics.

23. On the basis of the second division, theoretical philosophy consists of 7 parts, with music in the center. The underlying view is that the theoretical sciences by themselves complete philosophy or science, or that only the theoretical sciences are philosophic. But this view is the view of "the ancients" (60, 11-14 and 61, 16-17): it is not the true view. It is a pre-Aristotelian and even a pre-Socratic view. (Cf. Fārābī's *Plato*, loc. cit.) Cf. the report on "the ancient opinion" of the Pythagoreans and their "musical" philosophy in *Guide* II 8. It was the Pythagorean doctrine which offered a solid justification for arithmology. After the refutation of Pythagoreanism by the discovery of the irrational numbers, arithmology ceased to be unqualifiedly serious and became a serious play. Maimonides obviously does not share "the ancient opinions." Cf. *Guide* III 23 (49b).—In his first enumeration of moral virtues in the *Eight Chapters* (II), Maimonides mentions 7 moral virtues; the section of his Code dealing with ethics (H. De'ot) consists of 7 chapters.

24. Cf. Munk, *Le Guide des Égarés*, III, p. 8 n. 1. See also the statement on theology in *Logic*, ch. 14.

concerning divine things and things similar to the divine, and to the point of knowing the practical part of philosophy.[25] The question of whether the Talmudic Sages were men of science or not is identical with the question of the relation of "the account of the chariot" to metaphysics: the mystical meaning of "the account of the chariot" was vouched for by the Talmudic Sages.[26]

Maimonides' one-page statement on political science is a masterful epitome of the problem of revelation as it presents itself from the point of view of the philosophers, i.e., from the most sublime point of view to which pagans could rise. Once we realize this, we are on our way toward solving the other riddles of the *Logic*—for instance, the strange reference to the Sabean Abū Ishāq in Chapter 4 and the related strange definition of substance in Chapter 10. Maimonides pursued the philosophic approach up to its end because he was "the great eagle" who, far from fearing the light of the sun, "by virtue of the strength of his sense of sight, enjoys the light and longs to fly high in order to get near to it,"[27] or because he was animated by that intrepid piety which does not shrink from the performance of any duty laid upon us in the prayer "Purify our heart so that we can serve Thee in truth." If he had not brought the greatest sacrifice, he could not have defended the Torah against the philosophers as admirably as he did in his Jewish books.

---

25. Introduction to the Commentary on the Mishnah (E. Pococke, *Porta Mosis*, Oxford 1655, 147). Cf. Commentary on Berakot IX 5 and *Guide* III 22 (46b).

26. Cf. *Guide* III 5.

27. Cf. Albo, *Ikkarim* II 29 (190, 5-6) and *Guide* III 6 end.

VII

ON THE BASIS

OF HOBBES'S

POLITICAL

PHILOSOPHY

We begin by wondering why we should study Hobbes. This question implies that we doubt whether Hobbes's teaching is the true teaching. It implies, therefore, that our perspective differs from his. Hence our possible study of Hobbes is exposed to the fatal danger of subjectivism. Following the view which seems to be most acceptable today, we assume that we can avoid that danger by falling back on the inter-subjectivity of the present generation. Why then is Hobbes important to the present generation?

We are inclined to believe that Hobbes is studied at present by respectable people with greater sympathy than ever before. By respectable people, we mean people who are unlikely to be exposed, not only to social ostracism, to say nothing of criminal prosecution, but even to suspicion of serious unsoundness—people who cannot reasonably be suspected of harboring improper thoughts. To see with the necessary clarity the change in the appreciation of Hobbes, one need merely contrast the present attitude toward him with that which prevailed in the past. In the seventeenth century Hobbes's name was, together with that of Spinoza, as even Locke said, "justly decried." Yet while, according to Hobbes's most valuable testimony, Spinoza was much bolder or more offensive than Hobbes, Spinoza was rehabilitated much earlier than Hobbes. Spinoza had become acceptable by about 1785: by then the break with theism and even with deism had become acceptable. Furthermore, on the eve of the French Revolution there was no longer a political objection to Spinoza, the first philosopher who had championed liberal democracy. Spinoza became the father of a church whose creed was pantheism and whose order was liberal democracy—an order in which, as it was hoped, the mercantile patriciate would predominate. Hobbes, on the other hand, remained offensive because his dry atheism was not redeemed by anything which could be regarded as intoxication with God or even as hatred of God, and because he had constructed the soulless state-mechanism of eighteenth century enlightened despotism. How Hobbes's fate differed from Spinoza's appears most clearly from the different treatment accorded the two philosophers by Hegel and Nietzsche.

In the meantime, serious interest in Spinoza has considerably decreased and serious interest in Hobbes has proportionately increased. We have already indicated the causes of this change. Through the efforts of Schopenhauer and of Nietzsche, pantheism has lost its glamor and atheism has become respectable in Europe. Furthermore, respect for morality, or for what some people call traditional morality, has so far declined that Hobbes's moral teaching now appears in a very favorable light. To a generation which was successfully exposed to the gospels of the blond beast, of the class struggle, and of the redemptive virtue of toilet training, Hobbes must appear as the incarnation of old-fashioned decency. He never wavered in his adherence to the golden rule and he refused to speak about carnal pleasures because they are too well known—some of them even sordid. And as for the political objections to Hobbes, they were bound to fade into insignificance with the emergence of the tyrannies of the twentieth century. No sober man could hesitate to prefer Hobbes's enlightened and humane absolute king to the contemporary tyrants whose rule rests on obscurantism and bestiality and fosters these diseases of the mind.

The rehabilitation of Hobbes would seem, then, to be due to

the progressed weakening of the moral and religious tradition—to a further progress of modernity. But this explanation is manifestly insufficient. The progress of modernity consists precisely in the emergence of doctrines which are much more decidedly modern than is Hobbes's doctrine. The mere progress of modernity would condemn Hobbes to oblivion everywhere but in the pantheon where the bones of the originators of modernity rot. Hobbes's doctrine would not be alive, it would not be studied seriously, if the progress of modernity were separable from the decay of modernity. Modernity has progressed to the point where it has visibly become a problem. This is why respectable people, to remain silent about others, turn again to a critical study of the hidden premises and hence the hidden origins of modernity—and therefore to a critical study of Hobbes. For Hobbes presents himself at first glance as the man who first broke completely with the pre-modern heritage, the man who ushered in a new type of social doctrine: the modern type.

One cannot ignore Hobbes with impunity. Nietzsche, who abhorred the modern ideas, saw very clearly that those ideas are of British origin. The admirer of Schopenhauer thought it equitable to look down with contempt on the British philosophers, in particular on Bacon and on Hobbes. Yet Bacon and Hobbes were the first philosophers of power, and Nietzsche's own philosophy is a philosophy of power. Was not "the will to power" so appealing because its true ancestry was ignored? Only Nietzsche's successors restored the connection, which he had blurred, between the will to power and technology. But this connection is clearly visible in the origins of that philosophic tradition which Nietzsche continued or completed: the British tradition.

It has become necessary to study Hobbes as the originator of modernity, i.e., to take his claim seriously. That is to say, if we understand ourselves correctly, we see that our perspective is identical with Hobbes's perspective. Modern philosophy emerged in express opposition to classical philosophy. Only in the light of the quarrel between the ancients and the moderns can modernity be understood. By rediscovering the urgency of this quarrel, we return to the beginnings of modernity. Our perspective becomes identical with that of Hobbes, in so far as his perspective is not limited by his answer, the acceptance of the modern principle, but extends to his question, which is the quarrel between the ancients and the moderns.

M. Raymond Polin[1] goes directly into the midst of things. As a consequence he looks at Hobbes's thought from a present-day point of view. He approaches Hobbes in the perspective of philosophies of "history," "personality," "values," and "development of one's individuality," i.e., of conceptions which become legitimate only after one has accepted Hobbes's principle—the modern principle—and after one has become dissatisfied with Hobbes's own interpretation of that principle. Polin thus unnecessarily complicates the task of giving a lucid account of a doctrine which, as he is well aware, does not lack grave obscurities. The right procedure consists in imitating, within reason, that movement of Hobbes's thought for which he has accepted responsibility. Hobbes presents himself as a radical innovator. One must therefore start with a clear and coherent presentation of the traditional position which he attempted to replace. One must see that position both as it is described or caricatured by Hobbes and as it presents itself in its classic expositions. Thereafter one must listen most patiently to what Hobbes explicitly says about the deficiencies of the traditional doctrines. One must make a distinction between their radical deficiencies (their lack of exactness and their overestimation of the power of reason) and their derivative deficiencies ("anarchism"). Furthermore, since Hobbes's doctrine is not free from considerable ambiguities, not to say contradictions, the student is in need of a canon that would enable him to decide in a responsible manner which of various conflicting statements by Hobbes must be taken as expressing his considered view, and which may be neglected as remarks that are provisional, timid, loose, and so on. The need for such a canon is all the greater since none of the four or five versions of Hobbes's political philosophy (the *Elements of Law*, the *De Cive*, the English and the Latin versions of the *Leviathan*, the second half of the *De Homine*) can be regarded as simply superior to the others. Other considerations apart, Hobbes never said or indicated that one of those different versions is the most authentic. The canon in question can only be found by reflection on Hobbes's

---

1. *Politique et philosophie chez Thomas Hobbes*, Presses Universitaires de France, 1953, XX, 262 pp. If not otherwise stated, figures in parentheses will indicate the pages of Polin's book.

explicit declarations about his intention, as well as by reflection on the characteristic reasons which prevented him from ever giving a sufficiently clear account of his teaching. One may doubt whether Polin has taken these precautions. In spite of this he has succeeded, thanks to his unusually great familiarity with Hobbes's writings and sympathy with his doctrine, in bringing to light certain important aspects of Hobbes's doctrine which hitherto have been neglected or ignored.

Polin's thesis may be summarized as follows. Hobbes radically transforms the traditional understanding of man as the rational animal: man is the animal which invents speech and "the faculty of reasoning [is] consequent to the use of speech." Since speech is the human fact *par excellence,* man is the animal which is the author or maker of itself (5-7, 12-13, 25, 99). Hobbes is therefore emphatically a humanist (148-9). His understanding of speech as man's invention and therefore his novel understanding of reason creates a fundamental difficulty to which he did not find a solution. If, as he contends, the bases of all reasoning are arbitrary definitions, it is hard to see how reasoning can disclose to us the true character of reality. Since it is not sufficient to say that he had a naive faith in the rationality of reality, Polin has recourse to Hobbes's "phenomenalism" and "mechanism." Hobbes's "phenomenalism" is regarded by Polin, not unjustly, as a crude anticipation of Kant's transcendental idealism. Hobbes's "mechanism," as it is presented by Polin, reminds one vaguely of Spinoza's doctrine according to which the order and connection of ideas is identical with the order and connection of things (43-52). Since Hobbes holds that the specifically human is artificial, he is led to replace "the perspective of the interpretation of the past" by "the perspective of the construction of the present and the future," without however ceasing to be a conservative (93, 100-01, 150). For the same reason he is enabled to effect a reconciliation between the individual and society which is superior to Locke's, since according to Hobbes all natural rights are absorbed in the artificial Leviathan (109, 114, 128). His reflections on virtue culminate in the view that all those and only those actions are virtuous which are favorable to the state: the state, or the reasonable state, is the necessary and sufficient condition of virtue. Hobbes anticipates Hegel (173-175). He does this especially by breaking with the traditional conception of natural law which was still adhered to by Grotius. The tradition had assumed that there is a human nature which is given, not made. By rejecting this assumption, Hobbes was forced or enabled to deny all moral or juridical significance to the right of nature, and to contend that there is no natural law prior to the establishment of civil society or independent of the command of the sovereign (182-90). The reconciliation of the individual and the state, or the absorption of morality by the state, finds an adequate expression in Hobbes's notion of the state as a "person"—a notion of which he is the originator (224-30, 237-38).

Polin has then brought out very clearly, in particular by his anticipatory references to Kant and Hegel, "the discontinuity which characterizes [according to Hobbes] the situation of man with regard to nature" (23) or the radical distinction which Hobbes makes between the natural and the human or the political. Hobbes testifies to this dualism in a particularly striking manner by reserving the term "law" to commands addressed to men or by refusing to speak of laws ordering non-human beings (179). The human world is a state within a state. This means however that the human world is a part of the universe and must be understood as such. Since according to Hobbes every part of the universe is body, the human and the non-human have this in common, that they are bodies or properties of bodies. The fundamental distinction of bodies is that into bodies natural and bodies politic. Bodies, or their properties, are understandable only as generated. Therefore the bond uniting the human with the non-human may be called "generation" or "motion" or, as Polin prefers to say, "mechanism." The problem which Hobbes has to solve concerns then the relation between "the mechanism of nature" and "the social mechanism" (53, 55, 61, 66). Man belongs to the natural mechanism and yet escapes it. Hobbesian man, through his nature, successfully revolts against nature (XVIII, 7, 9, 99). The link between the two mechanisms is speech. The power of speaking is "given by nature" (9). It appears to be something irreducible or not susceptible of being understood as the product of a "generation." The power of speaking is the natural power of arbitrarily naming things. The exercise of this power, i.e., arbitrary actions of man, is the origin of the social mechanism (5-9). But arbitrary actions are as necessary, as determined by precedent causes, as any other events. Hence the social mechanism is as natural as the natural mechanism. The social mechanism is a prolongation of the natural mechanism: the continuity of the natural and the social mechanism is in no way broken (9, 61). The social mechanism is a part, or a kind, of the natural mechanism: that kind of natural mechanism which presupposes, and necessarily follows from, the natural power of arbitrarily imposing names. The social mechanism is that natural mechanism which originates in man, whereas the so-called natural mechanism is that natural mechanism which originates in non-man. Man's activity may appear as a conquest of nature or as a revolt against nature; but what takes place in fact is that a part of nature revolts by natural necessity against all other parts of nature.

We doubt whether one can ascribe to Hobbes the view that speech is a natural power or a "gift" (10). We likewise doubt whether one can ascribe to him, as Polin also seems to do, the related view that man is the only earthly being which is capable of thinking the future or of thinking teleologically (8-10). For while it may be true that the distinction between the natural mechanism and the social mechanism, or between natural bodies and political bodies, presupposes an essential difference between the nature of man and the nature of brutes, it is also true that Hobbes tends to conceive of the difference between the nature of man and the nature of brutes as a mere difference of degree.[2] The reason for

---

2. *Leviathan*, chs. 3, 4 and 12 (beginning). Cf. *De cive*, I, 2 (We are driven toward the delights of society, i.e. the gratification of vanity, "by nature, i.e. by the passions inborn in all living beings"); *ibid.*, V, 5 (vanity is distinctly human). See the parallel in *Leviathan*, ch. 27 (Blackwell's Political Texts ed., 194). Cf. also Polin's own interpretation of the *videtur* in *De homine*, X, 1 (6).—According to Hobbes, the only peculiarity of man's mind which precedes the invention of speech, i.e., the only natural peculiarity of man's mind, is the faculty of considering phenomena as causes of possible effects, as distinguished from the faculty of seeking the causes or means that produce "an effect imagined," the latter faculty being "common to man and beast": not "teleological" but "causal" thinking is peculiar to man. The reason why Hobbes transformed the traditional definition of man as the rational animal into the definition of man as the animal which can "inquire consequences" and hence which is capable of science, i.e., "knowledge of consequences," is that the traditional definition implies that man is by nature a social animal, and Hobbes must reject this implication (*De cive*, I, 2). As a consequence, the relation between man's natural peculiarity and speech becomes obscure. On the other hand, Hobbes is able to deduce from his definition of man his characteristic doctrine of man: man alone can consider himself as a cause of possible effects, i.e., man can be aware of his power; he can be concerned with power; he can desire to possess power; he can seek confirmation for his

Hobbes's wavering is this: there is a tension between the assumption that there are "natures" (of man, dogs, horses) and the view held by Hobbes that all properties can only be understood adequately as effects of generations (cf. *Leviathan*, Chapter 46, beginning, in both versions), and ultimately as effects of the most universal kind of generation. However this may be, in ascribing to Hobbes the view, e.g., that speech is a gift, Polin goes beyond what Hobbes himself says, as he seems to admit (6-7). We are very far from blaming him for going beyond what Hobbes himself says. We take issue with him merely because in going beyond what Hobbes says, he has stopped too soon, or, in other words, because he has not reflected sufficiently on why it is necessary to go beyond what Hobbes says. In the example under discussion, Hobbes can be seen to waver between a tendency to admit an essential difference between the nature of man and the nature of brutes, and a tendency to conceive of the essential difference between men and brutes as due entirely to human invention. Polin justly refuses merely to reproduce Hobbes's wavering. He does not attempt, however, to ascend to the reasons for Hobbes's wavering, and he thus fails to lay bare the fundamental difficulty with which Hobbes unsuccessfully grappled. To turn to another example, Polin may be said to come close to what Hobbes suggests by contending that there is both a discontinuity and an unbroken continuity between the natural mechanism and the social mechanism, or that man both escapes and does not escape the natural mechanism (7, 9, 23, 51-2, 99). In this case Polin merely reproduces or preserves the fundamental ambiguity of Hobbes's teaching. If one faces this ambiguity, one is confronted with the necessity of choosing one of two alternative interpretations of Hobbes's political science and of acting on this choice in a consistent manner. These alternative interpretations may loosely be called the naturalistic and the humanistic interpretations. It is better to say that the student of Hobbes must make up his mind whether he is going to understand Hobbes's political science by itself or whether he is going to understand it in the light of Hobbes's natural science.

---

wish to be powerful by having his power recognized by others, i.e., he can be vain or proud; he can be hungry with future hunger, he can anticipate future dangers, he can be haunted by long-range fear. Cf. *Leviathan*, chs. 3 (15), 5 (27,29), 6 (33-36), 11 (64), and *De homine* X, 3.

We shall try to show as simply as possible why one cannot leave it at reproducing Hobbes's political science as he himself stated it. According to Hobbes, speech, whether a natural gift or a human invention, is peculiar to man. Speech presupposes "thoughts" and "passions."[3] The original of all thoughts is sense, and the original of all passions may be said to be pleasure or pain. Yet sense and pleasure or pain are "nothing really but motion [within the head and about the heart] . . . but seemings and apparitions only," although "seemings" "made by nature." For "that which is not body . . . is nothing" and the mental in so far as it is not identical with the bodily, is nothing.[4] What is not corporeal is "phantastical."[5] Speech consists of "names," and names are not bodies nor accidents of bodies (*Leviathan*, Chapter 4). There is no reality in accidents (English *Works*, IV, 306; *De Corpore*, VIII, 2 and 20). The body politic is a fictitious body (222-3); for "it is impossible for any man *really* [*De Cive*, V, 12: *Naturali modo*] to transfer his own strength" to the sovereign, i.e., to the "soul" of the body politic (*Elements*, I, 19, sect. 10): the real is the natural, i.e., the bodily. But are even bodies real? Is Hobbes not eventually forced into "phenomenalism"?

In the light of Hobbes's natural science, man and his works become a mere phantasmagoria. Through Hobbes's natural science, "the native hue" of his political science "is sicklied o'er with the pale cast" of something which is reminiscent of death but utterly lacks the majesty of death—of something which foreshadows the positivism of our day. It seems then that if we want to do justice to the life which vibrates in Hobbes's political teaching, we must

---

3. "Thoughts" and "Passions" together correspond to Descartes' and Locke's "ideas." Cf. *Leviathan*, Introduction and ch. 6 (38). Hobbes's hesitation to adopt a single term designating all "perceptions of the mind" (Hume) deserves notice. Hobbes found the oneness of man in the body, not in the "consciousness."

4. Hobbes seems to have thought that this view supports sufficiently his contention that only the pleasures and pains of the body are genuine, whereas the pleasures and pains of the mind are vain or fantastical; cf. *De cive*, I, 2, and *Leviathan*, ch. 27 (195) with *Leviathan*, ch. 6 (34). Or, in other words, he seems to have thought that his corporealism legitimates the polarity of reasonable fear and unreasonable glory.

5. *Elements*, I, 2, sect. 10 and 7, sect. 1; *Leviathan*, chs. 6 (33), 27 (195), and 45 (426); *Obj. IV, In Cartesii Meditationes*. Cf. Tönnies, *Hobbes*, 3rd ed., 128-29.

understand that teaching by itself, and not in the light of his natural science. Can this be done?

Hobbes published his *De Cive*, the third part of the *Elementa Philosophiae*, in 1642, more than a decade before he published the first two parts (*De Corpore*, 1655, *De Homine*, 1658). To justify this irregularity, he says, in the Preface to *De Cive*, that the understanding of that book does not require knowledge of the preceding parts of the *Elementa*: political science, being based on principles of its own which are known through experience, is not in need of natural science. Similar remarks occurring in the *Leviathan* (Introduction, Chapter 1 and Chapter 32, beginning), in *De Homine* (Ep. Ded.) and in *De Corpore* (VI, 7), allow us to express Hobbes's thought as follows: the science of man and human things, being based on principles of its own which are known through experience, is not in need of natural science.[6] Still, neither these remarks nor certain statements occurring in the first chapter of *De Corpore* to which Polin refers, justify one in saying, as he does in one place, that according to Hobbes there is no natural or logical order of philosophic or scientific inquiry (XII-XIII; cf. however 38-39). For in the very remark in the Preface to *De Cive* to which we have referred and which Polin quotes in Sorbière's French translation, Hobbes speaks of "ce renversement de l'ordre" which is implied in the fact that the publication of *De Cive* preceded the publication of the first two parts of the *Elementa*. However, Hobbes's repeated admission that his science of man and of human things is independent of his natural science, is invaluable. And Polin seems to be prepared fully to profit from it. He says in his Introduction: "Nous entendons, avec Hobbes, par *politique*, ce qu'il appelait aussi 'philosophie civile' et que nous appellerions de nos jours 'science politique' . . . La politique donne le ton de la philosophie Hobbienne ainsi que les schémas de comprehension par rapport auxquels tous les autres domaines peuvent etre compris" (xiii).

---

6. Only the study of the passions (as distinguished from the study of "thoughts") belongs essentially to political science in Hobbes's sense (cf. *De corpore*, VI, 6-7, and I, 9). This means that the *De cive*, supplemented by the remarks about the passions and related subjects which occur in the *Elements*, the *Leviathan* and the *De homine*, comes nearer to being an adequate expression of Hobbes's political science as an independent discipline than do the *Elements* and the *Leviathan*.

Certain statements occurring later in Polin's Introduction (xvi, xviii) even read as if Hobbes's natural science must be regarded as no more than a postulate of his political science: it answers the question of how the universe must be so that men can live as they ought to live according to Hobbes's political science. This interesting quasi-promise of the Introduction is not fulfilled by the body of Polin's work.

Polin's hesitations are easily intelligible. While Hobbes's political science cannot be understood in the light of his natural science, it can also not be understood as simply independent of his natural science or as simply preceding it. The reason for this is not that Hobbes's political science is based on his determinism as well as on the principle of inertia (*Leviathan*, Chapter 2 beginning, Chapter 6 [39], Chapter 21 [137-38]). For one might say with Hobbes himself that these principles in so far as they are relevant to the understanding of human life, are known to everyone by his own experience of himself (*De Homine*, XI, 2). And one might add that the humanly relevant meaning of these principles—especially the denial of the possibility of a *summum bonum* and of the efficacy of moral appeal—was realized by Machiavelli a century or so before the emergence of the new natural science. Considerations like these give additional strength to the assertion that Hobbes's political science stands on its own feet because it understands man as a being that has a character of its own by virtue of which it can oppose itself to nature as such (XVIII, 41) and because the substance of what it teaches about man is conceived in an *esprit de finesse* rather than in an *esprit de géométrie*. This does not mean that the substance of his political science is completely unrelated to his natural science. The relation between his political science and his natural science may provisionally be compared with that between theological dogmatics and theological apologetics. What Hobbes discovered about human things by reasoning from his experience of man, is put forth as indubitably true; but it must be defended against misconceptions of man which arise from vain opinions about the whole (*Leviathan*, Chapter 46 [442]; end of Chapter 47 in the Latin version). Therefore Hobbes must oppose the true view of the whole to those vain opinions. The true view of the whole is not proved by the fact that it, and it alone, agrees with the true political science: Hobbes's natural science is more than a postulate or projection of his political reason. We may even grant that his view of the whole precedes his view of man and of human things according to the necessary order of philosophy, provided we understand this precedence in the following manner. Hobbes's view of man, as far as it is essential to his political teaching, expresses how the new view of the whole affects "the whole man"—man as he is understood in daily life or by the historians and poets, as distinguished from man as he is to be understood within the context of Hobbes's natural science. "The eternal silence of these infinite spaces frightens" man: the mood generated by the truth, the true mood, is fear, the fear experienced by a being exposed to a universe which does not care for it by properly equipping it or by guiding it. The true mood, or the true view, can arise only after man has made a considerable effort. At the beginning, there was utter darkness, not illuminated by any natural light: "men have *no other means* to acknowledge their own darkness, but *only* by reasoning from the unforeseen mischances, that befall them in their ways" (*Leviathan*, Chapter 44 [396]). By nature man is blind concerning his situation. He regards himself as somehow taken care of by the first cause or causes, by spirits invisible, not to say as a favorite of Providence. The blinding passion *par excellence* is then glory or presumption or pride. The most extreme form of pride which a man can have is the belief that the first cause of the whole has spoken to him. Yet since man originally regards himself as utterly dependent on the arbitrary will of spirits invisible, he is both presumptuous and abject. Once he realizes his true situation, his "natural condition concerning his felicity and misery," he becomes filled with fear indeed, but with a kind of fear which points the way toward its overcoming: the stupendous whole which oppresses him lacks intelligence. The polarity of fear and pride in which Polin sees the core of Hobbes's teaching about human passions and therefore the core of his teaching about man (59, 103-04, 132-33), can be understood directly as the consequence of the new view of the whole for man's "common sense" understanding of himself. To the extent to which Hobbes attempts to replace that "common sense" understanding by a scientific understanding of man, he endangers his political science as a normative science and prepares the "value free" political science of our time.

This suggestion is by no means sufficient for removing the

fundamental obscurities of Hobbes's teaching. As Hobbes indicates by assigning specific subject matter to the *Elements of Law*, the *De Cive* and the *Leviathan* as to works which are meant to be intelligible and demonstrative by themselves, as well as by explicit statements, he assumes a fundamental bipartition of the sciences and therewith of things. But he is uncertain as regards the precise character, or the ground, of the fundamental bipartition. He refers to the bipartitions into body and mind, and into the non-voluntary and the voluntary. These bipartitions do not satisfy him because they do not bring out the fundamental difference between the non-human and the human, to leave here open whether they are not made questionable by his corporealism and his determinism. As for the specific difference between man and the brutes, Hobbes seems to see it in speech rather than in anything else. But he conceives of speech as a human invention. This means that the fundamental bipartition of things originates in man, through man's making: not so much man's nature as man's making is irreducible to anything else. The fundamental bipartition into that which exists independently of man's making and that which exists by virtue of man's making, resembles the bipartition into the natural and the artificial, a bipartition which Hobbes uses in distinguishing between natural bodies and artificial bodies (i.e., states). But the resemblance conceals a most important difference: according to Hobbes, the artificial embraces not only all artifacts proper and civil society but above all, the principles of understanding as well (we understand only what we make). Hobbes thus tends to assume that the artificial is not only irreducible to the natural but even primary. At the same time, his conception of understanding as making forces him to conceive of man and all his works as products of universal motion. The difficulties which we encounter in trying to understand Hobbes's teaching may be expressed by saying that his doctrine is the origin of both the monistic positivism of the nineteenth and twentieth centuries and its opposite, the philosophy of freedom of the same epoch. But Hobbes wavers not only between corporealism and what we may call constructionism; he is also uncertain whether the non-corporealist beginning has the character of arbitrary construction or of "data of consciousness."

The most important element of Hobbes's view of the whole is his view of the deity. Polin states without any ambiguity that

Hobbes was an atheist (xv, 139-40). Since his thesis is by no means universally accepted, it will not be amiss if we indicate how it can be established. If we limit ourselves first to natural theology, we have to say that Hobbes is an atheist according to his own definition of atheism. To deny, as the Sadducees did, the existence of spirits or angels, "is very near to direct atheism." But natural reason knows of no other spirits than "thin bodies, as the air, the wind . . ." and "the imaginary inhabitants of man's brain." It knows nothing of "angels substantial and permanent," to say nothing of incorporeal substances. "The names of *man* and *rational* are of equal extent." The Sadducees were right. Belief in spirits is superstition. Natural reason is then "very near to direct atheism."[7] Furthermore, to say that God is the world or a part of the world, means to deny the existence of God. But "the world . . . is all" and therefore that which is not the world and "which is no part of it, is nothing."[8] Hobbes teaches then "direct atheism." However, the definition of atheism which we have just used belongs to the context of Hobbes's discussion of "attributes of divine honour," i.e., of attributes which are not meant to express the truth but merely the desire, true or feigned, of honoring God.[9] We must therefore inquire whether natural reason as such, as distinguished from natural reason operating in the intention of honoring God, knows anything of God's existence and other attributes. Hobbes seems to contend that man can know through natural reason that there is an eternal and omnipotent God of whom we can have no idea or image or conception, or whose "greatness and power are unconceivable" or unimaginable. From this it would follow that there cannot be a true religion, since true religion is fear of power invisible "when the power imagined, is truly such as we imagine."[10] More precisely, if God is omnipotent, he is the cause of everything, of good as well as of evil; he is in particular the cause of sin. It is for this reason that the right of God's sovereignty cannot be derived from his graciousness, his goodness or his providence. Providence is a matter of belief, not of knowledge. Men believe in God's

<hr/>

7. *Leviathan,* chs. 4 (20), 6 (50), 12 (71), 27 (195-96), 34 (259-61, 264), 45 (420).
8. *Leviathan,* chs. 31 (237) and 46 (440).
9. *Leviathan,* chs. 12 (71), 31 (237), 34 (257), 45 (424-25), 46 (444).
10. *Leviathan,* chs. 3 (17), 6 (35), 11 (69), 12 (70).

goodness because, in order to gain the favor of the omnipotent God, they have to honor Him, and honor consists in the opinion of power and of goodness; it is on this opinion, as distinguished from knowledge, that natural religion is based. For the reason indicated, natural reason knows nothing of God as the author of the moral law, i.e., the law of reason, and the moral law does not contain any prescription of duties toward God.[11] But is God's omnipotence truly known? Is it not merely believed? Does the dogma of omnipotence not arise from the fact that men ascribe omnipotence to a being whose power, or the limits of whose power, are unknown to them? In other words, while the acknowledgment of an omnipotent God "may . . . be derived from the desire men have to know the causes of natural bodies," the actual "pursuit of causes" merely leads to the view "that there must be, as even the heathen philosophers confessed, one first mover,"[12] and the first mover is not necessarily omnipotent. But does natural reason know even of the existence of a first mover? The utmost one can say is that in the pursuit of causes one arrives eventually at a moved mover. Needless to say, God, the moved mover, is necessarily a body and therefore has parts and is "endowed with some determinate magnitude." He is a spirit, i.e., an invisible body: "a most pure, simple, invisible spirit corporeal." Since this is so, and since God must be either the universe or a part of it, God can only be a part of the universe. Being "a thin, fluid, transparent, invisible body," he can be "mingled with body of another kind" in such a manner that his parts retain their simplicity while changing the bodies of other kinds with which they are mixed. These would appear to be the Hobbesian remnants of omnipresence and omnipotence. The Hobbesian God is not distinguishable from the ether which is a most fluid body, filling every place in the universe that is not filled by bodies of other kinds. In a word, natural reason knows nothing of God. "Besides the creation of the world, there is no argument to prove a deity," and the creation of the world cannot be proved. Moreover, if the world in fact is not eternal, one would merely be led to "some eternal cause, one or more."[13]

11. *Leviathan*, chs. 15 (end), 30 (224, 232), 31 (233-37), 42 (340), 46 (445-46); *English Works*, IV, 390, 399, V, 210-12, 284.
12. *Leviathan*, chs. 11 (68), 12 (70-1), 37 (287), 45 (419).
13. *Leviathan*, ch. 3 (17); *De corpore*, XXVI, 1 and 5; *English Works*, IV, 302-3, 308-10, 313, 349, 427-28; *Obj. X. In Cartesii Meditationes*.

Hobbes might have regarded natural reason as unable to establish the existence of God and yet have been certain of God's existence because he was certain that the Bible teaches the truth. He does not hesitate to argue on the assumption that the Bible is the word of God. He does this especially in the Third Part of the *Leviathan* ("Of a Christian Commonwealth"). Some of the conclusions of his revealed theology deserve mention. There are angels but there are no devils. There are no immortal souls. The kingdom of God was and will be a kingdom on earth. It was "interrupted in the election of Saul" and it is to be restored at the Second Coming, when the dead will be resurrected. Until then, there exists no kingdom of God: the Christian is a man who intends to obey Christ after the Second Coming. After the Resurrection, the reprobate will be punished, not with hell fire (hell fire is a metaphorical expression) but by being "in the estate that Adam and his posterity were in" after the Fall: they will "marry, and give in marriage, and have gross and corruptible bodies, as all mankind now have" and then die again, whereas the elect will have glorious or spiritual bodies and will neither eat, nor drink, nor engender; all this will take place on earth. In order to be received into the kingdom of God, man must fulfill the laws of nature "whereof the principal is . . . a commandment to obey our civil sovereign," and he must believe that Jesus is the Christ. If the sovereign is an infidel and forbids the Christian religion, the command of the sovereign must be obeyed.[14]

The assumption on which this teaching is based cannot be established, according to Hobbes, by either the authority of the Church or the inner testimony of the Holy Ghost. Only reason, arguing from the antiquity of the Bible and from miracles, could conceivably prove that the Bible is the word of God. Hobbes denies all validity to the arguments taken from the antiquity of the Bible and from miracles. There is then no reason for believing in the authority of the Bible, and "where there is no reason for our belief, there is no reason why we should believe." The authority which the Bible possesses is derived exclusively from the fact that the Bible has been made law by the civil sovereign.[15] This being

14. *Leviathan*, chs. 34 (264), 35, 38, 42 (327), 43, 44 (410-11).
15. *Leviathan*, chs. 7 (42), 26 (187-88), 27 (191), 29 (212), 32 (243-45), 33, 36, 37, 38 (296), 42 (326, 339-42, 345), 43 (386-87); *English Works*, IV, 339-40, 369.

the case, the civil sovereign has a perfect right to abolish the Christian religion. It is misleading to say that he cannot do this because the beliefs of men are not subject to control by the sovereign. For since faith comes from hearing, the sovereign can destroy the Christian faith of the coming generations by preventing the teaching of the Christian religion. Certainly the study of "the causes of change in religion" leads to the conclusion that Christianity can as well be abolished as paganism was before. It goes without saying that as long as his subjects strongly believe in the Christian religion, it would be extremely foolish of the sovereign to exercise the right mentioned: its exercise would have to wait until the subjects' eyes have been opened by enlightenment. But why should a sovereign in Christendom think of such an extreme policy, seeing that the Bible is susceptible of an interpretation, namely the Hobbesian interpretation, which makes it an excellent vehicle of any government, especially if care be taken that all Christian sects which are not seditious are fully tolerated?[16] However this may be, the sovereign is under no obligation to establish any public worship, i.e., it is not necessary "that the commonwealth is of any religion at all." The "opinion of a deity . . . can never be *so* abolished out of human nature, but that new religions *may* be made to spring out of (it)" after the decay of the old ones: there is no necessity for the "first seeds, or principles" of religion again developing into a "formed religion," i.e., into something which can legitimately be called a religion.[17]

The uncertainty of the revealed character of the Bible does not prove that the teaching of the Bible may not be true and above reason, and hence it does not prove that the teaching of the Bible cannot be believed. Hobbes however seems to deny this possibility, arguing as follows. ". . . sense, memory, understanding, reason, and opinion are . . . always and necessarily such, as the things we see, hear, and consider suggest unto us; and therefore are not effects of our will, but our will of them." But it is contended that belief can depend on our will, since there are cases when the cognitive faculties are not sufficiently moved one way or

16. *Leviathan*, chs. 12 (77-80), 40 (314-15), 42 (327-28, 333, 381), 43 (387, 395), 45 (427-30), 47 (454-56).

17. *Leviathan*, chs. 12 (77), 27 (188), 31 (240; cf. also the Latin version). The italics are not in the original.

the other. According to Hobbes, however, if "the things" do not supply a sufficient reason for assent, the understanding, if awake, necessarily doubts, and this doubt is not subject to the will: there is no sphere in which assent and withholding of assent are both possible; the very freedom of choosing between assent and non-assent would presuppose knowledge of the uncertainty of the theses proposed, and therewith assent to that uncertainty, i.e., doubt of the theses proposed, or withholding of assent to the theses proposed. Hobbes argues against the possibility of revelation also in this way: one cannot prove the possibility of revelation by its actuality, for its actuality is uncertain; therefore one cannot say whether revelation is possible unless one knows how it is possible, i.e., unless one has adequate knowledge of the causes of revelation; but revelation is by definition above reason.[18]

Hobbes attempts to refute revealed religion more specifically by attempting to prove that the content of the Biblical revelation is against reason. We mention here only what he indicates in regard to the relation between the Biblical teaching and "the morality of natural reason." So doing, we shall also show that he knew very well how untenable was that interpretation of the Bible which he suggested in order to make the bulk of his philosophic teaching acceptable to believers. If a Christian sovereign were to make laws suitable to the Biblical doctrine, he would bind men to certain actions which he ought not to command. He would take his bearings by the rule "whatsoever you will that men should do unto you, that do ye unto them," whereas the law of reason only commands "do not to another, that which thou wouldest not he should do unto thee." He would be guided by the counsel "sell all thou hast, give it to the poor." He would forbid his subjects to "company with fornicators," i.e., he would command something "that could not be without going out of the world." Rules of conduct such as those mentioned are not fit for large societies. The same consideration would apply to the prohibition against fornication itself. He would be more concerned with orthodoxy than with morality for, according to the Biblical doctrine, "God doth always accept (the will) for the work itself, as well in good as in evil men," but "only in the faithful," or man's justification

---

18. *Leviathan*, ch. 32 (243); *Obj. XIII. In Cartesii Meditationes.*

depends not on his efforts but on God's grace. By encouraging religious zeal in the Biblical sense, he would educate his subjects to "contempt of honour, and hardness of heart." The Old Testament set up the rule of priests, i.e., a form of government which is bound to issue in chaos, as the Old Testament record itself shows. The rule of priests was responsible for the fact that after the anarchy had induced the Jews to set up a king "after the manner of the nations," "generally through the whole history of the kings . . . there were prophets that always controlled the kings." That is to say, the Old Testament laid the foundation for the dualism of power temporal and power spiritual which is incompatible with peace, the demand *par excellence* of reason. As regards Christianity, it originated in rebellion against the civil sovereign and therefore was forced eventually to sanction the dualism of the two powers.[19]

Holding the view of the Bible which he did, Hobbes was compelled to try his hand at a natural explanation of the Biblical religion. The fundamental difference between paganism and Biblical religion consists in this: that whereas pagan religion was a part of human politics, Biblical religion is divine politics, the politics of the kingdom of God. Owing to the Egyptian bondage, the Jews had conceived an extraordinarily strong desire for liberty and a deadly hatred of the subjection to any human government: the kingdom of God which was established at Mount Sinai was meant to satisfy in the highest degree the desire for liberty. But the kingdom of God was in fact a government of priests, i.e., a singularly defective regime. In spite of its breakdown, i.e., the establishment of human kingship in Israel, the authority of the ancient regime remained so great that the Jews would "not allow their king to change the religion which they thought was recommended to them by Moses. So that they always kept in store a pretext, either of justice or religion, to discharge themselves of their obedience, whensoever they had hope to prevail." In the course of time their dissatisfaction took on the form of the hope for a Messiah, i.e., a human king who would restore the kingdom of God and administer it: the idea of the Messiah is a correction

19. *Leviathan*, chs. 12 (76), 25 (168), 35 (269), 40 (312, 314, 315), 42 (328, 333, 338, 349-50, 356, 369, 371-73), 43 (388-89, 393, 394), 46 (442), 47 (456), Conclusion (464). Cf. *Elements*, II, 6, sect. 2 and 4; *De cive*, XI, 6 and XVI, 15.

of the original idea of the kingdom of God, a concession to the
political realities which was forced upon the Jews by their bitter experience with the rule of priests. As a consequence of the Captivity,
the Messiah came to mean a human king who would liberate the
Jews and thereafter establish a universal monarchy, thus restoring
and more than restoring the original kingdom of God. This expectation was the root of Christianity. Jesus preached that he was the
Messiah in the Jewish sense of the term. Therefore his very
disciples "understood the Messiah to be no more than a temporal
king." This understanding of Jesus' claim led to his condemnation.
Christianity proper is an attempt to give an account of the failure
of a political movement which was inspired by fantastic political
hopes, the account running in terms of belief in miracles and the
dualism of substances spiritual and corporeal. Christianity reveals
its origin by the fact that the foundation of the Christian faith
is "the belief in this article, *Jesus is the Christ*," i.e., Jesus is the
Messiah in the Jewish sense. As for the success of early Christianity,
it was due, among other things, to the fact that "Christians lived
. . . in common, and were charitable," and to the temporary
abandonment of all thought of temporal power or of civil disobedience.[20] In brief, Hobbes has sketched that interpretation of
Christianity which was developed with utmost explicitness about
a century later by Hermann Samuel Reimarus.[21] But even Reimarus
did not publish that interpretation; he did not even disclose his
views to "her who slept at his bosom." We ought not to be surprised, therefore, if, on this subject and its premises, Hobbes
expressed himself with great caution in writings which he published
with his name on their title pages.

But enough of Hobbes's shocking over-simplifications, not to
say absurdities, which the most charitable man could not describe
more aptly than by applying to Hobbes, with the necessary modifi-
cations, a remark which he himself makes about Lucian: *Homo
blasphemus, licet sit author quamvis bonus linguae Anglicae.*[22]
Hobbes's unbelief is the necessary premise of his teaching about the

---

20. *De cive*, XVI, 8, 9, XVII, 1, 3, 7; *Elements*, II, 6, sect. 7; *Leviathan*,
chs. 12 (73, 75-76), 32 (245), 35 (269), 38 (301), 40 (308, 314), 41 (319-20),
42 (322-23, 364, 366), 43 (373, 381-82, 388, 391, 392), 45 (419); *English Works*,
IV, 388.
21. Lessing's *Werke* (Hempel), XV, 331-341, 348 ff., 394-95, 406, 414-15.
22. *Leviathan*, Latin, Appendix, cap. II.

state of nature. That teaching is the authentic link between his
natural science and his political science: it defines the problem
which political science has to solve by inferring from the preceding
exposition of the nature of man, and especially of the human
passions, the condition concerning felicity and misery in which
man has been placed by nature. More specifically, the teaching
about the state of nature is meant to clarify what the status of
justice is prior to, and independently of, human institution, or to
answer the question of whether, and to what extent, justice has
extra-human and especially divine support. One may express
Hobbes's answer by saying that independently of human institution,
justice is practically non-existent in the world: the state of nature
is characterized by irrationality and therewith by injustice. But
Hobbes has recourse to the state of nature in order to determine,
not only the status or manner of being of justice or natural right,
but its content or meaning as well: natural right as determined with
a view to the condition of mere nature, is the root of all justice.[23]
Polin's account of Hobbes's teaching on this subject may not be
quite satisfactory since he has not paid sufficient attention to the
novelty of the very notion of a state of nature as a condition which,
while antedating all human institutions, is characterized by the
existence of natural rights or natural duties in such a manner as
to point toward civil society as the home of justice. But he has
brought out with commendable emphasis the fact that the state
of nature as Hobbes understood it is not a mere supposition but
an actual fact of the past (87-89). The state of nature must
have been actual if the human race had a beginning and if that
beginning cannot be understood as creation in the Biblical sense:
the first men necessarily lived, if perhaps only for a short time,
without being subject to, and protected by, any superior power.
Accordingly, Hobbes occasionally speaks of "the first chaos of
violence and civil war."[24] One would, therefore, expect Hobbes
to believe that the state of nature was actual in the beginning,
"generally . . . all over the world." Yet Hobbes denies this: the
state of nature was actual in the past, but "never generally . . . all
over the world." Hence there must always have been civil societies

23. *Elements*, I, 14, sect. 1-2; *De cive*, I, 1, X, 10 (cf. Polin, 63 n. and 132);
Leviathan, chs. 13 and 14 (85).
24. *Leviathan*, ch. 36, end. Cf. *De homine*, I, 1, and *De cive*, VIII, 1.

in the world: civil law is coeval with the human race. The state of nature finds its place in the intervals between the dissolution of a civil society and the emergence of a new one, and it is the habitual state among savages.[25] Hobbes apparently presupposes that the human race, and hence the visible universe, is eternal.[26] However this may be, he encounters great difficulties in identifying the state of nature with the way of life of savages; he is forced to admit that savages already have government. If, as Hobbes contends, nature dissociates men, the state of nature must be pre-social. Yet, according to him, men living in a state of nature possess speech already, and consequently also some "true, general, and profitable speculations": how else could they leave the state of nature by obeying the dictates of reason? But how can pre-social men possess speech? This contradiction supplied one of the starting points of Rousseau's criticism of Hobbes, a criticism whose principle may be stated as follows: the state of nature, as Hobbes conceived of it, points toward civil society; since the state of nature is the work of nature, Hobbes admits here, contrary to his principles, a teleology of nature.[27] The nonteleological understanding of nature requires that the state of nature (just as childhood) be understood in such a manner as not to point beyond itself, or, in other words, that men's leaving the state of nature must be understood as entirely due to mechanical or accidental causation: the rejection of teleology requires that the state of nature be "good," or that it be not imperfect in itself; one can not say more than that the state of nature proves to be imperfect after man has been changed through accidental causation.

We have said that in Hobbes's state of nature justice is practically non-existent. This does not mean that it is simply non-existent in the state of nature: the root of justice must be found in the state of nature, and it reveals itself with perfect clarity only in the state of nature. The root of justice is the right of nature, a "subjective" natural right. Perhaps the greatest weakness of Polin's interpretation of Hobbes is due to his failure to grasp the meaning of Hobbes's doctrine of the right of nature. According to Hobbes, the rights of sovereignty, which are natural rights of a certain kind

25. *Leviathan*, ch. 13 (83); *De cive*, XIV, 14.
26. Cf. *Leviathan*, ch. 28, end, and ch. 29, beginning.
27. *Leviathan*, chs. 10 (61), 13 (82-3), 30 (223), 46 (436); *De corpore*, X, 7.

(Chapter 30 [221]), are derivative from the laws of nature, and the laws of nature in their turn are derivative from the right of nature: without the right of nature there are no rights of sovereignty. The right of nature, being the right of every individual, antedates civil society and determines the purpose of civil society. More than that: the fundamental right of nature persists within civil society, so much so that whereas the right of the sovereign is defeasible, the fundamental right of the individual is indefeasible. Polin on the other hand contends, at least in one set of passages (127, 166, 184 ff.; but cf. 243-45), that one does not find in Hobbes a doctrine of the rights of the individual: a right of the individual exists only in the state of nature, and even there it is only a pseudo-right and in fact not more than a simple natural power. This cannot be correct. Man has the natural power to act in the spirit of fear of violent death, i.e., of concern with his self-preservation, and he has the natural power to act in the spirit of glory, i.e., of concern with the gratification of his vanity. Yet, as Polin notes, fear is always legitimate, whereas glory is not (191-92). Fear and glory are both equally natural, yet fear is the natural root of justice and glory is the natural root of injustice. Unlike Spinoza, Hobbes does distinguish between what is natural and what is by nature right. This distinction is not affected by the fact that Hobbes traces that which is by nature right to that which is by nature necessary; for in so doing he in effect traces that which is by nature wrong to that which is by nature unnecessary (*De Cive*, I, 7; III, 27 n.). We may say that Hobbes makes use, not only of the "scientific" conception of necessity according to which everything real is necessary, but also of the "common sense" conception of necessity according to which not everything real is necessary. Natural right is practically non-existent in the state of nature because in the state of nature the just demands of self-preservation lead to the same course of action as do the unjust demands of glory: in the state of nature both the just man and the unjust man try to acquire everything and to subjugate everyone by every means at their disposal. But there is this decisive difference between the just man and the unjust man in the state of nature: the just man in the state of nature is already a potential citizen, i.e., he is already animated by the principles animating the citizen although he cannot yet act on those principles, while the opposite is true of the unjust man in the state of nature (*Elements*, I, 16, sect. 4). Furthermore the fundamental natural rights persist within civil society; they are the basis of the liberty of subjects to which Hobbes has devoted a whole chapter of the *Leviathan*. There could not be natural right in Hobbes's sense if there were not some natural property. Contrary to what Polin suggests (115, n.3), Hobbes recognizes that natural property, those "by nature private things" which even the communist Plato did not deny: the individual's body and his limbs (*Laws*, 739c7; *De Cive*, I, 7); and going beyond Plato, Hobbes extends the natural property even to the "inward thought, and belief of men." Man's natural property is extremely precarious in the state of nature: by this very fact natural property is the natural standard for civil society. In attempting to prove that, according to Hobbes, all rights are absorbed by the sovereign or are derivative from the sovereign, Polin goes so far as to say that, according to Hobbes, the individual ought not to have an opinion and hence that only the sovereign has opinions, whereas Hobbes merely says that men ought not to have an opinion that in certain cases they may lawfully resist the sovereign (210; cf. *Elements*, II, 8, par. 4). On this foundation—on the substitution of a period for a colon—Polin erects the doctrine that "dans une République parfaitement constituée selon la science hobbienne . . . il n'y a qu'une seule opinion possible et une seule opinion réelle . . . l'opinion du Souverain" (219), whereas, according to Hobbes, the power of the sovereign cannot possibly extend to "the inward thought, and belief" of reasonable men (*Leviathan*, Chapter 40 [307-8]). It is perhaps not superfluous to recall here the connection between the assertion that only the rights of the individual are primary and indefeasible and the assertion that only natural bodies are real.

The law of nature or the moral law as Hobbes conceives of it is not by itself, as Polin notes, a law properly speaking: man is under no obligation in the state of nature to act kindly or charitably. The natural law becomes a law only within civil society: only after kindness or charity have ceased to be manifestly dangerous is man obliged to act kindly or charitably. The sovereign makes his little world safe for obedience to the moral law; he does not, however, determine the content of the moral law. On the contrary, the moral law essentially precedes the sovereign: the obligation to obey the sovereign is a natural law obligation. The difficulty to which Hobbes's natural law doctrine is exposed can be stated as follows: the duty of obeying the positive law or of obeying the will of the sovereign cannot be based on positive law but must rest on a natural law foundation (*Leviathan*, Chapter 30 [220]); yet that foundation necessarily acts as a standard enabling and forcing one to distinguish between just and unjust laws, or between kings and tyrants, and therefore acts as a potential basis for civil disobedience. Hobbes therefore tries to reduce the demands of natural law to the single demand of keeping one's promise, i.e. of unqualified civil obedience; yet in order to justify that reduction he is compelled to admit, so to speak, all demands of kindness or charity, and he cannot exclude the possibility of conflict between the demand of civil obedience and the demands of kindness or charity; the utmost he can maintain is that in case of conflict between the two sets of demands, the demand of civil obedience necessarily takes precedence. This may be sufficient for all practical purposes; but it is certainly not sufficient for denying the possibility of distinguishing between just and unjust laws and between just and unjust rulers. In a word, by trying to give reasons for unqualified submission to authority, Hobbes makes impossible unqualified submission to authority; by appealing from authority to reason, as Socrates did, he is forced to repeat what he regarded as Socrates' fatal mistake, "anarchism." Hobbes accordingly distinguishes in fact between the state simply and the reasonable state. The reasonable state is the state whose sovereign performs his duties. If the sovereign does not perform his duties, and in particular if he commits iniquities, his rights are in no way affected; nor does his factual power necessarily suffer considerably, since his mistakes may well be cancelled out by the mistakes of his foreign or domestic enemies. The actualization of Hobbes's reasonable state is almost as little necessary as the actualization of Plato's reasonable state (*Leviathan*, Chapter 31, end). The difficulty with which Hobbes wrestled has practically disappeared in Polin's "étatiste" interpretation. According to Polin the *Leviathan*, as distinguished from the earlier versions, "does not even allude to the wicked king or the mad king" (247; cf. 210). The *Leviathan* alludes to these inconveniences sufficiently by saying that "it is an inconvenience in monarchy, that the sovereignty may descend upon an infant, or one that cannot discern between good and evil," that kings sometimes "reason not well," that "they that have sovereign power may commit iniquity," as David did when he killed Uriah, that "there is scarce a commonwealth in the world, whose beginnings can in conscience be justified," that "an offence against a private man, cannot in equity be pardoned, without the consent of him that is injured, or reasonable satisfaction," and that the subjects are "obnoxious to the lusts, and other irregular passions of him, or them that have (sovereign) power in their hands."[28] Polin also says that according to Hobbes "absolute power is identical with reason and virtue" (247) or that Hobbes's sovereign is exactly like Rousseau's, necessarily all that he ought to be: Hobbes "has nothing to say to the sovereign" (249). It suffices to refer to Chapter 30 of the *Leviathan* and especially to the distinction there made between just laws and good laws. Polin goes so far as to say that in the reasonable state as Hobbes conceived of it, "the citizen cannot but be virtuous, since his reason as well as his passions . . . induce him to act in conformity with the laws." By this remark Polin does not mean that in Hobbes's reasonable state the commission of any crime leads *ipso facto* to the loss of citizenship, for he says explicitly that in Hobbes's reasonable state "all actions are virtuous and all men are virtuous" (174). He must therefore think that while there will be prisons and gallows in Hobbes's reasonable state—for the maintenance of civil society depends on justice, and justice on the power of life and death, and other less rewards and punishments (*Leviathan*, Chapter 38, beginning)—their use will have withered away. Polin's Hobbes would appear to be a synthesis of Hegel and Marx.

The most satisfactory section of Polin's study is his critique of the attempt to trace in Hobbes's writings a development from an early recognition of "honor" as "aristocratic virtue" to a later rejection of this principle. That attempt was occasioned by the observation that Hobbes may have been responsible for the thoughts expressed in *Horae Subsecivae*, i.e., by the consideration of a problem which is still unsolved. Apart from this, one can hardly say, as Polin does, that there is no trace in Hobbes's writings of his ever having held the view that honor is a fundamental virtue nor that it constitutes the source of an aristocratic morality (161). As

28. *Leviathan,* chs. 18 (116, 120), 19 (124), 21 (139), 29 (210), 30 (225), Conclusion (463).

regards the first point, it suffices to refer again to *Elements*, I, 17, sect. 15 ("equity, justice, and honour contain all virtues whatsoever") in contrast with *De Homine*, XIII, 9 ("contineri autem virtutes omnes in justitia et charitate"). Polin's remark on this subject (163, n. 3) merely proves that the status of honor had already become questionable in the *Elements*, which no one, I believe, ever denied. Polin's remark does not prove that at the very beginning of his great literary career, Hobbes had drawn out all the consequences of this questioning with the necessary precision. Or, as we may also put it, Polin does not appreciate sufficiently the significance of the fact that in *De Homine*, XIII, 9, Hobbes simply denies that courage, prudence and temperance are moral virtues, while in the earlier versions he did not go so far. As regards the second point, it suffices to refer again to Hobbes's early statement that "honour and honesty are but the same thing in the different degrees of persons"—a statement which implies that differences in the degrees of persons do affect morality. Hobbes continued to recognize this fact in the *Leviathan* (Chapter 30 [226]): "The honour of great persons, is to be valued for their beneficence and the aids they give to men of inferior rank, or not at all." "Great persons" are capable of specific courses of actions of which other men are not capable (cf. also *De Homine*, XIII, 5, on the character of the rich, of old nobility and of new nobility). Furthermore, Polin goes too far in denying any truth to the contention that Hobbes sometimes tended to regard magnanimity as the origin of all virtue (161-62). He overlooks the three-fold reference in the *Leviathan* to generosity as a passion inciting men to justice (Chapters 14 [92], 15 [97] and 27 [195]).

It seems to us that Polin has not succeeded in laying bare the unity of Hobbes's thought, or that single fundamental problem whose complexity explains why he expressed himself with such ambiguity or contradiction on some most important subjects. On the other hand, Polin has succeeded unusually well in bringing to light a great number of Hobbes's ambiguities and contradictions. He thus can be said to have laid the foundation for the adequate interpretation of Hobbes's political philosophy which, we may hope, he or someone else will give us.

VIII

LOCKE'S
DOCTRINE OF
NATURAL LAW

Mr. W. von Leyden has done a service to the students of political thought by publishing for the first time Locke's recently discovered eight essays, or disputations, on natural law (John Locke, *Essays on the Law of Nature, The Latin text with a translation, introduction and notes, together with transcripts of Locke's shorthand in his Journal for 1676* [Oxford: At the Clarendon Press], 1954). These essays are the only coherent and the most detailed exposition of the doctrine of natural law which Locke ever wrote; he failed or refused to publish them. He completed them in 1664, i.e., more than two decades before he completed his *Essay concerning human understanding* and his *Two treatises of government*. In 1664 he was Censor of Moral Philosophy at Oxford, and it seems that he was lecturing in that year on natural law. Eight essays were completed; Locke set down the titles for yet three others which he never wrote. "In a continuous series Locke attached a number to each title, to those he merely contemplated as well as to those which have essays corresponding to them" (cf. p. 7 with pp. 134, 158 and 188). There are then eleven titles in all, the central one being "Can the law of nature be known from men's natural inclination? No"; the essay corresponding to this title was not written.

The essays may be said to consist of four parts. The first essay considers whether a natural law exists; the next six essays deal or would have dealt with whether and how the natural law is known; the following three deal or would have dealt with whether and to what extent the natural law is obligatory; the last essay deals with whether the private interest of each is the basis of natural law. The main thesis of the essays can be stated as follows. There exists a natural law which owes its obligatory power to the fact, known by the natural light, that that law is the will of God; the content of the natural law is known by the natural light which indicates what is conformable to a rational nature or to the natural constitution of man, and hence good. As a rational being, man is disposed to contemplate the wisdom and power of God in His works and to honor Him; as a being with a certain natural propensity to enter society, he has duties toward all other men, the law of nature not permitting that men be divided into hostile societies; as driven by an inner instinct to preserve himself, he has duties toward himself. All virtues (religion, obedience to superiors, truthfulness, liberality, chastity and so on) as well as abstention from robbery, theft, inchastity and murder are prescribed by the natural law. Obedience to the natural law leads men to that peak of virtue and happiness "to which both the gods call and nature tends." (110, 112, 140, 146, 156, 158, 162, 166.) In all these points Locke more or less follows the traditional natural law teaching, and in particular that of Thomas Aquinas whom he even mentions once (116). Accordingly he is almost completely silent in the essays about man's natural rights as distinguished from man's natural duties and about "the state of nature." He deviates from the tradition by denying that the natural law is inscribed in the minds of men and that it can be known from men's natural inclination or from the universal consent of men, to say nothing of tradition: the only way of knowing the natural law is by ascending from the sensibly perceived things to God's power and wisdom and to the necessary conclusions from these divine attributes as to what God wills man to do (124-130, 136-144, 158 n.3 and 160-178). The denial of the possibility of knowing the natural law from man's natural inclination is obviously of the greatest importance. That denial is reflected in the very passage, occurring near the center of the essays, in which Locke, tacitly following Thomas, indicates the essential connection between natural law and the threefold natural inclination of man: whereas Thomas speaks of man's natural inclination to know the truth regarding God, Locke speaks of man's proneness to contemplate God's works and His wisdom and power in His works; whereas Thomas speaks of man's natural inclination to live in society (or whereas Hooker speaks of "a natural inclination whereby all men desire sociable life and fellowship"), Locke speaks of "a certain natural propensity (of man) to enter society" (156-158; cf. Hooker I 10.1). Locke indicates his reason for denying man's natural directedness toward the virtues and justice near the end of the last essay: if one takes the principles of morality from man's natural inclination, one must observe what all men are actually inclined to; since there is a great variety among men in this respect, one cannot thus arrive at any principles of tolerable generality unless one starts from the natural inclinations of most men; most men are by nature inclined to their private advantage and even to their immediate private advantage; but this natural inclination is so far from supporting the virtues and justice that it rather subverts them (212). "Those who have no other guide than nature itself, those in whom the dictates of nature are in no way corrupted by positive customs, live in such ignorance of every law as if no attention whatever had to be paid to the right and honorable" (140). Or to quote from the *Essay concerning human understanding* (I 3.13): "Principles of action, indeed, there are lodged in men's appetites; but these are so far from being innate moral principles, that, if they were left to their full swing, they would carry men to the overturning of all morality."

As appears from Locke's reference to men's "ideas of particular sensible things" (146, 148), to say nothing of a reference to Descartes himself (136 n. 2), the author of the essays on natural law had already made the decisive break with the philosophic tradition by following the lead given by Descartes or, to make use of a much later statement of Locke, he already owed "to that justly admired gentleman (Descartes) the great obligation of (his) first deliverance from the unintelligible way of talking of the philosophy in use in the schools in (Descartes') time" (*The works of John Locke in nine volumes*, III [London, 1824], 48). Yet the young Locke also had already questioned Descartes' assertion that there is an innate idea of God (154; cf. Hobbes's *Objections to Descartes' Meditations*, X, end), and he had already denied the existence of any innate ideas: all principles, theoretical or practical, are acquired or derived from sense perception (144, 146, 148). Hence it would seem to follow that the very principles of natural law are not, as they are according to Thomas, indemonstrable, but themselves "but conclusions" as they are according to Hobbes. The influence of Hobbes on the essays on natural law appears most obviously in the rejection of universal consent as a source of knowledge of the natural law (cf. *De cive* II 1), to say nothing of the clear cut distinction between natural law and natural right (110).

The work of the editor and translator is of more than average solidity. The defects from which it suffers are not unconnected with his judgment on the subject of Locke's essays. That subject, he says, "is now regarded by many as obsolete" (p.v.). He himself follows those many. He is satisfied that "the notion of a law of nature . . . is derived from confused ideas . . ." or from the confusion of "the distinctions between rational demands, matter-of-fact propositions about reason, and the certainty of rational truth." More simply, natural law presupposes the confusion of "factual statements" (reason is an essential property of man) and "ethical assertions" (man ought to live according to reason) (44, 46). It is not improper to reply to a trite criticism by the trite observation that the notion of a law of nature is based on the distinction, and not on the confusion, between the nature of a being and the perfection or the end of that being. More particularly, the editor charges Locke with having confused "a matter of fact" (man is rational), "a way of knowledge" (man's reason leads to the discovery of the natural law), "a dogma" (the natural law is God's command) and "a logical truth" (the validity of the natural law can be proved in the same way as a geometrical theorem) (59). To say nothing of other things, it is impossible to call Locke's assertion of God's existence or of those divine attributes by virtue of which the natural law is necessarily a divine command, a "dogma" unless one shows first that Locke has not succeeded in demonstrating, as he claims he did, the existence as well as the attributes in question of God. Apart from this, the editor's judgment must be regarded as "unhistorical" in the sense of running counter to Locke's view of the state of the question unless one shows first that contrary to what Locke says he regarded the existence of a wise and powerful God as undemonstrated. It may or may not be true that "anyone attempting to study the relation between Locke and Hobbes would have to view it in its proper historical setting, against the background of the seventeenth-century battle against Hobbism" (38); it certainly is true that anyone attempting to study Locke's teaching must attempt to understand it as Locke himself understood it. As a consequence of his dogmatism, the editor's interest in Locke's teaching cannot but be purely antiquarian or must lack that philosophic concern without which the adequate understanding of philosophic teachings is impossible.

In a note to the second word occurring in the body of the essays, which is *Deus*, the editor says: "The spelling of this word in MS.A . . . and also in some of Locke's corrections in MS.B is *deus*; in this edition the word is capitalized wherever it stands for a truly theistic conception" (108 n.1). It would seem then that in MS.A, which is in Locke's handwriting, Locke invariably wrote *deus*. It is not clear from the cited note whether Locke invariably or only sometimes corrected the spelling *Deus* in MS.B, which is not in his handwriting, into *deus*, or whether he merely wrote invariably or only sometimes *deus* when he entered words or sentences in his handwriting in MS.B. However this may be, who has ever heard of such a thing? Locke wrote *deus*, and yet the editor permits himself the license of imposing on the readers his own spelling or his private opinion as to where Locke expresses "a truly theistic conception." His fault would have been less grave if he had told us clearly what he understands by "a truly theistic conception." He says in his Introduction: "*Deus* is capitalized by me throughout, except where the word stands for 'deity' in general or for a non-Christian god" (90). This would seem to mean that *Deus* is capitalized where it stands for the Christian God, the God known by the Christian or the Biblical revelation. But Locke explicitly refrains from reliance on revelation in the essays (122). The proper procedure would have been simply to reproduce Locke's spelling in the text and to translate *Deus* by "God" and *deus* when it occurs in the singular by "a God" (cf., e.g., *Essay concerning human understanding* I 4.8-9). Hereafter I shall put questionable renderings which are of some importance into angular brackets. After having asserted in the first sentence of his essays the existence of a God, Locke goes on to say that it is "wicked" [wrong] to doubt that "some deity presides over the world." Locke wished to make it quite clear that he regarded the doubt in question as a moral sin rather than as a speculative mistake. This is in conformity with the first sentence which reads as follows: "Since a God shows himself as everywhere present and, as it were, forces himself upon the eyes of men as much by the firm and uninterrupted course of nature now as by the frequent testimony of miracles in the past, I believe [assume] that there will be no one who has not decided in his mind that there is a God, provided he recognizes either the necessity for some accounting for [for some rational account of] our life or that there is something that deserves the name of either virtue or vice." Locke does not say that the existence of a God is evident to all men—he knew or believed to know of whole nations of atheists (174)—but only that it is evident to all morally concerned men. He thus seems to indicate that the status of a demonstration of the existence of God is not the same as that of geometrical demonstrations. If the recognition of virtue or vice is tantamount to the recognition of natural law (118), then the recognition of natural law is not only the consequence of the presupposed existence of God but the recognition of the existence of God also presupposes the previous recognition of natural law.

Our editor himself discerns in Locke a striving towards a natural law which does not presuppose the existence of God (52, 198). Near the beginning of the essays Locke says that the orderly character of all natural things and actions justifies one in wondering whether man alone of all natural beings is lawless or altogether his own master; "no one will easily believe this who has given thought to God the Best and the Greatest or to the universal consent of the whole human race at every time and in every place or finally to himself or to his conscience": in order to believe that man is subject to a law like all other beings, it is not necessary to reflect on God. Natural law may be said to have its source in nature rather than in God (132). "Speculative principles . . . do not affect moral things in any respect whatever" (178). This is not to deny that Locke says a few pages earlier that God and the immortality of the souls "must necessarily be presupposed if natural law is to exist," that "God and the immortality of the souls" are "principles" and that they are not "practical [moral] propositions" (172 f.): speculative principles affect moral things decisively. Let us not be shocked by this shocking self-contradiction but rather limit ourselves to noting that according to Locke's most frequent assertion it is only knowledge of the sensibly perceived things— of the matter, the motion and the visible structure and economy of this world—and not knowledge of virtue and vice which leads with necessity to the knowledge that some God is the author of all these things: "as soon as this (*sc.* the divine origin of the visible universe) is laid down, the universal law of nature [the notion of a universal law of nature] by which the human race is bound, necessarily follows [emerges]. . . ." Miracles are sufficient or necessary for establishing the existence of a divine positive law; the natural law can be established only by the ascent from the ordinary course of things: "Whatever obtains among men the force of law necessarily acknowledges either God or nature or man as its author; yet whatever either man has commanded or God has ordered by an oracle [by divine declaration], all this is positive law" (132). Natural law, we see, has its source in nature, the understanding of which is open to man as man. Here the question arises as to the way in which "the universal law of nature binds the human race." In his survey of the various names by which the natural law is known, Locke mentions the opinion of the majority according to which the natural law is that law which each can discover by the natural light and "to which (each) shows himself obedient in all points" (110). Here the editor notes "Text doubtful" but he does not suggest an alternative translation. His translation can be defended if one assumes that Locke admitted a natural law which no man ever transgresses because no man can transgress it. The universal consent of mankind does not prove, as Locke emphasizes in his thematic discussion of universal consent, the existence of a natural law which man can transgress; it may very well prove the existence of a natural law which no man does transgress (cf. 108).

Locke adduces five arguments in order to prove the existence of a natural law. Only in the third and hence the central argument does he refer to God or more precisely to "the wisdom of the first artificer" (116). The argument makes use of a statement of Thomas and of a statement of Hippocrates which occurs in Hooker (whom the translator judiciously follows) in this rendering: "each thing both in small and in great fulfilleth the task which destiny hath set down." Hooker uses Hippocrates' statement when speaking of the law which natural agents, i.e. agents "which keep the law of their kind unwittingly," observe, and he uses Thomas' statement when speaking of the law which "God hath eternally purposed himself in all his works to observe." The two statements, which occur in Hooker in entirely different contexts, are used by Locke in one and the same context, one in which neither citation occurs in Hooker, namely, in the context of a discussion of natural law. Locke's apparent misuse of the citations makes sense if one assumes that he is speaking of a natural law which cannot be transgressed, just as the laws spoken of by Thomas and Hippocrates cannot be transgressed. If, in the essays, Locke did not sometimes understand by the natural law a natural law of this kind, he could hardly have said that nobody has denied the existence of "some natural law" (130; cf. 114 and 200), for he says that Carneades and quite a few others denied the existence of the natural law in the sense of the moral law (204; cf. 112).

From the foregoing observations we draw two conclusions. In the first place, in his 53- or 54-page statement devoted exclusively to the natural law, Locke contradicts himself regarding the natural law in such a manner that what he did is most unlikely to have escaped his notice. He asserts that the existence of the natural law can be proved from men's consciences (108, 116) and he denies that the existence of the natural law can be proved from men's consciences (166, 168). He devotes a whole essay to refuting the contention that men give obedience to natural law by unanimous consent (160 ff.) and he asserts that men give obedience to natural law by unanimous consent (122, 108). He devotes a whole essay to refuting the contention that the natural law is inscribed or imprinted in the minds or the breasts of men (136 ff.) and he asserts that the natural law is implanted in our breasts (110) or that it is innate (116, 130). According to the editor, the last two self-contradictions can be taken care of by the assumption that Locke changed his mind while he progressed from his first two essays (108-134) to certain later essays (47 n.1). This, however, does not explain how a superior man, who regarded the problem of natural law as of utmost importance, could repeat and thus endorse statements of his which concern the essence of natural law and which he had come to see are wholly wrong. Apart from this, the editor's explanation does not account for other self-contradictions occurring in the essays, for instance that which occurs in one and the same essay regarding the need for speculative premises in moral matters. Locke asserts and denies in one and the same sentence that the existence of a deity which presides over "this world" can be proved from the testimony of the conscience and from the innate idea of God. The editor blurs the difficulty by saying that Locke "allows the cogency of two of the other arguments, namely the one from conscience and the one from the innate idea of God, but he remarks that their authority is not based on reason and sensation alone and, in fact, presupposes *a priori* notions which it is difficult to accept" (49). Here the editor reproduces Locke's self-contradiction without noticing it: arguments presupposing notions which it is difficult to accept cannot be cogent. More precisely, according to Locke, the two arguments "do not derive their whole force from our native faculties, namely, sense perception and reason," and the cooperation of sense perception and reason is the necessary condition for the production of cogent arguments (cf. 156 with 146 and 136 n.2). Locke says first that the two arguments in question prove the existence of God with certainty; and immediately thereafter he says in effect that, "as will perhaps appear to him who considers the matter more carefully," the two arguments do not prove the existence of God with certainty. Yet, as we have seen, Locke does not explicitly say in the negative part of his statement that the two arguments do not prove the existence of God with certainty. On the other hand, he does not unambiguously say in the affirmative part of his statement that the two arguments prove the existence of God with certainty; he says "in case the two arguments prove the existence of God with certainty" (*si . . . probet*). The editor and translator limits himself to saying that "*si* appears redundant" (154 n.2). The *si* certainly makes the sentence in which it occurs very awkward. We for our part would say that Locke regarded the two arguments as altogether weak but that he "was unwilling to show the weakness" of any argument allegedly proving the existence of God "since possibly by it some men might be confirmed in the belief of a God, which is enough to preserve in them true sentiments of religion and morality." (*Works*, III 53-54.) The editor has paid attention to Locke's spelling and to his Latin but only once to his manner of writing. In his Introduction he calls "attention to a slightly puzzling, yet obviously important, passage in essay V, where (he has) sought to give a coherent version without taking unwarranted liberties with the text" (91). The passage referred to reads as follows: "Such a consent (*sc.* unanimous and universal consent), I confess, could indicate a natural law but not prove it; it could achieve that I believe more ardently, but not that I know more certainly that the opinion (*sc.* which is held unanimously and universally) is a natural law; for I cannot know with certainty whether this (opinion) is the view of every individual by himself [I cannot know with certainty whether the opinion of each individual severally is a law of nature], for it (*sc.* my thought about another man's thoughts) is faith but not knowledge" (176). Locke refers here to a thought which was expressed by Descartes more clearly as follows: ". . . it seemed to me . . . that in order to know which were truly their opinions (*sc.* the opinions of those with whom I would have to live), I ought to pay attention to what they practiced rather than to what they said; not only because in the corruption of our morals there are few people who would say everything which they believe but also because some do not know it themselves." (*Discours de la méthode*, III.) Or, to quote from a fragment of Locke published for the first time by the editor: "if idolatry were nothing but terminating our worship, i.e. thought, on some thing that is not God, I do not see how there could be a law to punish idolators, seeing their thought cannot be known" (261). The student of Locke's thought must not disregard Locke's thought, or rather his exaggerated speech, on the impossibility of knowing other men's thoughts from their speeches: a man may deliberately contradict himself in order to indicate his thought rather than to reveal it.

Our second conclusion is that the proof of the existence of a wise "first artificer" is not sufficient according to Locke for establishing the existence of a natural law proper, i.e., of a natural law which man can transgress. In his thematic discussion of how reason can come to know the natural law, he explicitly distinguishes two presuppositions of the knowledge of natural law. The first is the

existence of some wise and powerful artificer of all sensibly perceived things including man—an artificer who can bring us forth,
preserve us and raise or destroy us as he sees fit and to whom
therefore we are rightly subject. The second presupposition is that
God has a will as regards what we ought to do or is concerned
with how we act (150-158). Without entering into the question
whether one can establish the existence of natural law without
establishing by this very fact the existence of knowledge of natural
law, we note that in demonstrating these two presuppositions of
the knowledge of natural law, Locke presupposes the existence
of natural law (cf. 146 top with 136 top). The ascent from the
sensibly perceived things leads to knowledge of "some supreme
deity," of the existence of "some powerful superior" who can treat
man as a potter treats clay or, more precisely, of "some artificer
of all these things whom it is necessary to acknowledge not only
as powerful but also as wise" and even as "most wise," who is in
fact a "most perfect and wise author" of all things. We note that
in his demonstration of the existence of God in the essays Locke
does not speak of God's omniscience and omnipotence although
he mentions these attributes elsewhere in those essays. That "most
wise" and "omniscient" are not identical would seem to appear
from the expression "omniscient and most wise" (182). One would
thus be justified in assuming a corresponding distinction between
"most powerful" and "omnipotent." "Power" as compelling power
belongs together with "right" and both seem to be characteristic
of God *qua* creator; wisdom seems to be characteristic of God *qua*
legislator (182, 186). Could the natural law which man cannot
transgress belong to God as creator and the natural law which
man can transgress belong to God as legislator? Yet it is precisely
God's infinite wisdom which is revealed in his creation, whereas
his infinite power extends beyond what he has in fact created:
"God could have created men so that they lacked eyes and did
not need them" (200). The translator has somehow become aware
of this difficulty. When Locke speaks of "that first fiat by which
(God) created and brought forth out of nothing this ornate structure" (160), the translator makes him speak of "that first fiat by
which He created and furnished this world, bringing order out of
chaos." He does this in spite of the fact that he renders literally
and correctly another reference of Locke to creation out of noth-

ing as distinguished from creation out of chaos (186). In this connection we may mention that whereas Locke speaks of "the majority of mortals who may not even once have thought about the (a) first man or his fall," the translator makes him speak of "Adam and his fall" (138; cf. *Treatises of government* I sect. 141); he does not consider that it is possible to assume "a first man" without knowing anything of the Bible.

According to Locke, knowledge of the natural law presupposes knowledge of God's will in regard to man's actions. Such knowledge of God's will is derived partly from the end or purpose of all things and partly from the constitution of man himself. Since all things are "the work of a most perfect and wise author, they do not seem to be destined by him for any other end than his own glory to which one must defer in everything." To speak less vaguely, man ought to perform all his actions with a view to the glory of God. Since man is not made fortuitously, the function of man seems to consist in the proper exercise of his natural faculties, not to say in acting according to his natural inclinations. Man being endowed by nature with the faculty of reason, his first and foremost duty is to contemplate God's works and His wisdom and power in His works, and then to give God the praise, the honor and the glory most worthy of Him (156). Knowledge of God and worship of God seem to be the first, the highest and the most weighty duties prescribed by natural law (cf. also 198). Yet there are whole nations of polytheists, and polytheism differs from atheism only by name, to say nothing of other nations which are manifestly atheist (174). Hence many nations must be regarded as criminal to the highest degree. This conclusion is not in harmony with the spirit of natural law which does not permit that men are divided into hostile societies (162). If the Greeks violate the spirit of natural law by regarding all other nations as barbarians, the Jews do the same by regarding all other nations as heathens and not sanctified (174). To overcome this difficulty Locke makes two suggestions. In the first place he says that "it is to be believed that religion becomes known to men not so much by the natural light as by divine revelation" (166). Locke here follows tacitly and perhaps unwittingly the Thomas Aquinas who says that it is not reason simply but reason informed by faith which dictates that God is to be loved and to be worshipped (*Summa theologica* I

2q.104.a.1.ad 3.), for the difficulty under consideration was as well known in the middle ages as it is in modern times. Since certain knowledge of divine revelation has not reached the majority of men or since revelation cannot be certainly known but is apprehended by faith (188), the majority of men cannot be regarded as criminal for failing to observe the duties of religion. Yet one obviously does not overcome completely the difficulty caused by the natural law prohibition against the worship of gods if one replaces that natural law prohibition by a prohibition based on revelation. Besides, Locke's suggestion implies that religion does not clearly belong to the virtues demanded by natural law. He suggests therefore in the second place that religion as a virtue demanded by natural law is not incompatible with the worship of gods. He speaks of the plunder of "temples of the gods" [divine temples] when enumerating crimes against "all right" (160), and he speaks of the absence of "temples of the gods" as proof of the disregard for a precept of natural law (190). On the same page on which he says that the majority of men do not possess knowledge of divine revelation, he also says that no one has denied the obligatory character of the revealed law. In fact he regards the uncontested admission of the obligatory character of the revealed law as so important that he builds on it his central argument for proving the obligatory character of natural law (188). This gentle procedure which consists in denying the existence of a serious issue and which wittingly generates tolerance together with confusion appears to be characteristic of Locke. For he also says that no one has denied the existence and the obligatory power of natural law (130; cf. 200 and 212) although he refers more than once to men who did and do deny the existence and hence the obligatory power of the natural law (112, 204). In the same way he says in the *Essay concerning human understanding* (II 28.8) "That God has given a rule whereby men should govern themselves, I think there is nobody so brutish to deny," although he had said earlier in that work (I 4.8) that there are men "who have enjoyed (the improvement of arts and sciences) in a very great measure who yet . . . want the idea and knowledge of God"; and in the *Reasonableness of Christianity* he says that the miracles of Jesus were never denied by anyone.

Locke says first that once it is established that there is a God who is the author of all sensibly perceived things, "the universal law of nature by which the human race is bound, necessarily follows" (132). He says next that knowledge of the natural law is based on two presuppositions, the existence of a wise and powerful author of all sensibly perceived things and his having a will as regards what we ought to do (152, 156). Yet these two presuppositions prove to be insufficient for establishing the existence or knowability of the natural law. Since "every law is in vain if there is no punishment" and, we must add, since the punishments available in this life do not suffice as sanctions for the natural law, the natural law is impossible without "the immortality of the souls" [the soul's immortality] (172, 174). Following the well known rule of reading according to which what a writer says only once is less important than what he says frequently, the editor says that in the essays Locke "noted, but he never stressed, the connection between God's law and the sanctions engaging men's obedience to it" (71): he does not speak of Locke's referring to punishment after death. It is more important to note that in the essays Locke does not even attempt to demonstrate the immortality of the souls although that immortality is a necessary presupposition of the natural law. We cannot help remembering here his later teaching according to which on the one hand the natural law stands or falls by rewards and punishments after death and on the other hand the natural light is unable to establish that there is a life after death. This state of things is obviously fatal to natural law. The editor's insufficient attention to the question of immortality is responsible for certain inadequacies of his translation. He does not sufficiently distinguish in his translation between *anima* and *animus* (cf. 148 and 126). Of a certain Lockian sentence he says he "cannot think of a satisfactory translation. I have taken *una* as an adverb." The difficulty disappears if one takes *una* as an adjective. Locke says: "This whole knowledge (*sc.* the knowledge accessible to man through his natural faculties), however great it is (and it certainly has made great progresses), which traverses the whole nature of things and, not confined within the limits of the world, enters Heaven [the sky] itself insofar as it contemplates it, and has investigated more carefully (*sc.* than was previously done) spirits and minds, what they are, what they do, by which laws they are bound—this whole knowledge, I say, which is one ["which is one" is omitted by the translator] reached the mind [here the translator adds "altogether"] from those three ways of knowing . . ." (122, 124). Locke expresses here exactly the same thought which he expresses in the last chapter of the *Essay concerning human understanding*: one and the same science, "Physica," is "the knowledge of things as they are in their own proper beings, their constitutions, properties, and operations, whereby I mean not only matter and body, but spirits also, which have their proper natures, constitutions, and operations, as well as bodies.—The end of this is bare speculative truth: and whatsoever can afford the mind of man any such falls under this branch, whether it be God himself, angels, spirits, bodies, or any of their affections, as number, and figure, etc." Even Thomas Aquinas was prepared to regard metaphysics as a subdivision of physics (*Commentary on the Ethics* I, lectio 1. and *Summa theologica* 2 2q.48c.). But when two men say the same thing, they do not necessarily mean the same thing. The translator also has some difficulty in understanding one of Locke's arguments allegedly proving that the natural law is not inscribed in the souls of men. Locke says: "If this natural law were inscribed in our breasts, why do the stupid and insane have no knowledge of this law? Since it (this law) is said to be stamped immediately on the minds themselves [on the soul itself] which (*sc.* the minds) depend in no wise [and this depends very little] on the constitution and the structure of the body's organs which (*sc.* the constitution and the structure of the body's organs) is admittedly [Yet therein admittedly lies] the only difference between the wise and the fools" (142). Locke appeals here to two generally accepted views, to the view that the intellect is not bodily and has no bodily organ, and to the view that the differences among men regarding the intellect are due to differences regarding the body (cf. Thomas, *Summa theologica* 1 q.85.a.7.c.). It is not impossible that the cited remark is the first sign of his later suggestion according to which it is "impossible for us, by the contemplation of our own ideas without revelation, to discover whether Omnipotency has not given to some systems of matter, fitly disposed, a power to perceive and think. . . . What certainty of knowledge can any one have that some perceptions, such as, *v.g.*, pleasure and pain, should not be in some bodies themselves. . . ?" (*Essay concerning human understanding* IV 3.6). In the essays he merely says that God can fill and stir the soul with sorrows or joy and the body with pain or pleasure (154; cf. 230).

In order to be a law, the natural law must be duly promulgated or sufficiently knowable to man as man. We have indicated the difficulty caused by the facts that according to Locke the natural law cannot be known by reason if reason cannot establish the immortality of the souls and that he does not even attempt to show that it can. In the penultimate essay he discusses the question of the proper promulgation of the natural law thus: can the natural law bind man as man seeing that whole nations are altogether unaware of it and that many nations are unaware at any rate of some of its precepts? Given these conditions, it follows either that there is no natural law at all or else that its obligatory power is not universal. In spite of this Locke asserts that the obligatory power of the natural law is universal (190, 192). He goes on to explain the meaning of this assertion. But nowhere in this discussion does he meet the issue which he had stated so forcefully at its beginning. He merely says that the natural law is so certain in itself that it is obligatory "although perhaps most men are so ignorant [lazy] and so thoughtless that for want of attention they ignore" the natural law which is so manifest (198, 200, 112, 128). Ignorance of the natural law is no excuse since that ignorance itself is due to criminal negligence. Everyone can know the natural law provided he applies his mind properly to its study (186). No one can ignore the natural law except him who loves blindness and darkness (188). Yet this does not dispose of the difficulty. In the penultimate essay Locke says: "it is hard to believe that the dictates of nature (*sc.* the natural law) are so obscure that they are hidden from whole nations" (190). But in the first half of the essays he says: "those who have no other guide than nature itself, those in whom the dictates of nature are in no way corrupted by positive customs, live in such ignorance of every law as if no attention whatever had to be paid to the right and honorable." As for the civilized nations, their moral opinions have the character of prejudices (which perhaps agree to some extent with the content of natural law) and therefore cannot be assumed to embody knowledge of the natural law (140, 142); a law which is merely believed in or known only by tradition cannot be the natural law (130). Where then do we find knowledge of the natural law? "Some acknowledge a different law of nature, others none, all an obscure one." This obscurity of the natural law cannot be explained by the Fall (138). Still less can it be explained, we may add, by any other kind of human guilt. The diversity of men's opinions about the natural law is due to the fact that that law "is not easy to know" (134). The natural law belongs to "the secrets of nature"; it is "remote and hidden." Not only vicious and dull witted men but also those who lack the leisure to occupy themselves with the study of the sensibly perceived things and with the higher knowledge which arises from that study, are necessarily ignorant of the natural law (cf. 112, 114 with 122, 124 and 134).

The natural light by which the natural law is said to be knowable "leads us to that peak of virtue and happiness to which both the gods call and nature tends." This statement seems to imply that by obeying the natural law man will reach his natural end, his natural happiness (146; cf. 214). Locke explicitly identifies the natural law with "the way which leads to happiness" (174). He is silent about man's supernatural happiness made possible by revelation although he says that "it must be believed that religion becomes known to men not so much by the natural light as by divine revelation" (166). Yet he also says: "nothing is so obscure, so concealed, so remote from every sense perception [from any meaning] that the mind, capable of everything, could not reach it by reflection and reasoning if it is assisted" by reason (the discursive faculty) and sense perception. Locke does not explain what he understands by "mind" (*animus*, in the context used synonymously with *mens*). But he seems to suggest that man's natural faculties are in principle sufficient for understanding everything. However this may be, in proportion as it becomes doubtful whether the natural law is sufficiently promulgated, it becomes doubtful whether man is capable of reaching happiness. After having proved the existence of God from the perfect order of the world, of which man is "not the lowest part," Locke shows parenthetically that man could not have been made by inanimate things and brutes nor by man himself: if man were his own maker, he would give himself, i.e. every human individual, everlasting existence, for man cannot be conceived to be so full of hate and enmity against himself as to deprive himself of all the charms of life (152). From this it would appear to follow that the creation of man as a mortal being which knows of its mortality cannot be due to a being which loves man. At any rate, man's condition, which is due to his mortality, is here presented as a condition of extreme misery, a condition which cannot be relieved by obedience to the natural law and which only a being inimical to man could have inflicted on him. Locke himself applies this thought to the problem of natural law. "Mankind would be very well off" if the natural law were inscribed in the minds of men and hence easily and very conveniently knowable; but nature— and, it would seem necessary to add, the author of nature—has not been so kind to man as to provide him with innate knowledge of natural law (124, 126) but rather withholds knowledge of the natural law like a secret (114, 228). Therefore if nature is supposed to demand obedience to the natural law from man as man, nature would be a most cruel tyrant and not at all the kind mother of all (190, 192). In other words, if nature were the most kind mother of all, she would wish that our duties are not only necessary but pleasant as well: there would be no need for heroic virtue (208; cf. 226). Nature is then not only not able but even not willing to establish a harmony between duty and pleasure. Nature promises man great happiness; she gives him none. She treats us like slaves or convicts: she gives us many laws and commands but no tranquillity and leisure. It is not certain that there is in us a small flame of heavenly origin but if there is, we owe it to Prometheus' theft rather than to Zeus' gift. (220.—Cf. also Locke's remark on the precise meaning of Genesis 1.28 in *Treatises* I sect. 25-26.) Nature has arranged that "it is impossible to take care of the interests of all at the same time," for the inheritance of the human race is one and always the same and does not increase in proportion to the number of the human beings born. The goods which nature provides do not grow with men's needs. The limits of the world do not extend in proportion as the need of man grows (210). The generosity of nature is extremely limited. This being the case, we may add, the large majority of men do not have the leisure required for becoming aware of the natural law, or their ignorance of the natural law cannot be due to their fault.

The foregoing observations compel one to look in the essays on natural law for suggestions of an alternative to natural law or at any rate to the traditional natural law teaching. After having admitted that the majority of men are ignorant of the natural law,

Locke asserts that human society is impossible without obedience
to the natural law (cf. 118 with 112) and hence without knowledge
of the natural law. Yet human societies exist and some societies
even flourish. Hence society is possible without natural law. Alter-
natively, one would have to say that the natural law without which
society is impossible is a natural law which men cannot transgress
at all or which they cannot transgress without suffering from the
consequences of their transgression in this life. Society, Locke
argues, is not possible if men do not keep the social compact, and
men are induced to keep the social compact because the natural
law obliges them to keep it. But he adds the qualifying remark that
unless there is a natural law obliging men to keep compacts, they
cannot be expected to keep the social compact "if a more convenient
condition were offered elsewhere." Thus the question arises whether,
generally speaking, the condition of life which is available outside
society is not so inconvenient that both interest and pleasure induce
man to keep the social compact and prior to that to make that
compact (cf. 118). As Locke notes elsewhere (160, 162, 164),
"men's common need and convenience" give rise to compacts and
in particular to tacit compacts. Whatever is agreed upon by tacit
compacts does not have the character of natural law since it is not
commanded by a law nor are men driven to it by some natural
instinct but it is suggested by common interests or by calculation.
We wonder then whether Locke does not intend to follow the
lead given by Hobbes and to replace the traditional natural law
teaching by a moral teaching which is grounded on the desire or
instinct for self-preservation. When speaking of what Thomas had
presented as man's three-fold natural inclination, Locke traces to
"an inner instinct" only man's proneness to preserve himself; only
of the proneness to self-preservation, as distinguished from the
proneness to religion and to social life, does he say that all men
are actually prompted to act in accordance with it (156, 158). But
even self-preservation is not hallowed by universal consent; its
power can be overruled by custom and custom-bred opinion (172),
as Hobbes had of course admitted (cf. *Leviathan* ch. 14 with ch. 29).
Yet, as precisely Hobbes had shown, if one takes self-preservation
to be the sufficient basis of morality, one cannot conceive of self-
preservation as commanded by natural law. If self-preservation is
therefore the fundamental right and not a duty, suicide cannot be

a crime. When enumerating certain things which are always forbidden, Locke remarks that "no one can stain himself with another's blood without incurring guilt" (194). If self-preservation is understood as the source and the principle of natural law rather than as a precept of natural law, even compliance with the natural law itself can no longer be conceived as the fulfillment of a duty but only as an act of expediency. Hence we can certainly neglect and violate the natural law without crime, although not without our damage, "whenever it pleases us to abandon our right," i.e., the right of self-preservation [whenever it pleases us to claim our right and give way to our own inclinations] (180).

The purpose of the last essay is to refute the assertion that "the private interest of each is the basis of natural law." The essay opens with a quotation reporting Carneades' assertion according to which there is no natural right but all men are driven by nature to seek their own interests. It goes on to remark that Carneades' contention has found adherents in every subsequent generation. Carneades was a man of very great sharpness of mind and eloquence. His successors on the other hand adopted his view with the greatest ardor or partisanship. They lacked the virtues and gifts of mind whereby they might pave for themselves the way to honors and riches; they traced their lack of honors and riches to the injustice of government; they asserted that they were debarred from the goods which are by nature common to all men; they clamored for the abolition of government and for the assertion of natural freedom: right ought to be determined not by other men's law but by every one's own interest (204). It would seem that the unphilosophic successors of Carneades, while pretending to deny natural law, appeal to natural law or at least to natural right. Locke rejects their opinion with contempt and takes the side of "the saner part" whom he will call in the *Treatises* "the rational and industrious." The saner part has little respect for what the quarrelsome and the lazy regard as their private interest or as their natural right. Locke does not even attempt to refute Carneades' assertion that each man is by nature driven to seek his own interest and not to act justly. He merely attempts to refute the assertion that the private interest of each is the basis of natural law. He proceeds as follows. He first identifies the basis of natural law with the basic natural law. Hence the thesis that the private interest of each is

the basis of natural law comes to mean that according to the basic
natural law, man is obliged above everything else to be concerned
with his private interests. Furthermore since no one can be a fair
judge of another man's interest, everyone must be allowed to be
the sole judge of his own interest; since most men understand by
their interest their immediate interest, those men at any rate are
under a sacred obligation, which overrides all other considerations,
to take care of their immediate private interest and they are forbidden to do anything which conflicts with their immediate private
interest (204, 206, 212; cf. *Treatises* II sect. 87 and Hobbes *De cive*
I 9). Hence the men who have been admired hitherto as models
of virtue must be loathed as the most wicked criminals unless one
were to say that they sacrificed their lives and fortunes for the
benefit of their country and mankind in order to earn immortal
fame (cf. 206, 208). Every act of generosity becomes a violation
of natural law unless one were to say that generosity pays or even
pays immediately (cf. 212, 214, 180). But let us concentrate on
Locke's central argument (210, 212). If everyone is by nature
obliged to be concerned above everything else with his immediate
private interest, it follows necessarily that everyone is by nature
at war with everyone else and that society is altogether impossible.
Hobbes had inferred from this that men must cease to think primarily of their immediate or present interest but must think rather
of their future or long range interest; thus they will realize that
they must seek peace and subordinate their immediate private interests to the requirements of peace; the natural law is nothing but
the moral conditions of peace (*De cive* III 31). In the same way
Locke replaces everyone's immediate private interest by everyone's
long range private interest. But he contends that if everyone's first
and overriding obligation is to be concerned with his long range
interest, there follows, not the demand for peace, but again the
war of everybody against everybody. The reason is the natural
scarcity of things which man needs for his long range interest or
for his self-preservation: it is better to fight with other men for
the barest necessities than to perish through starvation while keeping the peace. In order to see how Locke has overcome this difficulty, it suffices to remember the normal connection between
domestic peace and plenty. He leaves no doubt that there is a fundamental harmony between the private interest of each and the law

of nature (206, 214). The fact that there is a fundamental harmony between private interest and the law of nature (the law which dictates peace and therefore obedience to the government) does not mean that that harmony is complete. The most important practical consequence of this is the fact that if "manifest acts of tyranny . . . reach no farther than some private men's cases," "the body of the people do not think themselves concerned in it" and hence do not cause any difficulty for the government (*Treatises* II sect. 208). For all practical purposes it may therefore be better to say that the basis or end of society is not the private interest of each but the public interest, i.e., the interest of the large majority. To quote the motto of the *Treatises*: *Salus populi suprema lex esto.* This is not to deny that the root of the public interest is the private interest of each. Just as Machiavelli did before him, Locke therefore speaks once of "the common interest of each" (206; cf. Machiavelli, *Discourses* I near the beginning). Locke is closer to Machiavelli than he is generally said or thought to be.

Locke's early essays show clearly how doubtful he was, from the beginning of his career, of the traditional natural law teaching. That teaching derives man's duties from man's natural constitution or his natural inclinations; it assumes that man is by nature ordered toward virtue; it also presupposes that each man and each nation is ruled by divine providence, that men's souls are immortal, and that the natural law is sufficiently promulgated in and to the consciences of all men. Locke never elaborated his alternative to the traditional natural law teaching. In both the *Treatises* and the *Essay* he limited himself to combining a somewhat modified version of the traditional natural law principles with a natural law teaching which follows from the Hobbesian principles rather than from the traditional principles and to alluding to his objections to the traditional principles. In a passage of the *Essay* he almost contrasts the two different ways in which natural law or morality can be known or taught. The first way starts from the "ideas" of "a supreme Being, infinite in power, goodness and wisdom" and of "ourselves, as understanding, rational beings"; those two "ideas . . . would, *I suppose*, if duly considered and pursued, afford such foundations of our duty and rules of action as *might* place morality among the sciences capable of demonstration." The second way starts from the "ideas" of justice, property and government; it leads to propositions like "Where there is no property, there is no injustice" and "No government allows absolute liberty." (IV 3.18; the italics are not in the original.) Why Locke's exposition of the first way is defective has been shown above at great length. His exposition of the second way is defective because it too is silent about the sanctions of morality; or more particularly it is silent about the compelling reason for which property and government are necessary and hence good. That compelling reason is the fundamental need or right of self-preservation.

In conclusion we mention some pecularities of the edition and translation for which we have not found a convenient place. "We do not investigate here what a man can know [experience] who is divinely inspired" (122). When used in this context, "experience" does not today necessarily suggest knowledge. "(Most men) are guided by opinion and praise [by belief and approval], not by the natural law" (128). It is dangerous to identify opinion and belief, as can be seen from a comparison of Thomas, *Summa theologica* 2 2q.1.a.5. and Locke, *Essay* IV 17. "No ground can be assigned why one man [the translator adds "of the older generation"] rather than another maintaining quite the opposite should be credited with the authority of the tradition of the ancestors" [the translator omits "of the ancestors"] (128, 130). "Those barbarous nations" [those primitive races] (138). "Customs" [morals] which are "remote from virtue" (140). ". . . if we would review the classes of virtues and vices—and nobody doubts that they (*sc.* the virtues) [this classification] are [is] the law of nature itself . . ." (166). Here the editor tries to translate Locke's original version, which Locke himself corrected, "thereby confusing the sentence"; but it is unlikely that man's duty should consist in classifying the virtues and vices whereas it makes sense to say with Locke and the translator that the virtues are "precepts of the law of nature" (128) and that justice is "an outstanding law of nature" (168). On page 166 the editor wisely uses in his English translation a variant reading which he relegates to a note in his Latin text. In connection with this he obscures the manner in which Locke has numbered his arguments; by numbering his arguments and the parts of his arguments, Locke enables those readers who count all the numbers in one series, regardless of whether the numbers indicate a whole argument or part of an argument, to discern the true center of an essay. "Habits" [sentiments] (194). Locke does not suggest as the translator makes him suggest that "it depends on our ability" but that "it rests within our power" (194) whether for instance we marry or not. It is hard to believe that Locke would have meant to write that the natural law obligates men to the extent to which it is "delightsome" (*laeta*) to them; it is more likely that he meant to write that the natural law obligates men to the extent to which it is proposed or given (*lata*) to them (196). For no reason the translator renders in one and the same sentence *virtutes* first by "moral virtue" and then by "virtuous actions" (212). "For what justice is there where there is no property [personal property] or ownership, or what property where everyone may not only possess what is his own but where that is a man's own which he possesses, which is useful to him [where what he possesses is his own, merely because it is useful]. But [In truth] one may observe here briefly that the upholders of this view derive the moral principles and the rule of life rather from men's desire and their natural inclination [natural instincts] than from legal obligation . . ." (212). In quoting the beginning of that passage of the *Nicomachean Ethics* which deals with natural right, Locke apparently made a slip (112 n.3); he certainly understood the passage in exactly the same way in which it had been understood by Averroes.

IX

ON A FORGOTTEN
KIND OF
WRITING

Recently, a student at the University of Chicago told me that a suggestion which I have made both in the classroom and in print has proved to be of interest to some of his friends but that it is not sufficiently clear to them. This student mentioned that it would be helpful if I were to write a note on the matter for the *Chicago Review*. In order not merely to repeat what I have written elsewhere, I believe it will be best if I discuss here those objections to my suggestion which have been made publicly. I suspect that these objections arose out of difficulties similar to those that various students have felt.

I should begin by briefly summarizing my suggestion. In studying certain earlier thinkers, I became aware of this way of conceiving the relation between the quest for truth (philosophy or science) and society: Philosophy or science, the highest activity of man, is the attempt to replace opinion about "all things" by knowledge of "all things"; but opinion is the element of society; philosophy or science is therefore the attempt to dissolve the element in which society breathes, and thus it endangers society. Hence philosophy or science must remain the preserve of a small minority, and philosophers or scientists must respect the opinions on which society rests. To respect opinions is something entirely different from accepting them as true. Philosophers or scientists who hold this view about the relation of philosophy or science and society are driven to employ a peculiar manner of writing which would enable them to reveal what they regard as the truth to the few, without endangering the unqualified commitment of the many to the opinions on which society rests. They will distinguish between the true teaching as the esoteric teaching and the socially useful teaching as the exoteric teaching; whereas the exoteric teaching is meant to be easily accessible to every reader, the esoteric teaching discloses itself only to very careful and well-trained readers after long and concentrated study.

The crucial premise of this argument is the proposition that opinion is the element of society. This premise is accepted by many contemporary social scientists. They teach that every society rests, in the last analysis, on specific values or on specific myths, i.e., on assumptions which are not evidently superior or preferable to any alternative assumptions. They imply, therefore, that social science reveals and stresses the arbitrary character of the basic assumptions underlying any given society; social science desires to be "objective" and "undogmatic." They fail to see, however, that this state of things creates a tension between the requirements of social science (knowledge of the truth and teaching of the truth) and the requirements of society (whole-hearted acceptance of the principles of society): if I know that the principles of liberal democracy are not intrinsically superior to the principles of communism or fascism, I am incapable of whole-hearted commitment to liberal democracy.

My suggestion consists, then, fundamentally of two questions: the historical question as to whether there ever were any great thinkers who held the view about the relation of philosophy and society which I have just sketched and who acted on it; and the philosophic question whether that view is simply false or simply true, or true if qualified (e.g., "opinion is the element of all non-liberal societies"). The two questions are obviously of importance; and they are not trivial in the sense that they are discussed in every textbook. One might go further and say that it is a considerable time since they have been discussed at all. My young friends expected, therefore, that the suggestion mentioned would arouse some interest in scholarly circles. But young people are bad judges in matters of this kind. Only four or five scholars of my generation did become interested. One of them is a man of high reputation in his field who understands the contemporary dangers to intellectual freedom well enough to realize that these dangers are caused, not only by men like Senator McCarthy but by the absurd dogmatism of certain academic "liberals" or "scientific" social scientists as well. He expressed the lesson which I had tried to convey by the words, "there is hope."

Professor George H. Sabine has reviewed my book, *Persecution and the Art of Writing*, in the April, 1953, issue of *Ethics*. He begins by wondering whether the canon for reading certain great books which I suggested "provides a workable rule for historical interpretation or an invitation to perverse ingenuity." This doubt is perfectly justified, especially prior to any investigation: there is no method which cannot be misunderstood or misused. Did the principle that one ought to understand the teachings of the great thinkers in terms of their social backgrounds not also become, in more than one case, "an invitation to perverse ingenuity"? Sabine says that I make "the argument somewhat too easy when [I put] the case of a 'master of the art of writing' who 'commits such blunders as would shame an intelligent high-school boy,' because that kind of writing would not deceive even a careless reader." I shall not complain about Sabine's manner of quoting. I merely note that the quotation is a part of one sentence out of seven sentences which are meant to indicate some rules of reading. The complete sentence runs as follows: "If a master of the art of writing commits such blunders as would shame an intelligent high-school boy, it is reasonable to assume that they are intentional, especially if the author discusses, however incidentally, the possibility of intentional blunders in writing." As regards Sabine's remark on the passage which he quoted, I regret to say that I know of more than one case where commentators who are not exceptionally careless did not even notice blunders of this kind. Readers who do not notice blunders of this kind are not the only ones deceived. Also deceived are those who notice them but take them simply as blunders of the sort that everyone commits from time to time. Contradictions are one species of the blunders I had mentioned. "The limits of permissible or probable contradiction in an author are really very difficult to determine." Those limits are impossible to determine because the meaning of "an author" is so vague. Things which are true of the highest intellects are wholly inapplicable to others. The case of authors who explicitly say that they intentionally contradict themselves in order to indicate a secret teaching to an elite among their readers, is entirely different from that of authors who neither say nor indicate anything of the kind. Sabine cannot but admit that it is sometimes necessary to read between the lines, but he trivializes this admission by refusing to consider its implications. In particular, he evades the question of the criteria which would allow us to distinguish between guessing at and knowing what an author indicates between the lines. He raises the question, "Is reading between the lines characteristically the unraveling of an elaborate system of contrived deceptions?" This objection suffers again from lack of definiteness. I would rejoin: characteristic of whom? If a present-day American economist, of average intelligence and average power of expression, would indicate between the lines of an article a preference for planned economy while in the lines evading the issue "planned economy vs. the free enterprise system," I would hesitate to assume that he is using "an elaborate system of contrived deceptions"; but writers of another caliber might well use such a "system." Still, even the most casual writing between the lines make unconscious or half-conscious use of those very principles of expression the fully conscious use of which presupposes "an elaborate system of contrived deceptions." Sabine is doubtful whether I mean to say that "at least in political philosophy, a distinction between an esoteric and an exoteric meaning is the typical form of interpretation." I never committed this absurdity. He asserts that "a society can hardly be imagined that does not put restrictions on what an author may say, or on the circumstances under which he may say it, or on the choice of persons to whom he may suitably say it." I assert that societies in which men can attack in writings accessible to all both the established social or political order and the beliefs on which it is based can not only be imagined but have existed, e.g., the Third Republic in France and post-Bismarckian Wilhelminian Germany. I do not know what Sabine thinks of the wisdom of such extreme liberalism. Be this as it may, I admit of course that there were and are societies which were and are not extremely liberal. The issue concerns the conclusions which the historian must draw from the fact that not all literate societies were and are liberal. If a society prevents writers from freely discussing its principles, one is entitled to raise the question as to whether a writer who belongs to such a society and who makes himself the mouthpiece of its principles expresses these principles because he is convinced of their soundness or because he cedes to superior force. The question takes on some urgency if the writer in question is a great mind who expressly says that it is not wrong to teach doctrines which one regards as erroneous. It becomes still more urgent if his writings abound in enigmatic features which one easily overlooks if one is not attentive.

After stating his general criticism, Sabine turns to my chapter on Spinoza's *Theologico-Political Treatise*. He grants that that work "is well adapted to the use of Strauss's method" and that I am not entirely wrong in what I say about Spinoza's attitude toward revealed religion. If I understand him correctly, he means to say that while the rejection of revealed religion is a necessary consequence of Spinoza's *Ethics*, Spinoza was perhaps not fully aware of this consequence, whereas I had maintained that he was fully aware of it. I cannot discuss this criticism, which is not more than an unsupported assertion that my detailed argument, based almost entirely on the *Theologico-Political Treatise*, is perhaps faulty. Sabine does not leave it at expressing the opinion that my conclusions are perhaps uncertain. He tries to show that they are "in one respect . . . paradoxical." Spinoza, I had contended, used certain literary devices in order to conceal his seriously held views from the vulgar; but, Sabine says, "the vulgar whom he had most occasion to fear, namely, the Calvinist theologians" "were just the ones who were not deluded." I thought I had left no doubt about this point: I had spoken of Spinoza's extraordinary boldness. His whole enterprise consists of what one might call an open attack on all forms of orthodox Biblical theology. He could dare to make this attack because he could count, within certain limits, on the sympathy of liberal believers or, more precisely, on the sympathy of those who regarded the moral teaching, as distinguished from the teaching about dogma and ritual, as the chief teaching of divine revelation as accessible in the Bible. The explicit theses of the *Theologico-Political Treatise* may be said to express an extreme version of the "liberal" view. But there are strong reasons for doubting that Spinoza himself agreed with that extreme version of the "liberal" view. Spinoza attempted to appease not any orthodox theologians but those who were more or less inclined toward a liberal Christianity. He concealed his partial, but decisively important, disagreement not with the orthodox theologians but with liberal believers of various shades.

In speaking of another "paradox" of mine, Sabine suggests that I regard the commentators as even less penetrating than the vulgar. This suggestion is not entirely wrong: I regard many present-day commentators as less penetrating than the vulgar of the seventeenth century, because the latter had a much greater awareness of the serious character of the theological problem and even of its details than do men brought up in the belief that enthusiasm for science and progress constitutes a form of religion. When Sabine says that Spinoza knew "that a frontal attack on Calvinist theology was impossible," I can only ask him whether Spinoza does not make a frontal attack on the belief in any miracles and whether a doctrine of a certain miracle (the miracle of resurrection) is not the very center of Calvinist theology as Spinoza knew it.

Sabine "should have preferred to believe that Spinoza was quite honest when he said that the chief aim of his book was to advocate freedom of speech and of investigation, rather than 'to refute the claims which have been raised on behalf of revelation throughout the ages' as Strauss says." The chief aim, or, according to the full title of the *Theologico-Political Treatise*, the sole aim of that work is to advocate freedom of philosophizing. But, as Spinoza says in the preface, he cannot successfully defend that freedom without drawing the reader's attention to the chief prejudices regarding religion, i.e., especially to the prejudice that philosophy must be the handmaid of theology: he must advocate the radical separation of philosophy and theology. But such a radical separation appeared to him unreasonable if theology or the Bible could be assumed to teach theoretical truth. He was therefore compelled to try to show that the Biblical teaching has no cognitive value whatever: he was compelled to try to refute the claims which have been raised on behalf of revelation throughout the ages. It is legitimate to designate as the chief aim of a book that aim which the author consciously pursues in a very large part of the book, provided his having attained that aim is the necessary and sufficient condition for his other aim or aims becoming defensible. "If Spinoza was fully convinced that revelation ought to be refuted, he certainly knew that if toleration waited until there was general agreement on that point it would wait forever." Hence, I concluded, he argued exoterically on the assumption that, through the Bible, God has revealed to man, not indeed knowledge of things spiritual or natural, but the right principles of action, and that these principles demand toleration.

Sabine notes that my "argument about the esoteric interpretation of philosophical writings is combined with, and complicated by, another argument against . . . 'historicism,' " but he does not see a "close logical relation between the two arguments." The strict connection is this. Esotericism necessarily follows from the original meaning of philosophy, provided that it is assumed that opinion is the element of society; but historicism is incompatible with philosophy in the original meaning of the word, and historicism cannot be ignored today. One can illustrate the connection between the two arguments as follows: Historicism may be said to be the view, accepted by Sabine, that "there are presumptions implicit in what Carl Becker called the 'climate of opinion' of an age that no contemporary ever fully grasps, precisely because they are so deeply ingrained in the texture of his thinking." In other words, even the greatest minds cannot liberate themselves from the specific opinions which rule their particular society. This view can be established more easily if all explicit statements of all great thinkers must be taken to express their private thoughts than if this assumption is questioned.

As regards my argument against historicism, Sabine doubts if he follows it. What I meant to say was that if one does not take seriously the intention of the great thinkers, namely, the intention to know the truth about the whole, one cannot understand them; but historicism is based on the premise that this intention is unreasonable because it is simply impossible to know the truth about the whole. I never said, as Sabine believes I did, that reading old books can support the truth of the statement "that, unless there is a single true account of the whole, no account of anything in particular can be true." I merely said that reading old books is today indispensable as an antidote to the ruling dogma that the very notion of a final and true account of the whole is absurd. I never said that "a historian must proceed on the supposition that philosophers, even original and important ones, always know the presuppositions and consequences of all the statements they make." I merely said that the historian must proceed on the supposition that the great thinkers understood better what they thought than the historian who is not likely to be a great thinker. Sabine however believes that "there are presumptions implicit in . . . 'the climate of opinion' of an age that no contemporary ever fully grasps." He seems to imply that the historian may grasp fully the presuppositions implicit in the "climate of opinion," say, of early fourth century Athens which Plato, accepting those presuppositions, did not fully grasp. If Sabine had given an example he would have enabled his readers to consider whether he is right. I do not know of any historian who grasped fully a fundamental presupposition of a great thinker which the great thinker himself did not fully grasp.

The attitude of Sabine contrasts with the open-mindedness characteristic of M. Yvon Belaval's review in the October, 1953, issue of *Critique*. Even if Belaval had known only Renan's *Averroès* and the *Encyclopédie*, he would have been prevented from rejecting my suggestion *a limine*. He realizes that that suggestion gives unity and force to some fragmentary and scattered remarks which serious students of certain earlier thinkers could not help making. He realizes above all that my suggestion is not incompatible with compliance with the demands of historical exactness.

Belaval begins his criticism with the remark that my suggestion is based on the anti-positivist view "that the philosophic truth is untemporal" or on "a classical and rationalist conception of truth." He raises the question whether there is no contradiction between this view and my apparent concern with making historical inquiries independent of every philosophic postulate. I did not suggest that one can make the study of the history of philosophy independent of every philosophic postulate. History of philosophy necessarily presupposes the persistence of the same fundamental problems. This, and this alone, is the trans-temporal truth which must be admitted, if there is to be history of philosophy. On the other hand, history of philosophy is endangered if the historian starts from the acceptance of any solution of the fundamental problems: if he knows in advance that a given philosophic doctrine which he is studying is false, he lacks the incentive for studying that doctrine with sympathy or care. What I said does imply the rejection of positivism: posivitism is blind to the fundamental problems, and therefore the positivist as positivist cannot be a historian of philosophy; a man who happens to be a positivist can become a historian of philosophy only to the extent to which he develops the capacity for questioning positivism.

Belaval raises the further question whether every philosophy finds itself in conflict with politics or only dogmatic philosophies. I can only repeat that there is a necessary conflict between philosophy and politics if the element of society necessarily is opinion, i.e. assent to opinion; this condition can be admitted by skeptics as well as by dogmatists; if this condition is rejected, there can only be accidental conflicts between philosophy and politics, conflicts arising from the fact that philosophers sometimes reach positive or negative results which are at variance with the principles of a given society. Belaval notes that non-official dogmatisms sometimes provoked the opposition of religious authorities rather than of political authorities. We do not have to consider whether every authority proper is not in the last analysis political. It suffices to say that political men frequently welcomed the support of able unbelievers against religious fanatics who seemed to endanger the statesmanlike handling of affairs. But this fact—the fact, in other words, that philosophers generally speaking have preferred the rule of non-priests to the rule of priests—obviously does not prove that there is no fundamental tension between the requirements of philosophy and the requirements of political society. Belaval wonders whether in speaking of such a fundamental tension I did not "systematize a partial view," i.e. the "Averroistic" view. The "Averroistic" view is no more partial than its contrary: both are total views about the relation of philosophy and politics. I would have to be much more ignorant than I am, and in fact than anyone is, if I had

been unaware of the existence of the alternative to "Averroism."
Belaval is quite right when he says that one cannot infer an
essential antinomy between philosophy and politics from the
factual persecution of philosophers by political authorities. I am
quite certain that I did not make this mistake. But I may add
that one cannot infer an essential harmony between philosophy
and politics from the factual recognition of a given philosophy,
or even of all philosophies, by certain societies: that recognition
may be based on capital errors. Belaval is also right when he
says that one cannot accept the "Averroistic" view if one believes
that M. Kojève teaches the truth.

Turning to the question of methods of reading, Belaval takes
issue with my "axiom" that one writes as one reads. He asserts
that very careful philosophers like Leibniz and Kant have not
been very careful readers. I had not spoken of careful philosophers but of careful writers. Belaval has not proved that the
Nouveaux Essais and the *Kritik der reinen Vernunft* are carefully
written in the sense in which the *Discorsi sopra la prima deca di
T. Livio* are carefully written, to say nothing of certain pre-
modern books. In the same context, he expresses the suspicion
that I might have mistaken the scholar for the philosopher, for
he believes that by starting from certain Jewish and Islamic
philosophers of the middle ages, I studied in fact scholars and
commentators rather than philosophers: the writers in question
were commentators on Plato and Aristotle rather than original
philosophers. I doubt whether originality in the sense of discovery or invention of "systems" has anything to do with philosophic depth or true originality. Spinoza was much more original
in the present day sense of the term than was Maimonides; but
Maimonides was nevertheless a deeper thinker than Spinoza.

Belaval also questions the "axiom" that, of two contradictory
statements the one that is the more subversive in the time of the
author is the more secret. I had said that if we find in writings
of a certain kind two contradictory theses, we are entitled to
assume that the thesis which is more secret, i.e., which occurs
more rarely, expresses the author's serious view. Belaval believes
that such a secret cannot be concealed at all. I must disagree. I
have noticed more than once that if an author makes a statement
on a very important subject only once, while in all other places

he either asserts its contrary or remains silent on the subject, students of the author invariably ignore the unique statement when presenting the author's doctrine: the unique statement is disregarded as unintelligible or unimportant. Belaval overestimates the carefulness and perspicacity of most readers. To prove his contention, he refers to the fact that the persecution of men like Maimonides and Spinoza began immediately after they had published certain books. This fact proves merely that they became immediately suspect of heterodoxy. It does not even prove that that suspicion was well-founded; there are examples of persecution of innocent men. It does not prove at all that their persecutors recognized how heterodox those great men were. Besides, these men or their causes had defenders who would not have been allies if the degree or the precise character of their heterodoxy had been known. It is also not irrelevant to refer to the relatively mild character of the persecution in the two cases mentioned and in other similar cases. It is not sufficient to say, as Belaval does, that the security of philosophers depended less on the cautious character of their writings than on the political support from which they benefited: a completely imprudent philosopher is beyond support if he does not have the good fortune to be regarded as insane.

The main objection of Belaval is to the effect that the method of reading which I suggest can never lead to absolute certainty. He is right in questioning my comparison of the deciphering of esoteric texts with the deciphering of cuneiform texts: that comparison occurred in what I thought was rather obviously an argument *ad hominem*. I shall limit myself to a counter-objection to Belaval's main objection: Do the alternative methods of reading lead to absolute certainty? Are not the alternative methods of reading based on the demonstratively false premises that in interpreting a book one may disregard completely what its author says about the necessity of secrecy or caution, and that one may disregard completely the unique or rare statements on important subjects in favor of what the author says most frequently or in all cases but one? As Belaval notes, M. Kojève, comparing my method to that of the detective, asserted that there is this difference: that my method cannot lead up to the confession of the criminal. My answer is twofold: I know of cases where the criminal confessed posthumously after having made sure that the detective would not condemn him; and I would be happy if there were suspicion of crime where up to now there has only been implicit faith in perfect innocence. At the very least the observations I have made will force historians sooner or later to abandon the complacency with which they claim to know what the great thinkers thought, to admit that the thought of the past is much more enigmatic than it is generally held to be, and to begin to wonder whether the historical truth is not as difficult of access as the philosophic truth.

X

KURT

RIEZLER

(1882-1955)

The Graduate Faculty has honored me with the request to speak in its General Seminar about the thought of our friend, the late Kurt Riezler. I feel with equal strength the obligation to comply with that request and my inability to comply with it sufficiently. I met Riezler for the first time in 1938, in this country, in this very building, when he was already well in his fifties and had already completed a distinguished career. And although two of my friends had spoken to me about him in terms of high regard, I had never read a line of his. It took him and me a number of years until a somewhat complicated relationship of colleagues grew into a simple and firm friendship. After I had left for Chicago in 1949, we met only at long intervals. During the last two years of his life, we did not see each other at all and we exchanged only a few letters. While he was alive, I had never found the time to read those of his writings which were published prior to 1941, with the exception of his *Parmenides*. During the last two months, I have read most of these writings, but I was unable to read them with the care which they deserve.

But I am embarrassed not only by my lack of knowledge.

Riezler was not only a thinker and writer. He was equally a man of action. He was, above all, a human being of rare breadth and depth. To speak adequately in his honor, one would have to do more than to analyze his thought. One would also have to narrate his actions and to bring to light and to life the man himself. I have never deplored as much as on the present occasion that I lack the gifts of narrative and of characterization.

Riezler represented to me, more than anyone else among my acquaintances, the virtue of humanity. I believe he was formed by Goethe more than by any other master. His interests and sympathies extended to all fields of worthy human endeavour. He could easily have become an outstanding scholar in a great variety of fields, but he preferred to be a truly educated man rather than to be a specialist. The term "professor" does not designate anything of him, but the term "gentleman" does. The activity of his mind had the character of noble and serious employment of leisure, not of harried labor. And his wide ranging interests and sympathies were never divorced from his sense of human responsibility. Nothing human was alien to him unless we reckon the sordid, the mean, the vulgar and the fanatical among the human. He could become angry but he never felt moral indignation. He could despise causes and even human beings but his contempt was never cut off from pity. He was a man of great warmth and tenderness but he was utterly unsentimental. He disliked words like duty and fatherland but he was singularly free from levity and he retained until his end a certain Bavarian sturdiness that had become transfigured into an unpretentious strength and greatness of soul. In his long and varied career he could not help hurting other human beings but there was no trace of cruelty in him. He had strong likes and dislikes but they bore no relation to self interest or vanity. He was sometimes unjust but he never was petty. In company he was altogether pleasant: neither heavy or moody nor frivolous or half absent. He was a man of rare intelligence but only a crude man could call him an intellectual. His speech was in perfect harmony with his being: direct, weighty, of a manly grace, and free from every kind of the spurious or affected. He did not derive pleasure from winning arguments. When I try to see vividly what distinguishes wisdom from cleverness, I think of Riezler. His political judgment was not misguided by passion or by system or by prejudice: in the few cases where I believed at the time that he was wrong, his judgment was vindicated by what happened or what transpired afterwards. All important points which were made after the Second World War on the basis of more or less secret information by Chester Wilmot, were made during that war on the basis of information accessible to everyone by Riezler.

Not having been as unpolitical in his youth as the young Thomas Mann, he was protected against ever becoming as simplistically political as the middle aged and old Thomas Mann. I encountered the young Riezler for the first time some weeks ago when I read his *Grundzuege der Weltpolitik in der Gegenwart* (Outlines of Contemporary World Politics) which he published under the pseudonym of J. J. Ruedorffer. For the proper understanding of the book one must bear in mind the fact that it was published shortly before the outbreak of the First World War by an influential official of imperial Germany. Riezler attempted to clarify the character which foreign politics had taken on during the long period of peace among the great European powers after 1871. He traced that character to the nature of foreign politics on the one hand, and the particular conditions of the period on the other. The most massive political fact was the conflict among nations: each nation concerned with self preservation and expansion, and driven by unlimited selfishness. But national conflict was not the fundamental conflict. Nationalism was challenged by cosmopolitanism. Both nationalist and cosmopolitan tendencies were growing in force, and so was their irreconcilable hostility. Riezler faced the question whether peace among nations or war among nations is according to nature. He saw this alternative: either the nation is the highest form of human association, with the consequence that there is "eternal, absolute enmity" among the nations, friendship among nations being enmity postponed or common enmity to other nations, or else humankind as a whole stands above the nations assigning them their role and place and legitimately limiting their aspirations. He decided without hesitation in favor of nationalism. The conflict of ideas, he argued, reflects the conflict of living forces; the question of the truth of an idea is therefore the question of its power. Now we only have to look around us in order to realize that the thoughts and sentiments of the nations are dominated by the national idea not by the cosmopolitan idea. And history teaches us that while nationalism and the nation state are of fairly recent origin, their earlier equivalents were always more powerful than cosmopolitanism. Riezler was not impressed by the cosmopolitan professions of faith of which there was no scarcity. He was certain that if these professions were put to the test, even the socialist workers would go with their countries. Nor was he impressed by the belief that if the nations only knew each other better by seeing more of each other, enmity among them would cease: increase of acquaintance does not necessarily improve feeling. But the power of nationalism, i.e., its power in the present and the past, was not the only reason why Riezler preferred it to its opposite. He thought that nationalism stands for something more noble than cosmopolitanism, i.e., than that cosmopolitanism which is politically relevant. The politically relevant cosmopolitanism was supported by the modern economic-technological-scientific development. But this development did not strengthen, it rather weakened, the human in man. It increased man's power but not his wisdom. One could see with special clarity in Germany that this development was accompanied by a decay of the spirit, of taste, of the mind. It compelled men to become ever more specialistic, and at the same time it tempted them with a sham universality by exciting all kinds of curiosities and stimulating all kinds of interests. It thus made ever more difficult concentration on the few things on which man's wholeness entirely depends. Riezler found the intellectual root of the politically relevant cosmopolitanism in what he called the modern ideal. He discerned in that ideal three elements. The first was the belief that human life as such, i.e., independently of the kind of life one leads, is an absolute good. The second, derivative from the first, was universal and unqualified compassion or humanitarianism. And the third was "materialism," i.e., an overriding concern with pleasure and unwillingness or inability to dedicate one's life to ideals. This analysis is not very much liked today but it is historically correct. To see how it leads on to the defense of nationalism, we shall express Riezler's thought as follows. The modern ideal does not leave room for reverence, the matrix of human nobility. Reverence is primarily, i.e., for most men at all times and for all men most of the time, reverence for one's heritage, for tradition. But traditions are essentially particularistic, and therefore akin to nationalism rather than to cosmopolitanism.

It would appear then that Riezler's decision in favor of nationalism rested entirely upon experience, on the experience of the power of nationalism in the present and in the past, and the experience of the low character of actual cosmopolitanism. One might say that that decision did not do justice to the possible future, the promise, the ideal of cosmopolitanism. This neglect of the future is the more remarkable since Riezler taught at the same time that the nation is never what it is actually but that it is always what it is, by virtue of its future. The difficulty is hardly overcome by what Riezler suggests regarding the essence of the nation. According to him, both the individual man and the nation are living beings, genuine wholes. But whereas the individual necessarily dies, there is no necessity for the death of nations; nations can live in the hope of eternal life, whereas the individuals cannot. Therefore the individual partakes of eternity only through his nation, and hence his nation is the only true way for him. Riezler quotes in this context the following words of a character in Dostoievski's *Possessed*: each nation has its own god and its own conception of good and evil; there is no God for all nations, and no universally valid conception of good and evil. I regard this as unsatisfactory—if for no other reason than that, as Riezler himself admitted, there may be an essential necessity for the death of nations as of beings which have come into being. It is worthy of note that Riezler did not attempt to establish the metaphysical dignity of the nation by having recourse to the connection between thought and language. There were probably two reasons for this. In the first place, he seems to have thought that language is not the matrix of the truth towards which thought is directed. And besides, he saw too clearly that there is no necessary connection between the community created by the unity of language and the political community, as is shown by the modern examples of Switzerland on the one hand and of the United States and Great Britain on the other. One may wonder whether there is another alternative to cosmopolitanism than the political philosophy of Plato and of Aristotle who taught that the natural political community is, not the nation, but the city; the nation would thus appear as a half-way house between the polis and the cosmopolis, and any attempt to bring out the truth underlying nationalism, but not adequately expressed by nationalism, would have to be guided by the insight embodied in the classical preference for the polis over against cosmopolis. However this may be, Riezler later on abandoned the nationalism of his youth, and he studied with ever increasing devotion the *Republic* of Plato.

While nationalism is as such theoretically unsatisfactory, it may still supply us with the best available framework for understanding the present political situation and for enlightening political action within a world that is dominated for all the foreseeable future by nationalism. Nationalism is certainly superior for these purposes, not only to the constructs of the legalists, but likewise to a certain sociology which is guided by the notions of "society" and "growth." For that sociology is apt to make us forget two things which the nationalist never forgets. Societies are still, and for the foreseeable future, national or imperial societies, closed off from other societies by unmistakable and formidable frontiers which have been established by wars rather than by other means; and if societies "grow" there is no guarantee whatsoever that they will not take away the light of the sun from others: he who preaches "growth" without thinking of the term of growth, of the peak beyond which there cannot be growth, preaches war.

Riezler too spoke of the nation as of a being that, as long as it is healthy, always desires to grow. But he was far from concealing the fact that growth is most visibly growth in size, expansion: as long as it is healthy, the nation has a tendency toward empire, toward world rule. Yet, he held, extensive growth leads to disastrous hollowness if it is not accompanied and prepared by growth in intensity, depth, inwardness and consciousness, or in "culture." He opposed therefore the nationalists proper, i.e., those who understood by growth nothing but expansion or who overestimated "the power of force" and underestimated the power of ideas. This was not the only point at which he left the way taken by the official Germany of that time. Nationalism, as he understood it, deprived the antagonism of monarchism and republicanism of its former importance, and therefore it made him indifferent to the German-Prussian monarchy. His nationalism was fundamentally republican and at least on the verge of becoming soberly democratic. The imperialism which he favored was a farsighted, enlightened, sober, patient imperialism, an imperialism fashioned on the British model. Looking in this spirit at the political scene, he reached the conclusion that the national interest of Germany, as well as the national interests of all the other great European powers, required for the foreseeable future the preservation of peace, and he tried to enlighten his fellow citizens and especially his superiors about the possibilities of avoiding that war which we now call the First World War. He paid special attention to the fact that there was still sufficient room for the parallel, not conflicting, expansion of the white race in Asia and Africa. He even visualized the possibility that the end of the period of parallel expansion might coincide with the emergence of a state of things in which war would have become altogether impracticable because all great powers would have to lose much more from war than they could possibly gain from it. He saw the greatest danger to peace not in the big armaments and in the system of alliances as such, for he thought that by making calculations of victory extremely difficult, they would incline calculating statesmen towards a policy of caution, but rather in the weakness of the governments of the countries in which there were strong nationalist movements, and in the replacement of "the system of slowly shifting alliances . . . by an inflexible system of two camps" (the Triple Alliance and the Entente). War could be avoided in the foreseeable future if the possibility of maneuver remained open, and that possibility could be kept open provided the national interest, and not prestige or demagoguery, determined the handling of foreign affairs. Riezler returned to these problems forty years later in his Walgreen Lectures, *Political Decisions in the Modern Mass Society of the Industrial Age.* In comparing the statements made in 1953 with those made in 1913, I am struck by the similarity of approach. I seem to observe a slight shift of emphasis: the experience of forty years seems to have given Riezler greater clarity about the source of the weakness of modern non-tyrannical governments *vis-à-vis* demagoguery.

Nationalism or imperialism, as Riezler defended it, reminds at more than one point of the political views of Max Weber. The fundamental difference between Riezler and Weber consists in

this: the Christian teaching regarding war and peace, more precisely, the Sermon on the Mount, created less of a problem for
Riezler than it did for Weber. Whether this difference is connected with the fact that Riezler came from a Catholic family
and Weber from a Protestant family, I am unable to say.

It is not possible to summarize Riezler's analysis of the world
political situation of 1913. But it ought to be said that that clear
and broad analysis is an excellent model from which students of
international relations could learn an important part of their craft.
If I had to compile a Reader in International Relations, I would
incorporate into it Riezler's analysis. It reminded me of Burke's
analysis of the European situation in 1791 in his *Thoughts on
French Affairs*.

The young Riezler was a nationalist politically. He was not a
nationalist *tout court*. He distinguished genuine cosmopolitanism
from spurious and superficial cosmopolitanism, and he discerned
the root of the former in the depth of the individual. The individual is part of his nation, but he is not merely part of his nation:
"he has his own task, his own goal, and his own value." The
nation is then not the only way to eternity. Only individuals, and
not nations, can engage in the quest for truth, and this quest unites
individuals belonging to different nations. The genius, while being
the son of a nation, belongs to mankind. To quote from an essay
which Riezler published thirty years later, "the voluntary and cheer-
ful outcast who refuses to conform but bears no grudge . . . is
the salt and pepper of any society, and its most important member,
though he does not regard himself as a member. He is the spur
of the horse that likes to fall asleep." But this genuine cosmopolitanism does not affect the fundamental relation among the nations.

Imperial Germany went down in defeat and collapsed. At that
time people began to talk of the decline of the West. During the
Weimar Republic Riezler published, as far as I know, only one
writing which could be called political, *Ueber Gebundenheit und
Freiheit des gegenwaertigen Zeitalters* (On Fatality and Freedom
in the Present Age, 1929). Its theme is the future of western man.
Despite the great differences of the prospect and of the subject
matter, the two political writings composed by Riezler in Germany
have something in common: in both cases Riezler opposes "the
prophets of gloom" and attempts to show that there is hope if sanity

prevails. In fact insanity prevailed again. Led politically by Hitler and intellectually by Heidegger, Germany entered the Third Reich. Riezler had to leave Germany. The Third Reich and its biggest achievement, the Second World War, confirmed the prophecy of the decline of Europe. During the Cold War which follows the Second World War, Riezler was compelled to write his third and last political work, his Walgreen Lectures. The message remained unaltered: there is hope for western man, the western world is not doomed, if sanity will reassert itself as it is still able to do. For there is a difference which is not negligible between stigmatizing the expression of sanity as "controversial" and completely suppressing it.

Political analyses were the foreground, the by no means negligible foreground, of Riezler's philosophical studies. His analysis of the world political situation in 1913 was based on the assumption that political life cannot be understood with the means of science, of natural science. He assumed a dualism of methods, of the methods of natural science and those of historical understanding. He traced the dualism of methods to what one may call a metaphysical dualism. He developed his philosophical premisses in *Die Erforderlichkeit des Unmoeglichen, Prolegomena zu einer Theorie der Politik* (On the Indispensable Character of the Impossible, Preface to a Theory of Politics) which he published at about the same time as the *Grundzuege*. Since that book was not accessible to me, I turn to his second philosophical book, *Gestalt und Gesetz, Entwurf einer Metaphysik der Freiheit* (Form and Law, Project of a Metaphysics of Freedom) published in 1924. That book is devoted to the problem posed by metaphysical dualism.

Gestalt und Gesetz is a document of the fermentation characteristic of German thought during the first decade after the First World War. There was a strong dissatisfaction with the established academic positions and a groping for a new way of thinking, i.e., a feeling that a return from those academic positions to the great epoch of German thought (the epoch from Kant to Hegel) would not suffice. There was awareness of the general direction in which, as was believed, one had to move but there was no clarity and certainty about the way. One would discern two disparate intellectual sources of the prevailing dissatisfaction and unrest: Kierkegaard and Nietzsche. There existed at the end of the First World War three significant academic positions, which I shall enumerate in the order of their emergence: the neo-Kantianism of the school of Marburg, Dilthey's philosophy of life, and phenomenology. It is somewhat surprising that while Riezler's aspirations had least in common with the tenets or tendencies of the school of Marburg, he was more impressed by it than by its rivals. From conversations with Riezler I gathered the following reason: the founder of the school of Marburg, Hermann Cohen, surpassed all other German professors of philosophy of the period between 1871 and 1925 by the fire and power of his soul. Passion and power of the originator of a doctrine do not establish the truth of a doctrine, but they were the indispensable conditions for Riezler's paying serious and sustained attention to a doctrine. As regards the transacademic forces which agitated the German mind, we note that Riezler was not touched at all by Kierkegaard, but was touched deeply by Nietzsche.

In the book under consideration, Riezler starts with accepting a fundamental dualism which he expresses to begin with as Law and Form, the inorganic and the living, nature and mind, necessity and freedom. He rejects the view that one of the two opposites can be reduced to, or deduced from, the other: mind cannot be understood as a product or effect of nature, nor can nature be understood as a derivative from mind. He likewise rejects the view that the fundamental dualism can be conceived as a mere dualism of points of view: the unity of man who partakes of both nature and its opposite, demands a single point of view from which he in his unity can be grasped. For fundamentally the same reason one cannot solve the difficulty by ascribing one of the two opposites to the phenomenal world and the other to the Thing-in-itself: both opposites belong to one and the same world. What is required is then not merely a theory of knowledge or even a critique of the human mind, but a metaphysics whose theme is the whole of the one world as of a world characterized by a fundamental dualism. But, Riezler adds, this metaphysics must be critical. Critical metaphysics, in contradistinction to the obsolete ontological metaphysics, is based on the Kantian insight that things *qua* things depend on human knowledge, are constituted by human knowledge, or, in other words, that the whole conceived of as a totality of things cannot exist. "The central question" of metaphysics is therefore "the question of the subject, the Ego, the soul, or the monad." Riezler does not speak here of reason or mind; he conceives of reason or mind as part of the subject or the soul. In other words, the spontaneity which is characteristic of the subject, is spontaneity not only of reason or understanding, as Kant had taught, but of the senses as well. This does not mean however that the subject is man. It is merely due to human pride that men regard man as superior in dignity to plants and to brutes. Nor is the subject God. However this may be, critical metaphysics, being essentially concerned with the subject or the soul, is "metaphysics of freedom."

If critical metaphysics is metaphysics of freedom, necessity must be understood as derivative from freedom: the dualism of freedom and necessity reveals itself as only provisional. Only in the peripheral perspective of man does a broader freedom appear as necessity. Necessity, fatality, determinacy is in truth nothing other than the mutual limitation of free, creative powers and the dependence of creative powers on their own creations. Similarly, other dualisms prove to be merely provisional. Thus one may receive the impression that Riezler simply suppresses the dualism from which he started.

No pair of opposites is stressed more strongly in *Gestalt und Gesetz* than that of Law and Form: the mathematical formula of the scientific law and its ancestor, the Platonic-Aristotelian idea or form, or rather general rules and the concrete gestalt. And yet this dualism too proves to be provisional. This does not mean that the extensive discussion which Riezler devotes to it is superfluous. The opposition of Law and Form, the movement from Law to Form, is indispensable if the true character of reality is to be understood. Thinking in terms of Law is inevitable for man but it is the obstacle *par excellence* to the understanding of reality. Yet one must also beware of the equally faulty opposite extreme which is that of conceiving of reality as a blind, creative will that lacks direction, meaning or a goal. The mean between those faulty extremes, Law and Will, is Form. It is only by the analysis of Form that Riezler discovers the pair of fundamental opposites and therewith, not indeed their reconciliation, but their essential inseparability. Form is generated by a process which has no other meaning than to generate forms, ever higher forms. This process does not precede form: the forming is always itself formed. Form is what it is by its own formative action. Every form, everything that is, points beyond itself, tends beyond itself. It is less than it ought to be. Reality is in between Is and Ought. The fundamental and eternal antinomy of the Is and the Ought constitutes reality. The world is eternal disharmony, striving, longing, endeavour, *eros,* and therefore eternal life. It strives for the infinite, permanent and perfect and achieves only the finite, transitory and imperfect. It is eternally imperfect: everything good is only by virtue of some evil; love is inseparable from hatred, joy from pain; every achievement is bought at the price of some failure; every coming into being is a perishing. There is no possibility of redemption by human or divine means: not even Heaven itself can be redeemed. But precisely for this reason, the world is eternally alive. In theological language, God is not, He is eternally becoming. Reality thus understood must consist of infinitely many forms, formative forms, subjects, or mortal monads, each of them qualitatively different from all others or unique. These monads are not isolated from each other. Each monad is, as it were, within others and by virtue of its unique striving in conflict with the others: reality is the eternal conflict of infinitely many monads. There is no harmony among them since there does not exist the one uncreated central monad. Every monad is the center, and therefore every monad is peripheral. Every monad longs for the impossible center; this longing is life. Every monad has its own perspective: reality is something different for every monad. Reality is an infinite process which gives rise to, or rather consists of, an infinite number of processes, i.e., of formation of forms, and which reveals itself only in infinitely many incompatible perspectives. In this infinity, everything is means and everything is end: reality is not a hierarchic order.

But does this "eternal relativity" not destroy the unity of the world? Does it not lead to the consequence that nothing is true and everything is permitted? Riezler denies this. There remains something firm and stable, there remains a unity, but this one and unchangeable cannot be found in any "absolute suchness" or in any form, to say nothing of number or law. The unity of the world is the unity of fate, i.e., of the fate of each of its parts: birth and death, striving and failure, and so on. In moving from neo-Kantianism to his critical metaphysics, from Law to Form and to the ground of Form, Riezler moved from the unity of method to the unity of fate.

From all that has been said, it follows that critical metaphysics is distinguished from the ontological metaphysics of the past, not only by its theme, but by its mode as well. It is not theoretical. It does not imply that one leaves the world of change for the permanent or eternal. Philosophy as critical metaphysics is aware of the limitation of philosophy. There is a disproportion between the breadth of the task of philosophy (to grasp the whole, the whole process) and the narrowness of its means (concepts). Philosophy needs concepts and must break through its concepts. The task of philosophy is unfinishable. The fate of philosophy is tragic—as tragic as the fate of every other manifestation of life. Thus while philosophy is unable to grasp the whole by its concepts, it copies or represents the whole by its fate: for the whole is that unity which is the fate of every part of the whole. The eternal antinomy at the bottom of everything cannot be looked at in detachment; it discloses its meaning only if it is experienced, i.e., if it is experienced in the anguish of the radically isolated individual, and if that experience culminates in an ultimate "And in spite of it"; philosophy means honorably to come to grief, obstinately to refuse the delusion of redemption, to say yes to, or to love, this world as the only world. In this way and only in this way does it appear that not everything is permitted.

The phenomena which led Riezler from Law to Form were the living beings and the works of art. But those phenomena are not sufficient to support his speculations about the ground of reality. In these speculations he was guided by what he regarded as the phenomenon of History: History as the creation of ever new forms, of ever higher forms. His metaphysics is an attempt to understand nature after the analogy of History. Accordingly he asserts that time, and not space, belongs to the core of reality, nay, is the core of reality: "time is the longing of the deity for itself."

It is only with a certain difficulty that I recognize in *Gestalt und Gesetz* the Riezler I knew. The differences between *Gestalt und Gesetz* and his later books may be traced to a single cause: his later thought was shaped by both the influence of Heidegger and the reaction to him. Not indeed Riezler's deepest tendency, but the way in which he expressed it or did not express it, was decisively affected by Heidegger.

It would be an understatement to say that Heidegger was the greatest contemporary power which Riezler ever encountered.

One has to go back to Hegel until one finds another professor of philosophy who affected in a comparable manner the thought of Germany, nay, of Europe. But Hegel had some contemporaries whose power equalled his or at any rate whom one could compare to him without being manifestly foolish. Heidegger surpasses all his contemporaries by far. This could be seen long before he became known to the general public. As soon as he appeared on the scene, he stood in its center and he began to dominate it. His domination grew almost continuously in extent and in intensity. He gave adequate expression to the prevailing unrest and dissatisfaction because he had clarity and certainty, if not about the whole way, at least about the first and decisive steps. The fermentation or the tempest gradually ceased. Eventually a state has been reached which the outsider is inclined to describe as paralysis of the critical faculties; philosophizing seems to have been transformed into listening with reverence to the incipient *mythoi* of Heidegger:

> Tum, pietate gravem ac meritis si forte virum quem
> Conspexere, silent arrectisque auribus adstant.

Riezler delivered his speech on *Gebundenheit und Freiheit des gegenwaertigen Zeitalters* in Davos before the same audience which immediately before had listened to a debate between Heidegger and Cassirer. Riezler took the side of Heidegger without any hesitation. There was no alternative. Mere sensitivity to greatness would have dictated Riezler's choice. Cassirer represented the established academic position. He was a distinguished professor of philosophy but he was no philosopher. He was erudite but he had no passion. He was a clear writer but his clarity and placidity were not equalled by his sensitivity to the problems. Having been a disciple of Hermann Cohen he had transformed Cohen's philosophic system, the very center of which was ethics, into a philosophy of symbolic forms in which ethics had silently disappeared. Heidegger on the other hand explicitly denies the possibility of ethics because he feels that there is a revolting disproportion between the idea of ethics and those phenomena which ethics pretended to articulate.

In *Gestalt und Gesetz*, we recall, Riezler had found the unity of the world, not in any "suchness" which as such would be accessible to a detached view, but in the fate of each of its parts, which fate was said to disclose itself only by being experienced in the anguish of the radically isolated individual; the parts of the whole were conceived of as mortal monads. One could say that Riezler had identified "the substance" with the fate, the specific finiteness, of the mortal monad. He thus was not unprepared for Heidegger's thesis according to which "the substance" is *Existenz*. Yet Riezler's mortal monad was not man in particular but any living being, i.e., any being, though man and man alone had supplied him with the clue to the other beings: he had attempted to understand the whole after the likeness of man or of History. What he learned from Heidegger was in the first place that such an attempt presupposes the clarification of what man is. But, as Riezler had stressed, the question of the What or of suchness does not go to the root; the fundamental question must concern the fate of man, or, as Heidegger said, his *esse*, his *Existenz*. Heidegger's analysis of *Existenz* is meant to be the fundamental ontology, i.e., "the first philosophy," for philosophy is nothing other than ontology. Riezler learned from Heidegger above all that philosophy is ontology. In *Gestalt und Gesetz* he had suggested that everything comes into being and perishes, or that nothing "is," but also that only coming into being and perishing "is." He thus had touched upon the ontological problem but at the same time he had rejected ontology as obsolete. In his later writings however he identifies philosophy with ontology. One can express Heidegger's notion of ontology most simply by using Platonic expressions in an un-Platonic sense. Ontology is concerned, not with beings, but with that which we mean whenever we say of anything that it "is," or with that by virtue of which beings are, or with that through partaking of which beings are and are said to be; this—*esse* as distinguished from *entia*—as the ground of all beings is not a being but beyond being and beingness. The distinction between *esse* and *entia* enabled Riezler to articulate what in fact had been the most fundamental distinction used in *Gestalt und Gesetz*: the distinction between fate which can never be a thing or an object and everything else which is or can become a thing or an object.

The first book which Riezler composed on this basis is his *Parmenides* (1934), the only book of his which is devoted to a subject belonging to the history of philosophy. The historical problem, the problem of the meaning of Parmenides' poem, was for

Riezler at one with the most important "systematic" problem. The ontological problem is to begin with not intelligible to us because we are the heirs to a tradition of many centuries which mistook the ontological problem (the problem of *esse*) for the cosmological problem (the problem of the totality of *entia*) or the theological problem (the problem of the highest *ens*) and which in its modern part had gradually lost the last vestige of memory of the ontological problem. All our habits of thinking, all the concepts that are at our disposal stem in the best case from the time in which the ontological problem had begun to be overlaid or to be superseded by the cosmological or the theological problem. The ontological problem appears clearly and purely only in the beginning of western thought, and in particular in Parmenides. To understand the ontological problem means then to liberate oneself from the shackles of a tradition which conceals the problem or to recover the origin of our tradition: the "systematic" problem is inseparable from the historical problem. In this Riezler follows Heidegger for whom the elaboration of the ontological problem is inseparable from the "Destruktion" of the philosophic tradition. Riezler deviates from Heidegger in a decisive point. Heidegger's return to the origin of western thought serves the purpose of overcoming the limitations of western thought and in particular of Greek thought. But Riezler held that early Greek ontology is the true and final foundation of ontology. According to Heidegger the essential limitation of Greek ontology shows itself in the fact that the Greeks understood by "to be" "to be present or near." Riezler however accepts the Greek view according to which only "to be present" is "to be truly." In his copy of the first edition of Diels's *Vorsokratiker*, he wrote the following words on the margin of the beginning of Parmenides' fragments: "Gegen dieses verstaubte Gold der Philosophie ist alles seit hunderten von Jahren nur vergoldeter Staub." ("Compared with this gold of philosophy which is covered by dust, everything else for centuries has been only dust covered by gold.") And at the end of his *Parmenides* he indicates his belief that among all post-Greek thinkers only Nietzsche would have been favored by Parmenides with an intimation of the right way: the same does not have to return eternally, for it is always wholly present.

It is necessary to explain briefly what Riezler understood by ontology. The most fundamental presupposition of all thought is what one may call the decision as to what it means "to be." For instance, modern science may be said to identify "to be" with "to be observable by everyone" or "to be a possible object" or "to belong to the spatial-temporal order." "To be" thus understood is relative to the observer, to any observer, to the anonymous observer. But we divine somehow that "to be" means above all "to be in itself" and not merely "to be relative . . .": "to be" means, above all and primarily, to be a subject and not an object. The anonymous observer would then "be" in a more fundamental sense than any or all of his objects. Furthermore, the anonymous observer "is" not according to that meaning of "to be" which is authoritative for him: we can observe only this or that observer who is always much more than the anonymous observer. The anonymous observer and everything that "is" only relative to him is an abstraction, and we divine somehow that "to be" means primarily "to be concrete." "To be concrete" means not merely to be a particular being but likewise to belong to a particular whole, to a particular dynamic context: a particular being divorced from its particular dynamic context is an abstraction. Every real observer belongs to such a dynamic context. In proportion as he leaves that context, as he looks at it from without, he misses the concrete: true reality is "reality seen from the inside." This implies that in order to be truly real, reality must be "seen": if there are no human beings there cannot be concreteness. However this may be, if "to be" means "to be concrete," the fundamental question cannot concern this or that concrete someone or something, nor the totality of concrete someones and somethings in their concrete contexts, but concreteness as such. More generally and more cautiously, the fundamental question concerns not this or that being, nor the totality of beings, but beingness. Beingness is distinguished from the beings as the One from the Many. This does not mean that beingness is the transcendent God whereas the beings are His creatures in this world: beingness is nothing but the ground of the this-worldliness of everything in this world; the One is only in the Many; beingness is not without beings and *vice versa*. Nor is beingness related to the beings as the whole to the parts. Beingness is the one fate, the one order, the one law of all beings, although we have access to beingness only in the case of man. The unity of beingness does not mean simplicity, but unity of the different: beingness has a complex articulation; it is a whole consisting of a variety of elements or "powers," each of which demands the others and is co-present in them; it is a texture in which each thread entails all others or in which the whole inheres in each thread. It is this whole texture by virtue of which any being "is." Whereas all beings come into being and perish, beingness is unchangeable, eternal, timeless. At the same time however beingness is said to be "occurrence": it is for this reason that Riezler prefers to use the verb *esse* rather than the noun "beingness."

In the light of ontology thus understood Riezler approaches the fragments of Parmenides' poem. It would be more accurate to say that having become aware of the ontological problem Riezler turned to Parmenides and that his ontology was partly shaped by what he learned from Parmenides. Parmenides' poem consists of two parts, the first devoted to the truth, the second to opinion. According to the traditional or vulgar interpretation, Parmenides taught in the first part that being is one and therefore that manyness and change do not exist or are mere appearance or opinion; even knowledge and being must be identical; in the second part he presents the general opinion of mankind, according to which manyness and change exist, by deducing that opinion from its false principle; that false principle is that being is not one but two (say, light and darkness); the world of appearance can be understood as a mixture of light and darkness, as Parmenides shows by presenting the genesis of the many and changing things out of that mixture. Riezler, who continues the way of interpretation that was opened by Karl Reinhardt, contends that Parmenides denies manyness and change not to the beings but to beingness; opinion consists, not in admitting manyness and change, but in being blind to the unchangeable unity which underlies and makes possible manyness and change; the unity of beingness is a unity of opposites; opinion consists in divorcing the opposites completely from each other or in being blind to the co-presence of one of the opposites in the other; opinion is aware only of that quality which is sensually perceived at a given moment—it is unaware of the opposite quality which is co-present but not sensually perceived at that moment: opinion identifies the truth with what is sensually perceived; opinion is surrender to sense perception. Hence, the fundamental error of opinion does not consist in assuming the two principles, Light and Darkness: both these principles and everything which flows from them belong to truth, and not to opinion. Accordingly, the second part of Parmenides' poem does not so much "systematize" opinion as supply the true explanation of opinion. In particular, one fragment of the second part (Fr. 16), rightly understood, gives us the decisive information, supplied nowhere in the first part, about the true relation of truth and opinion.

Riezler's interpretation is a high point in the modern study of Parmenides. One can hardly go further in the direction which he has followed, as long as one remains concerned with what Parmenides himself taught, as distinguished from what his poem may convey without his necessarily being aware of it. And Riezler has disposed of the vulgar interpretation more completely than others have done. The question that remains is whether the vulgar interpretation, which saw only the gulf separating the two parts of the poem, did not see therewith something which is now in danger of being overlooked. Riezler himself speaks of the "imagery" of the second part. The second part does not convey then the pure truth. But the same would apply to the first part, if, as Riezler contends, the first part does not contain the full truth: the first part is, to say the least, not very explicit about the unity of opposites in being or in beingness. The relation of the two parts would then not be identical with that of truth and opinion, but their relation would only reflect the relation of truth and opinion. Neither pure truth nor pure opinion would come to full view in the poem; and yet Parmenides makes us expect that they do come into full view in his poem. Perhaps Parmenides did not desire that the expectation should be fulfilled in an obvious manner. Were this suspicion proved correct, the vulgar and traditional interpretation according to which the first part sets forth the full truth and the second part mere opinion, might adequately render what one may call the immediately and universally visible meaning of the poem, and Riezler's interpretation would transcend that meaning in the direction of the hidden and serious meaning without however arriving at it. Here as elsewhere an intransigent return to the surface might be the indispensable condition for progress towards the center.

Riezler's critical metaphysics had claimed to be supported by the phenomenon of History and to articulate that phenomenon in a fundamentally adequate manner. When he turned from critical metaphysics to ontology, he ascribed to ontology the same support

and the same function as he had originally ascribed to critical metaphysics. Hence he was confronted by these two difficulties. 1)
There is a tension between the understanding of beingness as timeless law and order and the understanding of beingness as occurrence, between the understanding of beingness as trans-historical
and the understanding of beingness as historical. 2) All understanding of beings or the concrete was said to belong to a particular
dynamic context or to be itself concrete. Must the same not be
true also of the understanding of beingness or concreteness as such?
Or can the ontologist be an anonymous observer? If this is impossible, will ontology itself not become involved in the process and
therewith become relativized?

Riezler took these questions up in his *Traktat von Schoenen. Zur
Ontologie der Kunst* (Treatise of the Beautiful. Towards an ontology of art, 1935). The treatise was meant to prepare a fully
developed ontology, but only to prepare it: not the phenomenon of
art but the phenomenon of History would have to be the starting
point for a comprehensive ontology. The analysis of art is however
the most appropriate "prolegomenon to a doctrine of History"
because it brings the analyst into the proper mood for his larger
task. Art, and not thought or concept, is akin to beingness. Art, and
not nature, is the domain of the beautiful. Art, and not religion,
expresses man's self affirmation: art is religiousness without gods;
it does not need religion whereas religion needs art in order to be
truly religion. Last but not least, art is the supreme remedy for the
Christianity without God which, as Riezler suspected, limits Heidegger's perspective.

What then is, according to Riezler, the essence of art? Art is
expression but in such a way that the expression is somehow the
expressed. What is capable of being expressed, is never a thing;
things can only be described or denoted; only states of the soul,
only what we ourselves are or can be, can be expressed. For instance, the good painting of a stone, as distinguished from a mere
copy, brings out those qualities which are possible states of ourselves or possible manners of our being: the bright or the dark, the
rugged or the smooth, loneliness or togetherness, and so on; the
good painting of a stone brings out the stony which is, though in
different ways, both in the stone and in ourselves. More precisely,
it expresses, say, loneliness in such a way that togetherness is co-

present with it while on the surface being simply absent. The good
work of art lets us see togetherness within loneliness, or hauntedness
within serenity, i.e., serenity as a state of a being which can be
haunted. Trash or poor art is distinguished from high art by the fact
that it does not bring out the co-present opposite of the sweet, the
gruesome and so on. When we say of a work of art that it is
"alive" we mean precisely that it brings out possible states of the
soul as co-present with their absent opposites. Art expresses an in-
between of opposites. But it always expresses more than one in-
between: it expresses the in-between of many in-betweens. By this
very fact it expresses the soul, the texture of the soul, the beingness
of the soul, beingness as such. In the work of art beingness itself, the
mystery of life, comes to sight or into appearance. This is the reason
why the work of art is mysterious, inexhaustible and resplendent. If
the work of art makes visible beingness, beingness is as such visible
or concealed, and therefore also more or less visible or concealed.
Beingness is not indifferent to being visible or concealed; it has a
directedness towards coming to sight. A being is, or partakes of
beingness, more or less, according to the degree to which beingness
is visible in it. The stone as we see it ordinarily, does not reveal
beingness—it is just a stone. In the good painting the stone is no
longer a stone, i.e., something which we could not possibly be: in
the good painting the stone has become visible in its beingness; only
in the work of art is the stone truly. A soul is to a higher or to a
lower degree, the more or less it is aware of its beingness and therewith of beingness as such; only by being aware of beingness are we
truly. Beingness is only if it appears. But beingness appears only in
the work of art. Only in the work of art is beingness: only in the
expression is the expressed. The unchangeable texture is only as
occurrence. Reality is only if it is "seen." Or, as Riezler interpreted
the verse of Parmenides: beingness and awareness of beingness
belong inseparably together. But since beingness is occurrence,
there is no necessity why it should be actually seen, and if it comes
to sight, it appears in every case in a different manner, i.e., it *is*
in every case in a different manner.

These suggestions, of which I could barely give the roughest out-
lines, indicate the direction in which Riezler sought the ground of
History: the ground of History is beingness as occurrence. As far as
I know, he did not attempt to understand from this point of view the

history or the fate of ontology as he saw it—the appearance of the ontological problem in the beginnings of philosophy, the concealment of the ontological problem by the cosmological problem in the thought of Aristotle, the oblivion of the ontological problem in modern times, and its reappearance in the thought of Heidegger. In regard to the problem of art or of the beautiful Riezler says that the problem is an eternal problem but that it depends upon History whether it is raised and whether it can be raised. Each epoch which is sure of itself, has a specific understanding of what constitutes beauty or artistic excellence; each healthy epoch has a specific style which it regards as the only good style. Only epochs of decay can be fully open to the artistic excellence of all other times and spaces; in such epochs no style can claim any more absolute superiority. Only in an epoch of this kind can the question of what constitutes artistic excellence as such be raised adequately. It is then, as Riezler put it, a present need or predicament which imposes on him the raising of the problem of art. The present need in question is apparently a need which was never felt before: the eternal problem of art has become susceptible of being raised adequately for the first time now, in response to the present predicament. One is therefore compelled to wonder as to whether the relation between the present and unique need and the eternal problem is not a part of the eternal problem itself or in other words whether one can legitimately or strictly speak of an eternal problem. It certainly becomes necessary to reflect on the present need in its unique character. We find such a reflection in Riezler's speech on *Gebundenheit und Freiheit des gegenwaertigen Zeitalters.* There he referred to the relativism or nihilism which were the immediate consequence of the historical consciousness. Opposing this immediate consequence, he inferred from the relativization by the historical consciousness of every known Yes and No the demand for a new Yes and No. Since this demand arose out of the historical consciousness and was informed by the historical consciousness, one is led to expect that the historical consciousness, having reached full self consciousness, will point to a new Yes and No, prepare a new Yes and No, and perhaps even identify it. More precisely, since the historical consciousness is the insight into the root of all Yes's and No's, of all norms or ought's, it is the absolute insight; therefore it would seem that the historical consciousness cannot rest satisfied merely with a new Yes and No but must point to the absolute Yes and No, the final Yes and No. This would seem to be necessary also for the reason that, as one might think, only the absolute, and not the provisional can bind the conscience. In other words, the historical consciousness if it understands itself would seem to belong to the absolute moment in history and therewith to be beyond the relativity of history. Riezler rejects this line of thought altogether: History is an unfinishable process and therefore it does not allow of an absolute moment, an absolute Yes and No, but only of a new Yes and No. The new Yes and No cannot be found by philosophy but only by an act of History, of life itself. If I understand Riezler's thought correctly, he meant that philosophy cannot do more than to understand human life as historical, as dynamic context, as moving in a space which itself is moving, and therewith to understand the formal character of all possible Yes's and No's, without being able to deduce from this understanding any substantive Yes and No. Philosophy is limited to the task of bringing to light the eternal structure of life or History, "the eternal *humanum*," the immutable form of man's mutability. This is the eternal problem to which philosophy seeks the solution—a solution which, if it is to be adequate, cannot but be an eternal, an eternally valid solution. The eternity of the problem and of the solution does not depend on whether they are eternally accessible or not. Following this line of thought, Riezler was eventually driven to abandon the quest for a new Yes and No in favor of the quest for the immutable or eternal " 'good itself' which is the measure of all measures." In his *Physics and Reality*, in which he speaks through the mouth of Aristotle, he says: "knowledge of being itself . . . is in itself the end. Its perfection is Being's pure activity, the ultimate Whither through which all ends are ends."

If we are permitted to say that historicism is the view according to which at least all concrete or profound thought essentially belongs to a concrete dynamic context, and that Platonism is the view according to which pure thought, being "anonymous," transcends every dynamic context, we must go on to say that Riezler felt too strongly the difficulties of historicism not to be attracted by Platonism, but that he was too deeply impressed by both art and historical change resolutely to follow Plato. From the point of view of Platonism there can be only one type of classic art. Riezler how-

ever held the view which is much more plausible today that there
is classicity not only in Greek art but in Chinese art, medieval art,
impressionism, and so on as well. By conceiving of the classic as
the artistically excellent, he avoided the childish absurdities of
vulgar relativism or historicism. Riezler was far too intelligent and
too experienced in things beautiful to believe for a moment that the
application of the distinctions between art and trash, between
works of higher quality and works of lower quality is "merely subjective," or that the appreciation of artistic quality depends in any
significant way on historical or extraneous knowledge. The grasp of
"the eternal *humanum*" may not be sufficient for legitimatizing
one's preferring one Yes to another Yes or one's preferring, say,
classic Greek art to classic medieval art; it may not lead us therefore beyond what one may call a qualified relativism; but it is amply
sufficient for revealing fully the unspeakable absurdity of unqualified or vulgar relativism.

The impression of Riezler's thought which we received from
his German books is confirmed by his English books, *Physics and
Reality* (1940), and *Man: Mutable and Immutable* (1950). There
is a very close and very obvious connection between these two
books: *Man* begins where *Physics and Reality* ends. The character
of *Physics and Reality* is sufficiently indicated by its subtitle: "Lectures of Aristotle on Modern Physics at an International Congress
of Scientists, Cambridge, 1940." Riezler makes Aristotle subject
the physics of the modern centuries to a radical criticism. Modern
physics is in our time manifestly confronted with radical difficulties
which one cannot overcome by ascribing to the propositions of
physics a merely operational meaning, i.e., by abandoning the
original claim of physics that it reveals nature as it is in itself. There
is only one way out of the impasse, the way shown by Aristotle.
The primary theme of physics is beings in so far as they move or
change in time. Such beings are accessible not to modern physics
but to the modern physicists as well as to any other human beings:
"The nature you talk about as scientists is not the nature you mean
when you say 'I am.'" Aristotle approaches the phenomenon of
motion or change by never losing sight of, or even by starting
from, man's experience and understanding of himself as a being
that moves or changes in time. The more precise articulation of
this experience and understanding is the function of Riezler's *Man*:

Mutable and Immutable. The Fundamental Structure of Social Life.

As is indicated by the full title, the work is devoted to the analysis of man, of human life as radically social, or to the analysis of society or social life as radically human: the core of society is not institutions, interests, or even ideas, but passions and the striving for happiness, *la condition humaine* as occurrence, the heart and its logic, the life of the soul. In the language of the schools one would have to say that Riezler's doctrine of man and of things human is social philosophy as distinguished from political philosophy. His theme is "Society" as "the universe of response, the spontaneous culture" as distinguished from the State which is brought into being by Society for the service of Society. Nor is Society identical with the Nation although Riezler still contends that the complete or comprehensive society is the nation rather than "the doubtful unity of a 'civilization' comprising more than one nation." The Society which supplies the framework for Riezler's analysis of the passions is "the 'idea' of society" or what "any specific group can be" or "the scheme of a relational structure" which articulates "the human elements that in their mutual relationships constitute society as society." "As a scheme it is an abstraction." It abstracts especially from the purposes of society. Riezler opposes in this context the thinking in terms of means and ends and especially the notion that there can be a "single purpose to which everything else is . . . merely a means." From here we can understand why Riezler's social philosophy, as distinguished from the political philosophy of the past, does not contain an ethics proper: his central subject is not virtue and justice, but the passions (or the attitudes or the moods). In accordance with this, he discusses the relation of the I, the Self which can never become an object, with the Me, i.e., the I as object without even alluding to the conscience. Riezler is aware of the fact that one must not look at social phenomena in the light of questions or doctrines to which "no society pays any attention." But he does not draw from this the conclusion that social phenomena must be understood primarily in the way in which they come to sight in the perspective of the citizen or statesman. He does not begin at the true beginning of analysis, with the surface. The perspective of Riezler the analyst differs from the outset from the perspective of the citizen or statesman. Opposing "the man-environment scheme" which is the framework accepted by present day social science, he develops a much more solid and much more fertile scheme: not man confronting his environment of which other human beings as his objects are a part, but a We which constitutes itself by an I and a Thou mutually responding to each other and by distinguishing itself from a They, living "in" its world. Now while "we in our world" is more concrete than the Cartesian Ego which is shut up within "the box of its consciousness," it is nevertheless not more than a correction of the Cartesian starting point: the new starting point is as much a construction as the Cartesian one. The unnatural nouns, "the I," "the Me," "the Thou," "the We," reveal clearly this state of things. Riezler tries to proceed towards the concrete by starting from an abstraction. He thus does not arrive at the concrete. He does not ascend from the phenomena as primarily given to their principles.

The hidden and modified Cartesianism which is underlying the framework employed in *Man* is linked with the fundamental premise of Riezler's thought. That Cartesianism showed itself at the beginning in the monadological conception that was developed in *Gestalt und Gesetz;* for the monad is a transformation of the Cartesian Ego; it is distinguished from the Cartesian Ego especially by its spontaneity. In *Man,* the monad is in its turn transformed into "We in our world." The question guiding Riezler's monadology concerned the essential character of the monad or the essential structure of the life of the monad; it was not the question of what unites the infinitely many monads so that they form the world; this latter question, the question of the *kosmos* was regarded as unanswerable; the *kosmos* remained an x. Riezler's monadology (as distinguished from Leibniz's monadology) takes the place of cosmology, of speculative metaphysics because speculative metaphysics appeared to be impossible. When Riezler replaced monadology by ontology, his fundamental premise remained the same. Riezler stresses the fact that beyond any "world" which as such is the world of a "We," including both the "world" of a possible world society and the "world" of the anonymous observer, there is *the* world, but *the* world remains eternally an x. *The* world is then not the visible whole limited by the visible "starred heaven above me" and the visible firm earth. Heaven and earth and what is between them have lost their contours visible to the eyes of the body or the eyes of the mind, for those contours have been dissolved by the acid of modern natural science; and they can acquire visible contours, or "natures," again only by entering, as it were, into any of the many historical worlds: not those visible contours but only the fabric of beingness, and this means primarily the fabric of man's beingness has the dignity of the immutable. In spite of Riezler's appeal from modern physics to Aristotelian physics and from the historicist immersion in mutable man to the immutable in man, modern physics and its twin sister, "the historical consciousness," are the fundamental presuppositions of his ontology.

Yet however doubtful one may be as regards the fundamental premise of Riezler and the framework which he uses for his analyses of the passions and of misery and happiness, this doubt becomes almost irrelevant as soon as one is confronted by these analyses themselves and by the breadth, the earnestness and the delicacy which inform them. These analyses surpass by far everything which is at present attempted within psychology or any other discipline. With a view to the present state of the social sciences, one point needs to be mentioned with emphasis. Just as in earlier thought knowledge of the nature of the soul was seen to lead to knowledge of the right or good activity of the soul, i.e., of the good life, Riezler's understanding of the essential structure of human life leads him in a perfectly legitimate manner to non-arbitrary assertions about what constitutes the good life, about "the order of nature" as distinguished from convention. His analysis of the fundamental structure of society is only "apparently pre-moral." He thus shows that the common belief according to which there is no legitimate way leading from "facts" to "values" has no other basis than a shockingly narrow understanding of "facts." To understand the "fact" of language means to understand the unchangeable principles underlying the distinction between "perfect speech" and speech which is more or less imperfect. To understand the "fact" of laughter means to realize the variety of levels of laughter with the silly laughter of silly people about things which are not ridiculous at the bottom and divine laughter at the top. To understand the "fact" of friendship—a "fact" which is perhaps never fully a "fact"—means to realize the low or degrading character of loveless sex and the narrowness of hate as a passion which "knows no sky." By speaking humanly about the human passions, Riezler lets us see incidentally the powerful reasons why he could not have been mistaken or misled about the meaning of 1933. His analyses of the passions are also meant as a critique of the "narrow humanity" that informs Heidegger's analysis of *Existenz;* they point to the riddle posed by Heidegger's obstinate silence about love or charity on the one hand, and about laughter and the things which deserved to be laughed at on the other.

Riezler's analysis of the passions culminates in his analysis of shame and awe as respect for the vulnerable and the secret. Human dignity, Riezler suggests among other things, stands and falls by shame and awe because man's greatness is co-present in his littleness and his littleness is co-present in his greatness. It was ultimately because he grasped the meaning of shame and awe that Riezler was a liberal, a lover of privacy. By invading men's privacy one does not come to know them better—one merely ceases to see them. For man's being is revealed by the broad character of his life, his deeds, his works, by what he esteems and reveres not in word but in deed —by the stars for which his soul longs if it longs for any stars. Not anguish but awe is "the fundamental mood" which discloses being as being. Because he was animated by this spirit, he felt more at home in the thought of ancient Greece than in the thought of his time.

In pondering over Riezler's highest aspiration, I had to think more than once of Thucydides—of Thucydides' quiet and manly gentleness which seeks no solace and which looks in freedom, but not in indifference, at the opposites whose unity is hidden; which does not attempt to reduce one opposite to the other; and which regards the higher of the opposites not, as Socrates did, as stronger but as more vulnerable, more delicate than the lower. This is the treasure which Riezler divined, for which he longed and which he tried to bring to light again. We shall honor his memory best if we follow the light which he followed and to which he never ceased pointing.

Criticism:
Sixteen Appraisals

CROSSMAN, R. H. S. *Plato Today*. New York: Oxford University Press. 1939.

The intention of this book is described by the author in the following terms: "I am a democrat and a Socialist who sees Fascism rejected and democracy defended on quite inadequate grounds; and it is because I realize that our greatest danger today is not the easy acceptance but the easy rejection of Totalitarian philosophy, that I have tried to restate the *Republic* in modern terms" (p. 296). By making use of the teaching of the *Republic* the author is enabled to grasp with a clarity that is unusual in his camp the shortcomings of present-day democracies as well as of the political creeds and institutions of the Right and the Left. Yet he vigorously denies that Plato's work can supply us with an acceptable alternative to the solutions suggested by present-day movements: "The more I read it [the *Republic*], the more I hate it" (p. 292). The perfect government in the Platonic sense, the "dictatorship of the virtuous Right," is of necessity "transformed into a polite form of Fascism" (p. 285), and Plato himself was "a reactionary resolutely opposed to every principle of the Liberal creed" (p. 130). Accordingly, the last word of the author is: "It is Socrates, not Plato, whom we need" (p. 308).

Plato Today stands or falls with Crossman's distinction between a Socrates "who knew that he knew nothing" and a Plato who was "the systematic expounder of an authoritarian creed" (p. 90). But this distinction, as expounded by the author, coincides more or less with his distinction between two groups of Platonic writings: the *Apology of Socrates* and the *Phaedo* on the one hand, and the *Republic* and the *Seventh Letter* on the other. And he fails to inform his readers why he is so certain that the political teaching of the

Republic is Platonic and not Socratic, and that the "Orphic religious faith" expounded in the *Phaedo* is genuinely Socratic.

It would be most unfair to Crossman, however, to create the impression that his main concern was to write a detached or reasonably satisfactory interpretation of the Socratic or Platonic teaching. The valuable part of his book is the five chapters in which he shows how Plato would have judged, or might have judged, of the most important political facts of our time. He must be praised for the use which he makes of the device of reviving a dead hero and making him talk (or write). Plato's Socrates was unable to do full justice to Protagoras before he had resuscitated him. In a similar way Crossman, in the five chapters devoted to the resuscitated Plato, often makes visible the common sense and moderation of Plato which he implicitly denied him in the other chapters of the book by taking the *Republic* of the dead Plato quite literally. To mention only one example, Crossman's Plato says to a Member of Parliament: "I should assume in talking to you that your ideals are sound. Of course they are not, but they are less vicious than those of most other nations which I have visited" (p. 144). Statements of this kind come nearer to the intention of the *Republic* than anything Crossman says in his explicit account of that dialogue.

VAUGHAN, C. E. *Studies in the History of Political Philosophy Before and After Rousseau,* ed. by A.G. Little. Manchester: The University Press. 1939.

This is a new and cheaper edition of a work which was first published in 1925 and which occupied Vaughan from 1877 until his death in 1922. The studies of which it consists deal with the doctrines of Hobbes, Spinoza, Locke, Vico, Montesquieu, Hume, Burke, Kant, Fichte, Hegel, Comte and Mazzini. Vaughan was prevented by his death from elaborating, or finishing, chapters on Rousseau and on Bentham and the Utilitarians.

Vaughan's selection of topics, and also the way in which he treats them, are determined by his own political philosophy, which may be described as a liberal or progressive modification of Hegelianism. He starts from the assumption that "the central problem of political philosophy . . . is, without doubt, to secure the right relation between the individual and the State" (vol. 1, p. 2). Accordingly, what he called "a work on the History of Political Philosophy" (vol. 1, p. v) deals exclusively with the development since Hobbes, for it is only during that period that the central problem has been the focus of discussion (vol. 1, p. 3, and vol. 2, p. 278). "By the time of Rousseau and Burke, the solution to that issue was virtually accomplished" (vol. 1, p. 3), for the right solution presupposes the conviction, absent from the "individualist" doctrines of the enlightenment, that "the State is essentially prior to the individual" (vol. 2, p. 91). The specific task incumbent upon the thinkers after Burke was to solve the problems connected with nationalism and industrialism without forgetting that the issue "deeper and more vital" than those of nationalism and socialism is that "between the individual and the State" (vol. 1, p. 4). Accordingly, Vaughan devotes his attention mainly to the struggle between the "individualist" or "contractarian" view which prevailed in the period before the French Revolution, and the "communalist" view of the subsequent period (vol. 2, p. 64). His ultimate assertion is his belief in a continuous progress "towards a goal which itself is essentially progressive" (vol. 2, p. 275).

Vaughan is guided by a philosophy of history, but he is not a philosophic historian. He is a dogmatic historian. He starts from a settled and passionately asserted view concerning the problems of political philosophy and their solutions; and the various doctrines which he considers, he views primarily not in themselves but within the framework supplied by what one may call his personal views. Thus although his work is rich in extensive quotations, the voice of Vaughan is almost always more audible than that of the writers he discusses. And it is a monotonous voice. In his treatment of the doctrines of the various thinkers he does not take account of the peculiar literary character of their works; he hardly considers the fact that different weights have to be attached to the explicit statements of the scientific *Tractatus politicus* on the one hand and, on the other, to those of the popular-scientific *Leviathan*, the deliberately unscientific *Civil Government*, the voluntarily obscure *Esprit des lois*, or the rhetorical *Reflections on the Revolution in France*. Whatever may be ⁺he merits of such a treatment in other cases, it is strange, it is even hardly understandable, in the case of a writer such as Vaughan, whose watchword is "history," whose opposition to the doctrines of the enlightenment is decisively based on the alleged fact of the discovery, since that time, of "history." To express the same objection somewhat differently: while no dogmatic treatment of the doctrines of the past can be truly fruitful (for since the dogmatic historian knows the answer to the philosophic questions before he makes his historical studies, these studies will enhance his erudition but not his wisdom), probably the most disastrous form of dogmatism is that which proceeds from the belief in continuous progress; if that belief is sound, present-day views are, generally speaking, nearer the truth than earlier views, and therefore no passionate interest in earlier views, no serious willingness to submit to the teaching of earlier thinkers, no serious effort at liberation from the prejudices of the present, no progress, can develop.

Yet an historian, even if he believe in continuous progress, and in addition holds that the first "inspired theorist" of the contractarian doctrine was Hobbes (vol. 1, pp. 12, 22), should regard it as his first task to present coherently the pre-Hobbesian, the traditional, the uninspired, form of that doctrine. Otherwise he is unable to grasp the profound change effected by Hobbes, a change which paved the way for the contractarian doctrines of Locke, Rousseau and Kant in particular. Vaughan does not even attempt to raise this question. As a consequence, his account of Hobbes' "preposterous system" (vol. 1, p. 22) which, he feels, was based on what was "after all, nothing more than an ill-tempered caprice" (vol. 1, p. 161), is a caricature. Since he fails to grasp the historical significance of Hobbes' basic distinction between the right of nature and the law of nature, and even to allude to his doctrine of the liberty of subjects, Vaughan arrives at the conclusion, contradicted elsewhere in his work, that *Leviathan* "has remained, and deserved to remain, without influence and without fruit: a fantastic hybrid, incapable of propagating its kind" (vol. 1, p. 37). One is tempted to apply to this remark of Vaughan's the following judgment which he passes on Comte's remarks on the Reformation: "It is not, however, the injustice of this view, nor its lack of historical insight, that we are here concerned with. It is the impossibility of squaring it with those ideas of evolution and historical continuity in which Comte professes to find the basis of all positive enquiry. If evolution in human history means anything, it is that the development of mankind must be taken as a whole, and that each marked stage to be traced in it has contributed something essential to the general result" (vol. 2, p. 230). It is a consequence of the manner in which he treats Hobbes that Vaughan's account of the "far less vicious" (vol. 1, p. 161) doctrines of the subsequent thinkers, in spite of being more sympathetic, is fundamentally just as inadequate.

One example must here suffice to justify to a certain extent the foregoing criticism. Vaughan interprets Burke's opposition to the principles of the French Revolution as opposition to the "individualist theory," to the doctrine which is based on the assertions of a state of nature, of natural rights and of the social contract. In giving an account of Burke's opposition Vaughan imputes to him "the theory of the State as an organism," although Burke "studiously avoids the metaphor of the organism" (vol. 2, pp. 25 ff.); Vaughan does not even attempt to prove that Burke's avoidance of that metaphor was studious, or to explain why he avoided it. He goes even so far as to trace Burke's conservatism to his holding the organismic theory (vol. 2, p. 30). As a consequence, he must interpret Burke's acceptance of the doctrines of the state of nature and the rights of man and the social contract as occasional and unfortunate slips, as regrettable "admissions"—"an admission, repeated afterwards, *it must be confessed*, in his assaults on the French Revolution" (vol. 2, pp. 3 ff.). In another equally revealing statement Vaughan, after having quoted two passages from Burke, goes on to say that "both passages admit—*it would be more true to say that they loudly assert*—the existence of natural rights" (vol. 2, p. 18; italics mine in both quotations; similar remarks are to be found on pp. 40, 42, 54 ff. and 60). It was known before the discovery of "history" that a man who wants to understand the opinions of other men, either living or dead, must start from, and not merely admit as an afterthought, those men's "loud assertions," rather than from doctrines which they failed to assert. And it was known that one cannot impute to an author a doctrine which he does not assert, if one does not prove both that the doctrine is the obvious implication of explicit statements of his, and that there were compelling reasons which induced him to refrain from stating the implication explicitly.

LÖWITH, KARL. *Von Hegel bis Nietzsche.* Zürich, New York: Europa. 1941.

This book should be of interest to all who wish to understand the emergence of European, and in particular of German, nihilism. Its subject may be said to be the transformation of European humanism, as exemplified by Goethe and Hegel, into German nihilism, as exemplified by Ernst Jünger. Its thesis is that the philosophic development proceeding from Hegel, which was of "deadly logical ruthlessness," offers the clue to what is happening in present-day Germany (p. 530). It would not be easy to find another book touching so many controversial topics of a political character which is equally remote from partisanship. It is written *sine ira et studio*, without sentimentality or vagueness, and with competence and a natural grace. The treatment is narrative and meditative rather than disputative or analytical. At times, for instance when describing Goethe's "Christian paganism" and Hegel's "philosophic Christianism," the author, adapting himself to the character of his subject, seems to draw rather than to speak.

We can recall the time when the period between the death of Hegel and the return to Kant after 1860 was considered more or less a vacuum in German philosophy (p. 162 ff.). That time has passed: since the end of the World War, full justice has been done to the historical importance of the older Schelling, Kierkegaard and Marx by many people who imitated, wholly or in part, the model development leading from Hegel to Nietzsche. Löwith, having from his youth followed the postwar development with passionate attention and critical sympathy, and having arrived at a point almost beyond its reach, sums it up and takes leave of it by presenting to us a lucid and sober account of the model development.

The development discussed is the transformation of philosophy from a consideration of all beings *sub specie aeternitatis*, into an analysis of one's time from the point of view of one's time—a transformation followed by Nietzsche's attempt to restore the original meaning of philosophy (Part I); and the transformation of the ideals of the independent citizen, of work, *Bildung*, *Humanität* and Christianity into so many "problems" and finally into objects of disgust (Part II). While by no means neglecting the experience of his generation, the author has the courage to look at these transformations from a point of view which is not of the present time nor of the period immediately preceding it; and in choosing his point of view he has shown not only courage but discretion. His understanding of Goethe enables him to see that the way leading from Hegel through Marx, Kierkegaard and historicism to Nietzsche and beyond is necessary, not absolutely, but only on the basis of Hegel. He indicates the reason why he no longer believes in the absolute necessity of Hegel's system—that is, in its superiority to any doctrine not presupposing it—by contrasting Hegel, whose influence was overwhelming and is still very great, with his older contemporary, Goethe, who, in the words of Nietzsche, was "in the history of the Germans an accident without consequences." To Hegel's construction of the history of the mind as the Absolute, he opposes Goethe's perception of the "Urphänomene" of nature, a perception which is the basis of an unbiased and adequate understanding of "historical" phenomena as phenomena belonging to "the realm of human arbitrariness," not constituting by themselves a genuine whole or wholes (p. 239 ff. and p. 290 ff.). This confrontation implies that not humanism as such, as some theologians would have it (see p. 35 ff., p. 263, p. 528 ff.), but only a specific humanism ultimately led to nihilism. (Compare the emphatic conclusion of the chapter on *Humanität* with the conclusions of the other chapters in Part II.)

The book ends with the suggestion of a return to Goethe, and the assertion that a return to Goethe or to anyone else is impossible "in der Zeit." This rather cryptic statement probably means that so far as the "time," the "historical reality," is concerned, no return to an earlier "historical reality" is possible: once certain customs, beliefs or institutions have ceased to be an unquestioned element of human life, no deliberate effort can ever restore their original force. But what holds true of such public things does not apply to insights: those of former thinkers may be forgotten, and they can be recovered by unremitting effort. While a return to the "time," to the "world" of Goethe—to "Weimar"—is impossible, a return to his insights and his approach may be a necessity. One cannot, I confess, be certain that this interpretation of Löwith's intentions is correct. (It seems to be contradicted by remarks on pp. 13 note 1, 52, 112, 270 ff., 463 note 31, 493 and 529.) If it is correct, the book as a whole would be even more than a remarkable expression of the crisis of historicism: it would be a contribution to liberation from it.

The unity of thought which underlies the book is somewhat obscured by the fact that the fruitful confrontation of the nineteenth century development with the attitude and views of Goethe is restricted to Part I. In "Das Problem der bürgerlichen Gesellschaft," the first and basic chapter of Part II, Löwith contrasts Hegel and his successors not with Goethe but, pertinently enough, with Rousseau. But while his interpretation of Goethe is not fettered by the prejudices of the nineteenth century, his interpretation of Rousseau keeps within the limits of the tradition established by Hegel in particular. He identifies what Rousseau still considered the eternal and final contradiction between *humanité* and *patriotisme* with the historical and soluble antinomy between the ideal of Christianity and that of classical antiquity (p. 317 ff.). He does not realize that Rousseau's primary concern is with the fundamental difference, recognized by the philosophic tradition but obliterated by the predominant trend of the nineteenth century, between "nature" and "convention." (Accordingly, an analysis of the *Elective Affinities* would have been an almost equally appropriate introduction to the chapter in question.) As a consequence, his presentation of the politicizing of philosophic thought in the nineteenth century is not as lucid as his presentation of the parallel process of historicizing. Similarly the otherwise excellent chapter "Das Problem der Arbeit" would have gained considerably if the Hegelian view of labor as a "negative behavior toward nature" had been contrasted on the one hand with the classical view of both mechanical and fine arts as imitation of nature, and on the other hand with Locke's doctrine of labor as the origin of private right. Löwith would thus have been led to bring to light the common origin, not only of the ideals of *Arbeit* and *Bildung* (p. 357), but also of the ideals of M. Homais and "l'art pour l'art." It testifies to the value of Löwith's book that these and similar additions would in no way necessitate a revision of the principles on which it is based.

McILWAIN, CHARLES HOWARD. *Constitutionalism, Ancient and Modern*. Ithaca: Cornell University Press. 1940.

This book surveys those stages in the growth of constitutionalism which are most relevant "to the political problems facing us here and now" (p. vii). There is a preliminary discussion, in which a sketch of the peculiar character of English constitutionalism is aptly inserted, of "some modern definitions of constitutionalism" ("the new definition of 'constitution,'" as we find it in Paine, and "the older view" as expressed by Bolingbroke and Burke). Then the author describes "the ancient conception of a constitution" (Plato's *Statesman* in particular); "the constitutionalism of Rome and its influence" (Roman and English constitutionalism); "constitutionalism in the Middle Ages" (Bracton and Fortescue); "the transition from Medieval to Modern" (the Tudor period); and "modern constitutionalism and its problems" (the constitutional struggle in seventeenth century England and its relevance to the questions of the present time). The final thesis is that "our ancient distinction between *jurisdictio* and *gubernaculum*," between "matter of law" and "matter of state" (see p. 127 ff.), "may still be a valuable help in making [an] analysis of our present-day problems." For the reconciliation of *jurisdictio*, which "is essential to liberty," and *gubernaculum*, which must not be enfeebled by political "checks and balances" if there is to be efficient government, "remains probably our most serious practical problem, just as it was in seventeenth-century England" (p. 142 ff.).

Professor McIlwain's reinterpretation of the history of constitutionalism may be said to be directed against that school whose foremost representative was von Gierke. "A generation or two ago it was the fashion to trace all our constitutional liberties back to the institutions of the Germanic tribes as described by Tacitus" (p. 43). Over against this view, the author asserts that the origins of modern constitutionalism must be sought in the republican city of Rome rather than in the woods of Germany (see p. 45). One may wonder, however, whether he goes far enough in opposing the "romantic"

Criticism: Sixteen Appraisals

view. He seems to follow this view when he divides the history of constitutionalism into two main phases—"an earlier and much longer" phase lasting up to the eighteenth century, "in which constitutions were thought of not as a creation but as a growth," and "the 'self-conscious' phase, in which the people are thought of as creating their constitution by direct and express constituent action" (p. 23). This division is more or less convincing as long as one confronts modern views with those of the Middle Ages; but it cannot be maintained when considered in the light of the classical doctrines. Aristotle could not have attached practically equal significance to "blue-prints" of constitutions and to actual constitutions if he had thought of them as "a growth."

According to another opinion, which the author evidently prefers, the dividing line "between the ancient and the modern conception of constitutionalism" (p. 40) "must be sought . . . in the period between Aristotle and Cicero" (p. 45). To illustrate this "modern" view, of Roman or Stoic origin and alien to the Greek —or the pre-Stoic Greek—mind, he quotes with emphasis Cicero's statement "that no state can ever enact any binding law in derogation of [the] law of nature," "a statement that no Greek of the fifth or fourth century B.C. could have dreamt of making, even supposing that he could have understood it" (p. 40; see also p. 37 ff.). This judgment does not seem to be warranted. One may wonder whether the dividing line separating ancient and modern constitutionalism, and ancient and modern political thought in general, must not be sought in the period in which political philosophers consciously opposed to the ancient (and mediaeval) doctrines a doctrine which they themselves considered fundamentally novel, that is, in the latter half of the sixteenth and in the seventeenth century. Professor McIlwain's description of the difference between mediaeval and modern constitutionalism is apt to confirm rather than to weaken that suspicion.

POWELL, ELMER ELLSWORTH. *Spinoza and Religion.* Boston: Chapman and Grimes. 1941.

An adequate understanding of Spinoza's philosophy in general and his political philosophy in particular presupposes clarity about his attitude toward religion. Has the first part of the *Ethics* to be taken at its face value, that is, as speculative theology, or is it merely an exoteric presentation of what in esoteric presentation would be perhaps a "first philosophy," in the sense of Bacon or Hobbes? This is the question which the reader of Professor Powell's book cannot help raising. The book is the second edition of a study first published in 1906, but its thesis is as challenging today as it was, or should have been, thirty-six years ago.

The author treats his subject with remarkable candor, lucidity and seriousness. His book is a frontal attack, "from the standpoint of religion," on the opinion, widely held since the last decades of the eighteenth century, that Spinoza was a religious thinker, a "pantheist" or "mystic." The author maintains these theses: Spinoza was an atheist; he knew that he was an atheist—"of the title 'God-intoxicated philosopher,' he would certainly have been ashamed" (p. 242); his dominant interest was purely theoretical and "unmixed with anything which may be called the religious interest"; the many religious utterances of his which apparently contradict this characterization are due to his prudent accommodation to the views prevalent in his time; his "excessive timidity," his lack of courage, which was "his most serious defect of character" (pp. 6 and 44), is explained by the environment in which he grew up (he was a descendant of those Spanish-Portuguese Jews who had sacrificed their Jewish convictions by externally accepting Christianity in order not to lose their homes and fortunes).

It does not detract from the author's originality if one notes that his main thesis is merely a restatement of what was the generally held view until the late eighteenth century (*cf.* p. 243). What seems to have been almost self-evident to philosophic readers of the seventeenth and eighteenth centuries, who had a clear grasp of the theological essentials and, besides, an immediate experience of the influence of censorship and persecution on literary techniques, is today an almost shocking paradox. Accordingly, where these earlier readers could trust their flair, the modern historian needs, and demands, demonstrably correct rules of procedure. Powell is fully aware of this necessity; he prefaces his interpretation with reflections on Spinoza's manner of expression, and on the right manner of reading Spinoza's writings—reflections that are among the most valuable parts of his book. They culminate in the hermeneutic rule, appropriately italicized, that "*whenever two passages contradict each other, one of them expressed in religious terminology and the other not, we are bound to regard the latter as conveying Spinoza's real meaning*" (p. 65).

Certain readers will think that the author has begged the decisive question by defining "religion" as "a personal attitude" to "a higher personal power or higher personal powers" (p. 327). While I consider this definition as sufficient for all practical purposes, I feel that his expositions would have been more convincing if they had been based not on his own views, however sound, about religion, but on Spinoza's views, in other words, if the author had started from a coherent discussion of Spinoza's explicit teaching concerning *religio* and *pietas*.

The least acceptable of Powell's theses is that which concerns Spinoza's "excessive timidity" (pp. 37 and 62). Spinoza's timidity, if such it was, was not excessive. What contemporary of Spinoza was bolder than Hobbes? And Hobbes admitted that he had not dared to write as boldly as Spinoza (see Aubrey's *Lives*, vol. 1, p. 357). In view of all the evidence it is more correct to speak of Locke's "excessive prudence" (Thomas Fowler, *Locke*, p. 50) or of Rousseau as "timidity incarnate" (Alfred Cobban, *Rousseau and the Modern State*, p. 55) than of Spinoza's "excessive timidity." The author's error is due to the fact that he limited his observations to Spinoza, and thus assigned too private a cause to a phenomenon that was of a typical character. "Boldness formerly was not the character of Atheists as such. They were even of a character nearly the reverse; they were formerly like the old Epicureans, rather an unenterprising race. But of late they are grown active, designing, turbulent, and seditious" (Burke, *Thoughts on French Affairs*). "Atheists as such" became "active and designing," they ceased to be "timid," when they ceased to believe in the social necessity of the belief in God; prior to that crucial event they were, to quote Burke again, "not gregarious." Spinoza still believed in the social necessity of religion (*cf.* pp. 64 and 260). Accordingly, what appears at first sight as excessive timidity or lack of courage, or at best as "excessive tact" (p. 302), was actually not merely "justifiable prudence" but the performance of the duty of the citizen, or of the duty of man.

De Laudibus Legum Angliae. By Sir John Fortescue. Edited and Translated with Introduction and Notes by S. B. Chrimes. Cambridge: At the University Press; New York: The Macmillan Co., 1942.

This volume which contains, above all, what may be called the first critical edition of Fortescue's *De laudibus legum Angliae*, will be of considerable interest to students of comparative jurisprudence, of the history of political thought, and of English legal and constitutional history. Fortescue's little work is a dialogue between "the chancellor" (Fortescue himself) and "the prince" (Edward, the only son of Henry VI) in which the former demonstrates to the latter the excellence of the English form of government and of the English laws by comparing them with absolute monarchy and the civil laws respectively. The legal topics discussed are: procedure of proof, legitimation by subsequent matrimony, succession, guardianship of minors, theft, freedmen, legal training, and delays in courts; the section centering around the comparison of the English procedure of proof by juries with the Roman procedure of proof by witnesses makes up more than a third of the whole.

The setting stands in a somewhat melancholy contrast with the content: the conversation in which the English institutions are so highly praised, takes place while the two participants are in exile owing to the civil war then raging in England. The young prince, who is entirely given to martial exercises, has to be convinced by the aged chancellor that he ought to make himself

reasonably familiar with the laws. He seems to have a prejudice
in favor of the civil laws, a prejudice presumably caused by their
absolutist implications which are naturally pleasing to him as a
prince. And he certainly has a prejudice against comparisons
which, he feels, are odious as such. He wonders whether he
should study the laws of England or the civil laws: after all, "the
people should not be governed but by the best laws," and the civil
laws are more renowned than any others. It is in this context,
and with a view to the young prince, that the chancellor sets
forth his comparison of English and continental institutions, a
comparison which is made *ad hominem,* not to say *in usum Delphini,*
and is therefore not altogether free from deliberate inaccuracies
favorable to the English institutions (see the editor's remarks on
pp. 177, 206, ci, and ciii). It is interesting to note that the
chancellor does not retort at once—as the editor (p. xcvi) seems
to believe—that the laws of England are superior to the civil laws.
Instead, he shows first that the king of England has no right to
change the laws of his realm (*sc.* even if they are defective),
because his power is "regal and political" and not simply regal,
or, in other words, because in England the legislator is neither the
king alone (*dominium regale*) nor the citizens alone (*dominium
politicum*), but the (hereditary) king and Parliament jointly (see
the editor's notes to chs. 10 and 11). According to a somewhat
different formulation, the source of political kingdoms is not, as
the source of kingdoms merely regal, the will of the king (his
greed of dignity and glory in particular), but "the intention of
the people;" accordingly, "the solid truth by which that community (*sc.* the political kingdom) is maintained," are the subjects
whose rights are guaranteed, or whose bodies and goods are
protected, by the laws which the king cannot change. While the
chancellor being a good Aristotelian admits that the rule of a
good absolute king can be as satisfactory as the rule of a king
ruling "politically" (chs. 9 and 32), his statements leave hardly any
doubt as to his preferring the *dominium regale et politicum* not
only because it happens to be English, but because it is intrinsically
better. This judgment is probably connected with, although it
does not altogether depend on, his conviction that "liberty is
instilled by God into the nature of man" [*cf.* ch. 42 (104, 6ff.)

with ch. 12 (28, 21)]. After thus having been reminded of the limits of his future power, the prince no longer asks whether or not the civil laws are absolutely preferable to the English laws, but whether the latter are as good for the government of England as the civil laws are supposed to be for the government of the whole world (*cf.* end of ch. 14 with end of ch. 7 and beginning of ch. 9). The chancellor does not limit himself to answering that question in the affirmative; he goes much beyond this by demonstrating the absolute superiority of the English laws. His discussion of the first example (the English jury-system) compels the prince to admit the superiority of the English law and to wonder why the reasonable English procedure is not accepted everywhere. The chancellor suggests that the jury-system presupposes a fairly wealthy rural population, and that this condition is met by England in contrast with France in particular. The prince is satisfied by that explanation which tallies with his dislike of odious comparisons: connected with that explanation, the praise of the English law seems not to entail a blame of the civil law (end of ch. 28 and 29). But the chancellor avails himself of the earliest opportunity for making it clear that the different economic conditions of England and France in their turn are due, in a large measure, to the fact that England is ruled by a regal and political government, whereas France is ruled by a government merely regal which impoverishes the rural population (ch. 33). What Fortescue suggests is then, not so much an "explanation of legal and constitutional institutions in terms of comparative economic and social conditions" (p. 177), as an explanation of economic conditions in terms of the political set-up.

As regards the translation, Mr. Chrimes has been guided by the commendable intention "to avoid rendering the Latin text into what might justly be described as normal twentieth-century prose" and "to translate into plain English as closely as [he] could the letter and the spirit of Fortescue's words." (p. lvi). In many cases, his performance lives up to this standard. In the following critical remarks, which do not by any means claim to be complete, figures indicate pages and lines of the text, words in quotation marks Mr. Chrimes' translation, and words in angular brackets the correct translation.

4, 31 and 6, 2: *timor servilis* "abject fear" [servile fear], *timor filialis* "a son's fear for his father" [filial fear]; the expressions are technical (see Thomas Aquinas, *S. th.*, 2 2, qu. 19, art. 2 e.g.). Cf. 18, 2 and translation.

10, 26-31: *Iusticia particularis* "Justice . . . of the kind" [particular justice or justice in the narrower sense]; *particularis virtus* "(sort of) virtue" [particular virtue, special virtue]; (*omnis virtus* "Virtue [the whole virtue]), *cf.* Aristotle, *Eth. Nic.*, 1130a8-9.

12, 8: *omnis virtus* "of all virtue" [the whole virtue].

26, 14: *illa* (*sc. sinagoga*) *militabat* "and defended it" [it was struggling].

30, 22 f.: *populi illius* "of the people" [of that people, *sc.* of the people ruled politically].

30, 29: *communitas illa* "the community" [that community, *sc.* the community ruled politically].

30, 33: *proprias vires et propria alimenta* "proper strength and due nourishment" [the powers belonging to them and the nourishment belonging to them]; *cf.* 32, 1 *substancias proprias*.

32, 24: *existimantes parendo legibus se beatos fore* "thought themselves fortunate in obeying the laws" [thought that by obeying the laws they would become happy].

34, 19 f.: *non alio pacto* "by no sort of agreement other". Cf. also 34, 6. Here, the translation seems to impute to the text a more technical meaning than it probably has (*cf.* p. XCVI); I would suggest "in no other manner".

36, 17 f.: *in constitucionem sive statutorum naturam mutantur* "are changed into a constitution or something of the nature of statutes". I would read *constitucionum* and translate "are changed so as to take on the nature of constitutions or statutes".

42, 16: *que legum illarum eos* (*sc. casus*) *melius iustiusque diffiniat* "which of the laws shows its superiorities better and more justly" [which of these laws decides these (cases) better and more justly].

DEWEY, JOHN. *German Philosophy and Politics.* [Revised Edition.] New York: Putnam. 1942.

That strength and gentleness, or efficiency and generosity, can be combined is a conclusion which only a bold man would draw from the political history of Germany during the last hundred years. Accordingly, no one familiar with the Anglo-Saxon way of life can help wondering why "Germany is different." The question is evaded by those who refer to the "Other Germany," to the Germany which is not "different," which takes its bearings not by blood and iron nor by blood and soil but by philosophy. For the question concerns precisely not the mere existence but the political existence, the political efficiency, of the "Other Germany." Dewey's wartime statement, far from being guilty of that evasion, raises the question of whether German philosophy itself does not in large measure explain the characteristic features common to the Germany of Bismarck, of William II and of Hitler. And it answers that question in the affirmative.

No one will object to Dewey's question, but it is necessary to object to the way in which he arrives at his answer. The procedure which seems most natural is to describe as exactly as possible the characteristic features of the predominant German political spirit in the period under consideration (a peculiar mixture of authoritarianism, bellicism, nationalism); and then to discover how far a basis for that spirit is afforded by the political teaching of those philosophers who, in Germany, were generally considered most representative of German thought. The result would, I believe, partially confirm Dewey's thesis. But it would contradict that thesis as far as Kant, in particular, is concerned; and if Kant is indeed, as Dewey holds, "the philosopher of Germany" (p. 137), much of the relevance of the thesis would be lost. Dewey has chosen to start from a questionable description of the phenomenon to be explained: "Surely the chief mark of distinctly German civilization is its combination of self-conscious idealism with unsurpassed technical efficiency and organization in the varied fields of action" (p. 69). This sentence is a restatement of a certain German "ideology" concerning the German spirit, rather than an adequate description. Could one not describe American civilization, for instance, in almost the same terms? Still more surprising is Dewey's explanation. He finds the "root idea" of the combination in question "in the doctrine of Kant concerning the two realms, one outer, physical and necessary, the other inner, ideal and free," and the primacy of "the inner" (p. 69). It is difficult in a review to discuss this comprehensive thesis on its own level. Fortunately Dewey summarizes what he considers the consequences for social life of Kant's doctrine, on the basis of Kant's own explicit statements: "In contrast with this realm of inner freedom stands that of civil and political action, the principle of which is obedience or subordination to constituted authority" (p. 76). The same conclusion was reached by men such as Descartes and Spinoza, who started from widely different ultimate assumptions.

Dewey is on much safer ground when he points out the connection between the depreciation by German philosophers of "happiness" and the ensuing overemphasis on the aspect of self-sacrifice in morality, on the one hand, and militarism on the other: "That war demands self-sacrifice is but the more convincing proof of its profound morality" (p. 113). The phenomenon which he has in mind is that the German philosophers, opposing the unqualified identification of the morally good with the object of enlightened self-interest, insisted on the difference between the *honestum* and the *utile* to such an extent that they were apt to forget the natural aim of man, which is happiness: happiness and utility, as well as common sense, became almost bad names in German philosophy. The difference between duty and self-interest is most obvious in the case of one particular virtue—courage, or military virtue. Whereas it is actually advantageous to the individual to be just, temperate, urbane, meek, etc., what could be called the consummation of courage—death on the field of honor— is never rewarded so far as the individual himself is concerned. In defending menaced morality, that is, nonmercenary morality, the German philosophers paved the way for the glorification of military virtue to the detriment of the virtues of peace. While this approach, if consistently followed, would be helpful in laying bare what might seem to be one specific danger to which German thought is exposed—moralism unmitigated by sense of humor or sense of proportion—it should be enlightened by the important truth that self-denial is as a rule a safer guide to decency than is "self-realization," to use a term of German extraction.

In attacking German philosophy Dewey defends not simply the cause of democracy and international order, but a particular interpretation of that cause—his own philosophical doctrine. He seems to think that democracy is as much bound up with a belief "which is frankly experimental" as political absolutism is with "a philosophy of absolutes." No one will deny "that philosophical absolutism may be practically as dangerous as matter of fact political absolutism" (p. 113). But is it not also true that the "frankly experimental" "method . . . of success" (p. 142) has proved very dangerous in the hands of unscrupulous men, and that the belief in an "absolute" inspired the words "that all men are created equal, that they are endowed by their Creator with certain unalienable Rights"?

ROMMEN, HEINRICH A. *The State in Catholic Thought. A Treatise in Political Philosophy*. St. Louis: B. Herder. 1945.

Anyone who wishes to judge impartially of the legitimacy or the prospects of the great design of modern man to erect the City of Man on what appear to him to be the ruins of the City of God must familiarize himself with the teachings, and especially the political teachings, of the Catholic church, which is certainly the most powerful antagonist of that modern design. There are people who believe that they can dispose of the Catholic protest by pointing to the apparent opportunism of the policy of the Vatican. It is one of the merits of Dr. Rommen's book that it states without ambiguity the inflexible principles that the Catholic church has maintained throughout the ages by means of a most flexible policy.

An essential characteristic of Catholic thought about the state is that its emphasis on the different elements which it claims to reconcile, in a higher unity, changes with the change of circum-

stances. Rommen's book is an interesting example of the abandonment by Catholic thought of the romanticist, legitimist or
monarchist tendency with which it was allied as long as the fight
against the philosophic principles of 1789 was its primary polemic
preoccupation, and of its return to the more democratic views of
late scholasticism. Particularly valuable is Rommen's account of
the intra-Catholic controversy between the adherents of the less
democratic designation theory and those of the more democratic
translation theory of the origin of political authority (Chapters
19 and 20). In his presentation the only residue of what may
loosely be called the romanticist view is his use of the term
"organic," which in his work means hardly more, however, than
that political society is not simply and essentially egalitarian.

In thus reinterpreting the unity of its elements Catholic thought
does not refuse to learn from non-Catholic thought, or to incorporate such ideas of non-Catholic origin as can be reconciled with the
Catholic principles. The most outstanding example of this in
Rommen's book is his chapter about the content of natural law
(Chapter 7), in which he deals almost exclusively with natural
rights as distinguished from duties, although he is aware of the
fact that the shift of emphasis from duties to rights is of Puritan
rather than of Catholic origin (see pp. 423 ff., 556, 564 ff., 580).
Almost equally illustrative of the influence of the political situation
on the form in which the unchangeable principles are presented
is the chapter on the forms of government (Chapter 21), which
is devoted chiefly to an explanation of the anti-democratic attitude
of "the great majority of Catholic writers in political philosophy"
in the last century (p. 481).

Deviating from the somewhat questionable practice of certain
Catholic journalists, Rommen, who obviously has a strong bias
in favor of democracy, does not fail to point out that the acceptance of democracy or of any other non-tyrannical form of
government is not, and cannot be, the last word of Catholic
thought, but depends on the social or political situation of a
given country at a given time (pp. 3, 8, 69, 79, 412, 440, 477 ff.,
715). He is equally straightforward in distinguishing "the practice
of tolerance as a political expedient" from "the ideal status,"
which is "the union between Church and state whenever the
circumstances allow it" (that is, whenever "the people in over-

whelming majority are themselves Catholics"), and in making it clear that the union between church and state implies *inter alia* that the Catholic church is recognized as "the public and established religion" and that "the state laws censor and suppress the free circulation of heretical propaganda" (pp. 367 ff., 593 ff., 605). On the other hand he goes too far in saying (p. 337, n.) that "St. Thomas (*Summa theologica*, IIa, IIae, q. 10, a. 11) defends tolerance of Jews and infidels on the basis of the idea of the common good." In general Rommen succeeds in revealing the impressive unity that underlies the apparently heterogeneous elements which constitute Catholic thought about the state. He is sometimes less fortunate, however, in his account of non-Catholic positions, and he particularly fails to do justice to Rousseau, progressivism and the Third Republic of France.

The author is justified to a considerable extent in calling his work "a treatise in political philosophy." It consists of four parts: "Philosophical Foundations" (political anthropology, political theology, natural law); "The Philosophy of the State" (the origin and nature of the state, the common good, political authority, sovereignty, forms of government); "Church and State"; and "The Community of Nations." Today it is something of a surprise to come across a book on political fundamentals which is more than an open or disguised apology for democracy, and at least attempts to give an openminded and at the same time uncynical account of political principles. In this connection one must recommend especially Rommen's exposition of the scope of political philosophy (pp. 33 ff. and 49 ff.). Yet one cannot help noting a certain lack of clarity in what he says about the character of political philosophy. In his preface he claims that the political philosophy which he presents in his work is based on reason and not on revelation. Later on, however, he declares that "continuous respect for theology," nay acceptance of "faith and revelation," is of the essence of that very political philosophy (pp. 13 ff., 116). How little he succeeds in limiting himself completely to political philosophy proper, as distinguished from a political teaching based on revelation, may perhaps best be seen from his statement that "no state can live without the beneficent forces of divine religion" (p. 603; compare pp. 327 ff. and 708 ff.), that is, of the Catholic religion.

These critical remarks do not, however, detract from my opinion that Rommen's book is valuable, not merely because it clarifies the Catholic position, but above all because it states the issues of political philosophy with a comprehensiveness and a moral seriousness which are far from being common.

PEGIS, ANTON C., ed. *Basic Writings of Saint Thomas Aquinas.* [Annotated, with an introduction by the editor.] New York: Random House. 1945. 2 vols.

By this work, Professor Pegis has rendered a very great service to higher education in this country. He has made easily accessible in English translation the whole first part of the *Summa theologica* and such sections of its second part, as well as of the *Summa contra Gentiles,* as suffice for a general understanding of Thomas' "conception of the life of man within the divine government and of the principles, internal and external, which man needs and can find in working out his destiny." The translation is a revised version of the English Dominican translation. In his revision Professor Pegis has "aimed primarily at accuracy, and at preserving the uniformity of St. Thomas' technical terminology." As far as one can judge from an examination of a few selected passages, he has been remarkably successful. In particular, his translation seems to be unusually free of the vice that is common even in otherwise good translations of philosophic texts: that of unnecessarily departing from the literal. This is not to deny that there would be room for improvement in subsequent printings. For instance, in the translation of the *quaestio* dealing with the natural law (vol. 2, pp. 777 ff.), "apud omnes" is rendered without any reason by expressions as different as "in all men," "in all" and "for all," while "est de jure naturali" is translated "is a matter of natural law," "belongs to the natural law" and "is of the natural law." "Mutakallimin" should be replaced in all cases by "mutakallimūn."

In his introduction the editor discusses the intellectual background of the work of Thomas, his "spirit and significance" and his life and works. One could wish that he had devoted a few pages to the method of presentation used in the *Summa theologica,* a method which at first is bound to be bewildering, not to say unintelligible, to the general reader of our day. Pegis' summary account of the problem with which Thomas was confronted and of his solution is clear, sober and, on most points, convincing. He observes that "the basic issue at stake" was "the nature of wisdom," or, in other words, "the nature of philosophy itself," and that Thomas' achievement consisted in "freeing philosophy from the philosophers." This is certainly true in the sense that Thomas, in order "to make the Philosopher a worthy vehicle of reason in Christian thought," had to give to philosophy itself a meaning fundamentally different from its Aristotelian (or Platonic) meaning: in Thomas, as distinguished from the classical philosophers and certainly from their greatest follower in the Islamic world (Fārābī), philosophy is divorced from the conviction that happiness can be achieved only by, or essentially consists in, philosophy.

Pegis repeatedly grants that Thomas did not merely add a teaching based on revelation to the Aristotelian teaching based on reason, but that he directly opposed important elements of the Aristotelian teaching on the plane of the latter. He believes, however, that as regards the central question—the question of creation—the Aristotelian doctrine is not opposed to the Biblical doctrine, because "there is a considerable difference between not knowing the idea of creation and denying it." I fail to see the usefulness of this distinction in the case at hand. Is it made in order to suggest that one can reconcile the Aristotelian teaching with the Biblical teaching without abandoning the "spirit" of the former? But how can this be true in the light of the fact that Aristotle did not intend "to leave his explanation of the origin of the world unfinished," and did not leave it unfinished? Aristotle did not leave room, intentionally or unintentionally, for a revealed teaching which could be added to his rational teaching.

An introduction to the work of Thomas must point the way toward overcoming the typical present-day obstacles which prevent its genuine understanding. These obstacles are the two forces that dominate all present-day thought—science and history. With regard to science Pegis simply capitulates; he grants that there is "much bad science" in Thomas, yet he holds that this does not affect the value of his philosophy. Can one as easily as that get

rid of the enormous difficulty presented by the inseparable connection between Thomas' physics and his natural theology? It
would have been more fruitful to indicate why and how far the
questions raised by Thomist, or Aristotelian, physics retain their
full significance regardless of any progress that modern science
has achieved by raising questions of an entirely different type.

As for history, Pegis, while lucidly describing the attitude of
Thomas toward the philosophers who preceded him, refers to
his way of seeing "the history of philosophy," or of seeking "the
guiding thread of the history of philosophy," and asserts that
Thomas' "successful diagnosis of the history of Greek and Arabian
philosophy" freed "the thirteenth century of the danger of historicism in the presence of Greek and Arabian thinkers." Passing
over the strange implication that the danger of historicism existed
in the thirteenth century, I should say that it only contributes
to the prevailing confusion to interpret Thomas' critical study of
the teachings of his predecessors—a study closely akin to that
which a mathematician devotes, not to the history of mathematics,
but to mathematical literature—as a concern with the history of
philosophy. The confusion is apparently removed, and therefore
actually increased, by maintaining that "St. Thomas saw the
history of philosophy in the present" instead of saying that Thomas
studied the teachings of his predecessors with an exclusive regard
to their truth or falsehood, or that for Thomas only argument,
and not "history," could legitimately decide the fate of any
philosophic thesis.

OLSCHKI, LEONARDO. *Machiavelli the Scientist*. Berkeley:
Gillick Press. 1945.

"The scientific character of *The Prince* has been always noticed
and many times emphasized, but never correctly described and
accurately disclosed." According to a widespread opinion, Machiavelli was primarily "a teacher of practical statecraft" and "his scientific mind is . . . revealed by his realism." According to Olschki,
however, Machiavelli was primarily interested in elaborating "a

new science of man which anticipated in spirit and mental procedure Galileo's foundation of a new science of nature," and "his
scientific mind . . . is revealed . . . by the abstract quality of his
thought and his power of generalization." Olschki asserts that
Machiavelli was concerned with the "how," and not with the "why"
or the causes of political phenomena; that he made of politics "a
system of universal rules," that is, of "intrinsic laws to be discovered by an inductive method of thinking"; and that he succeeded
in this because he was able to reduce "the nature of [political]
phenomena to two principles or agents," namely, *fortuna* and *virtù*.

One cannot say that Olschki provides the analysis of Machiavelli's science which he almost promises in the sentence quoted at
the beginning of this review. He scarcely goes beyond the assertions summarized in the foregoing paragraph. No evidence is sub-
mitted to prove the contention that Machiavelli was a "scientist"
as distinguished from a teacher of practical statecraft. The fact (if
it is a fact) that the "lasting interest in his work" depends upon
his "scientific mind" in Olschki's sense of the term, does not, of
course, prove that for Machiavelli himself "science" as distinguished
from practical statecraft was the focal point. His constant preoccupation with what princes or republics should do, as distinguished
from what they frequently or generally do, seems rather to show
that Olschki's thesis is fundamentally wrong and that the distinction on which it is based is misleading.

As regards Machiavelli's allegedly exclusive concern with the
"how" as distinguished from the "why" or the causes, Olschki limits himself to asserting that a certain *perchè* in a certain letter of
Machiavelli's was "used in a modal and not in a causal sense"; he
does not discuss a single one of the innumerable passages in which
Machiavelli expounded the causes of political phenomena, although
he happens to quote one of them.

As regards Machiavelli's concern with "universal rules," Olschki
makes much of the fact that he used the term "regola generale,"
and he asserts that to Machiavelli this was fundamentally the same
as "natural law" in the sense of modern science. Olschki un-
doubtedly exaggerates the frequency of Machiavelli's use of this
term (p. 29 n.32: "*The Prince*, ch. 3 and *passim*"); if I am not
mistaken, it occurs twice in *The Prince* (chs. 3 and 23) and once in
the *Discorsi* (1 9). At any rate, it occurs very rarely, is never men-

tioned in passages in which Machiavelli explains the general intention of his political work, and its meaning is so little defined that
one cannot possibly build on it an interpretation of Machiavelli's
primary purpose. The utmost one might consider is this: whereas
Machiavelli understood by "rule" something to which one ought to
conform in order to act well, the normative element seems to be
absent from his "general rules." This would hardly entitle one to
identify his "general rule" with "natural law" in the sense of modern science. One's confidence in Olschki's assertions on matters of
this kind is not strengthened by his statement that "Leonardo da
Vinci is the first author who ever used the term of 'natural law.'"

Finally, as to the alleged fact that Machiavelli reduced the
nature of political phenomena to the two principles of *fortuna* and
virtù, it is obvious that the distinctions between the unchangeable
and knowable order of nature and the unpredictable ways of *fortuna*, between nature and *virtù*, rich and poor, public and private,
men and institutions, love and fear and so on, were no less important, no less fundamental for Machiavelli than the distinction between *fortuna* and *virtù*.

But in spite of its deficiencies Olschki's thesis is not without a
certain value. One or two generations ago it was taken for granted
that there is a fundamental difference between pre-modern political
philosophy and modern political philosophy, and that Machiavelli
played a decisive role in the emergence of the latter. Recent research has been inclined to see the "historical continuity" rather
than the break with the tradition—for example, the kinship of *The
Prince* with the traditional mirrors of princes, rather than the fundamental difference between them—and thus to blur the epoch-
making character of Machiavelli's work. Olschki rightly objects to
this tendency. But he does not do justice to its sound element, which
is the principle that Machiavelli's work must be understood historically, that is, in its own light, and not in the light, say, of nineteenth
century social science. Olschki denies the existence of any political
science worthy of mention prior to Machiavelli: "Machiavelli is the
first theorist of statecraft who wrote about that subject from first-
hand experience both as a politician and as a historian. None of his
supposed forerunners had any insight into governmental affairs of
any kind." Oblivious of the achievements of men such as Thucydides, Aristotle, Polybius, Cicero and Tacitus, he fails to see that

Machiavelli's achievement consists not in the discovery but in a radical transformation of the idea of political philosophy or political science.

This transformation is illustrated most strikingly by his concept of *virtù*, which in his political philosophy occupies a position comparable to that occupied by *virtus* in traditional political philosophy. Olschki asserts, without adducing any evidence, that this Machiavellian concept was derived from mediaeval medicine. It is true that Machiavelli sometimes used *virtù* in the sense of specific natural power (see his remarks about *occulta virtù* in *Discorsi* I 58 and II 32, and about *naturali virtù* in I 56), but he used it more frequently in the sense that it had in the political and moral literature of the past (see *Discorsi* I 60 and III 33, where *virtù* is used to render Livy's *virtus;* note especially the use of the term in *The Prince*, chs. 8 and 16). It is safe to say that Machiavelli's concept of *virtù* emerged from a transformation of Livy's or, more generally, of the classical concept of virtue.

Machiavelli's reinterpretation of virtue cannot be understood except in the light of his reinterpretation of tyranny. Within certain limits he accepted the traditional distinction between tyranny and kingship (or commonwealth). But at any rate in *The Prince* that traditional opposition ceases to be valid. According to Olschki, "tyranny is always condemned by Machiavelli. The popular view that *The Prince* is written as a manual for a tyrant is based on a superficial knowledge of the book." To describe *The Prince* as a manual for tyrants is certainly insufficient; but it is equally wrong to describe it as a manual for princes as distinguished from tyrants. The characteristic feature of the work is precisely that it makes no distinction between prince and tyrant: it uses the term "prince" to designate princes and tyrants alike. This is shown by the first sentence of *The Prince* (ch. 1).

The reason why the distinction between prince and tyrant ceases to be significant in *The Prince* is that the central purpose of the work is to bring to light the nature of "the new prince," that is, above all, the nature of the founder of "nuovi ordini e modi" (political, legal, moral or religious). Distinctions which are most important once an order has been established are inapplicable to the actual establishment and, we may add, to its "fringes" (especially foreign relations). Whereas traditional political philosophy took its bearings from the "normal" condition, that is, from the fully developed social order, the Machiavelli of *The Prince* was primarily concerned with what Hobbes would have called "the state of nature," or rather with the transition from "the state of nature" to "the civil state." It is for this reason that Machiavelli had to question the validity of the moral distinctions: he denied their applicability to what he considered the most important case, the case of him who establishes an order within which moral virtue of some kind can and should be practiced. He reinterpreted "virtue" to make it cover also and especially the specific excellence of the founder. One may say that he made the focal point the question of the roots of social order as distinguished from the question of its purpose. It would be most important to find out whether this change of orientation is akin to that effected by modern science with regard to the study of natural phenomena. This question cannot be answered, it cannot even be raised, as long as one accepts the untenable premise that Machiavelli was, or intended to be, a "scientist" in the nineteenth or twentieth century sense of the term.

FINK, ZERA S. *The Classical Republicans. An Essay in the Recovery of a Pattern of Thought in Seventeenth Century England.* Evanston: Northwestern University Press. 1945.

It was through a restoration, and transformation, of classical republicanism that modern republicanism came into being. This restoration in seventeenth-century England by the "classical republicans" (Harrington, Milton, Algernon Sidney and others) forms the central subject of Fink's scholarly study. His analysis of these men and their views of mixed government is prefaced by a sketch of the teachings of earlier thinkers, particularly Machiavelli, Thomas More and Gasparro Contarini. It appears from his presentation that the two most important sources of inspiration for the "classical republicans" were, aside from the authors of classical antiquity themselves, Machiavelli's *Discorsi* and the constitution of Venice as it actually was or was believed to be. Particularly valuable is what Fink has to say about the influence which admiration for Venice exerted on English thought and letters (on Shakespeare and Swift, among others) and, above all, his analysis of Harrington's *Oceana*. He concludes his discussion with an investigation of how the ideas of the "classical republicans" "entered in one way or another into the thought of the great English political parties," especially the Whigs.

As indicated by the subtitle of the book, the author is more concerned with the dependence of the "classical republicans" on classical models than with their transformation of them. His presentation nevertheless confirms the view that there is a fundamental difference between their teachings and those of classical political philosophy. The "classical republicans" were basically more democratic than their classical teachers, if only in their adoption of the principle of popular sovereignty (pp. 14 ff., 19, 53-60, 67 ff., 88, 100 ff., 119 ff., and 172 ff.). They had studied Machiavelli, and Machiavelli (as distinguished from Polybius, who had suspended judgment on the subject) had explicitly preferred the expansionist and hence relatively democratic Roman republic to non-expansionist and aristocratic Sparta, to say nothing of other democratic elements of his teaching which are not considered by the author. Characteristically, Machiavelli's approval of imperialism was also adopted by most of the "classical republicans" (pp. 81 ff., 156 ff., 172 ff., and 188 ff.).

Of the fundamental views mentioned in this study none is more important than the belief in the possibility of "the immortal commonwealth," that is, a political constitution whose perfection would enable it to last forever without undergoing any change. Fink finds "a classical counterpart" to this belief, which he avers was shared by most of the "classical republicans," in Plato's *Laws* (pp. 63 and 156). He does not, however, investigate the precise relation between the classical and the modern utopia. Harrington believed that the proper institutions would by themselves secure the state against dissolution from any internal causes. He could believe this because he held the opinion that the perfect character of the commonwealth is independent of the moral qualities of the citizens (p. 61). He thereby rejected the view of the classical thinkers, who defined the constitution not only in terms of institutions, but primarily in terms of the aims actually pursued by the community or its authoritative parts, and accepted the view advanced by Hobbes that man, as the "maker" of commonwealths, can solve once and for all the problems inherent in man as the "matter" of them. And he paved the way for Kant's assertion that the best, or the only legitimate, political order can be erected even in a nation of devils. In regard to the question of the relation between institutions and moral character, Richard Baxter (pp. 61 and 88) rather than Harrington was a "classical republican"—to say nothing of the fact that certainly Plato and Aristotle did not believe in the immortality of any commonwealth, however perfect.

Since the author is concerned with the restoration of classical ideals in seventeenth-century England, he is justified in disregarding the views of Thomas Aquinas and Calvin on mixed government. A glance at what these theologians had to say about the Hebrew state would have helped him, however, in elucidating the view of the "classical republicans" that that state was an example of mixed polity.

CASSIRER, ERNST, *The Myth of the State.* New Haven: Yale University Press. 1946.

In this posthumously published book, Cassirer utilizes his philosophy of symbolic forms in diagnosing the illness of our time. Agreeing with the self-interpretation of "some of our modern political systems," he notes the "preponderance of mythical thought over rational thought" in these systems (p. 3). Toward an understanding of the phenomenon thus interpreted, he discusses the nature of myth, the "struggle against myth in the history of political theory," and the "myth of the twentieth century." The book is at least as much a survey of the history of political thought as it is a discussion of the subject indicated in the title. But the title is justified inasmuch as the book's claim to attention rests chiefly on the sections in which the problem of myth is explicitly discussed.

Contradicting earlier students of myth, Cassirer contends that myth has no specific subject matter and hence its nature can be known only through the understanding of "its function in man's social and cultural life" (pp. 33 ff.). The function of myth is to interpret "religious rites." The function of these rites in their turn is to satisfy a "deep, ardent desire of the individuals to identify themselves with the life of the community and with the life of nature"; or, more precisely, since "to the primitive mind nature itself is not a physical thing governed by physical laws" and therefore "one and the same society—the society of life—includes and embraces" the life of the community and the life of nature, the rites satisfy the desire of the individual "to immerse itself into the stream of universal life, to lose its identity." What primitive man does in his rites in an "entirely unconscious" manner is interpreted in the myths. The myth turns the emotions, which find their first expression in rites, into images; "mythical symbolism leads to an objectification of feelings." Symbolic expression, however, "is no mere externalization, but condensation" and intensification. Myth, we may say, legitimates the rites and thus guarantees their survival (pp. 38 ff., 45 ff.). Inasmuch as myth legitimates the ritual, one may also say that the ritual is "based upon mythical conceptions" (p. 279).

However one may have to judge this view of myth, Cassirer is certainly right in negatively characterizing philosophy proper by its "struggle against myth." In Greek philosophy, he holds, that struggle found its culminating expression in the doctrines of Socrates and Plato. Socrates attacked "the mythical world in [its] center" by raising the "fundamental and essential" "question of good and evil" and by realizing that "myth has no answer to that question" (pp. 55, 60). But only Plato attacked myth at its root; since myth originates in man's "social experience," the only adequate alternative to myth is a "rational theory of the state" (pp. 38 ff., 61 ff., 76). It is true, "Plato did not entirely forbid mythical tales; he even admitted that, in the education of a young child, they are indispensable; but they must be brought under a strict discipline" (p. 67). It is also true that "we cannot think of Platonic philosophy without thinking of the Platonic myths," but Plato, Cassirer asserts, admitted myths only "into his metaphysics and natural philosophy," while in the field of "his political theories" he was "the professed enemy of myth"; he excluded myths "from his *Republic*, that is to say, from his system of education" (pp. 71 ff., 77).

The fight against myth had to start all over again after the victory of Christianity. In spite of their dependence on Greek philosophy, the scholastics, to say nothing of the church fathers, were unable to repeat the achievement of Plato, partly because "they only knew and acknowledged a symbolic truth" and hence, disregarding the literal meaning, "they tried to find out the *sensus moralis*, the *sensus anagogicus*, the *sensus mysticus* of the classical authors" (p. 88), and partly because "to doubt the fact of the original sin," which Cassirer terms a "definite mythical element," "was impossible for any medieval thinker" (p. 110).

A new liberation from myth was achieved by Machiavelli. The "constructive principle" that gives Machiavelli's new science of politics, his exact description of "facts," its unity or character, is the demand for the "full autonomy" of the state, a demand which presupposes the radical secularization not only of the state, but of religion itself as well (pp. 130, 137 ff., 154). To account for the limited applicability of his "general scientific principles"—"the axiom of the uniformity and homogeneity of nature"—to political affairs, Machiavelli had recourse to *fortuna*, that is, he apparently resorted to a mythical power. Actually, however, he secularized the "symbol of Fortune" by teaching that "Man is not subdued to Fortune," and thus introduced a "new element of thought and feeling which is specifically modern" (pp. 157, 159 ff.). But in order to assert the "autonomy" of the state, Machiavelli divorced the state not only from religion, but from morality as well. To complete his work it was necessary to restore the connection between state and morality without returning to myth. This was done in the social contract doctrines of the seventeenth and eighteenth centuries. On the one hand, "there is nothing less mysterious than a contract," and, on the other, the social contract presupposes, and guarantees, the "right to personality" by which man's humanity stands and falls (pp. 140 ff., 173, 175).

"All these great achievements were suddenly called into question" by romanticism, especially German romanticism. Its root was the "deep wish to go back to the sources of poetry," or "to 'poeticize' the world." But this led to a new interest in myth, which now became a "subject of awe and veneration." The political insufficiency of romantic aestheticism, in its turn, paved the way for the "realistic" political use of the myth in the twentieth century (pp. 179, 183 ff.).

The myth of the twentieth century—that is, chiefly the myth

fostered by national socialism—came into being by means of an amalgamation of hero worship, race worship, and state worship. In order to clarify its elements and to show their heterogeneity, Cassirer discusses the doctrines of Carlyle, Gobineau, and Hegel. Though he does not completely acquit these authors of indirect responsibility for national socialism, he insists on the fundamental difference between the teachers and their national-socialist pupils (pp. 216, 222, 232, 239, 243, 267, 273 ff.). National socialism cannot be traced directly to any one doctrine or combination of doctrines; its immediate source is man's myth-producing impulses which have never been "really vanquished and subjugated," and which reassert themselves with devastating results in extreme crises of social life. Since "civilized man . . . cannot entirely forget or deny the demand of rationality," the myth of the twentieth century is of course fundamentally different from all primitive myths; it is an "artificial thing," which was "fabricated by very skilful and cunning artisans" (pp. 277, 280, 281).

Space does not permit a detailed discussion of Cassirer's theses. All their deficiencies could perhaps be traced to his failure to account for the abandonment by romanticism of the social contract doctrines of the enlightenment. Possibly Cassirer believed that while the enlightenment was right in rejecting myth, it laid itself open to legitimate criticism by failing to give an adequate account of myth, and that, with his analysis of myth filling that lacuna, the fundamental moral-political thesis of the enlightenment no longer encounters serious difficulties. However this may be, if Cassirer were correct in his appraisal of the rights-of-man doctrine of the eighteenth century, an adequate answer to the challenge raised by the doctrines favoring the political myth of our time—for example, those of Spengler and Heidegger (pp. 289-93)—would have been not an inconclusive discussion of the myth of the state, but a radical transformation of the philosophy of symbolic forms into a teaching whose center is moral philosophy, that is, something like a return to Cassirer's teacher Hermann Cohen, if not to Kant himself. Considering the criticism to which Kantian ethics is open, this demand is not met by Cassirer's occasional restatements of Kantian moral principles.

Cassirer seems to trace the romantic revolt against the enlightenment to aestheticism. But is not aestheticism the essence of his own doctrine? With regard to Plato's attack on poetry, he says: "No modern writer would ever think of inserting his objections to poetry and art into a work dealing with politics. We see no connection between the two problems" (p. 67). But is not the obvious connection between politics and "art," according to Plato as well as other philosophers, that both must be subservient to morality?

A man of Cassirer's erudition could not discuss any historical subject that falls within the scope of his scholarly interest, however incidentally, without making some contribution to our historical understanding. The most valuable chapters of this book are those devoted to Machiavelli. Particularly useful is Cassirer's proof of the inadequacy of the current historicist interpretation of Machiavelli's teaching (pp. 124 ff., 142 ff., 151). The value of that proof is not diminished by the fact that in discussing what he rightly considers the central subject of *The Prince*—namely, the new principalities—Cassirer lapses into the historicist interpretation by practically identifying the new principalities with the modern state or modern tyranny (pp. 133 ff., 147 ff.). Cassirer has also realized the crucial significance of the eighteenth chapter of *The Prince* in which Machiavelli sets forth his interpretation of himself as another Chiron —that is, a half-human, half-bestial teacher of princes (p. 150).

VERDROSS-ROSSBERG, ALFRED. *Grundlinien der antiken Rechts- und Staatsphilosophie.* Vienna: Julius Springer. 1946.

It goes almost without saying that the picture drawn by Verdross of Greek political thought comes nearer the truth than the national-socialist version. This does not mean that Verdross' presentation is always, or even fundamentally, satisfactory. It is a presentation that must be characterized as conventional, and the convention it follows is the product, or the residue, of the studies made by nineteenth- and twentieth-century classical scholars, as well as of the tradition of classical political philosophy which has never been completely interrupted. Conventions of this kind are necessarily composed of true and false, of profound and superficial, of proved and hypothetical elements. Their greatest danger lies in the

fact that they inevitably breed a sense of familiarity with their subject matter—a sense of familiarity that in its turn leads one to underestimate the difficulties obstructing the understanding of the subject
matter. The beginning of understanding is a sense of the bewildering or strange character of the subject to be understood. Conven-
tion-bred familiarity is apt to preclude that crucial experience.

Verdross believes that he is breaking new ground. He complains
about the neglect of pre-Socratic political thought in earlier surveys, and regards as one great advantage of his book the attention
it pays to the development leading from Hesiod to the fifth-century
doctrine concerning democracy (p. v). Yet a case can be made for
the view, which he rejects, that the account of classical political
thought ought to start with Plato or Aristotle. The information we
possess about the doctrines of the pre-Socratics is fragmentary;
thus the dangers of misinterpretation, or of mistaking hypotheses
for facts, are unusually great. It would seem that the only non-
modern frame of reference for a philosophic understanding of the
fragments is supplied by Plato's and Aristotle's reports, and these
reports cannot be properly appreciated before the works, and
hence the teachings, of Plato and Aristotle have been sufficiently
understood. I believe that one arrives at the same conclusion, although by way of a somewhat different argument, when one considers the difficulties obstructing the philosophic understanding of
the political views of the classical poets and historians.

In any event, Verdross' attempt to start his account of Greek
political thought with an analysis of Hesiod leads him to substitute
for the only available classical frame of reference a modern one and
thus to state, for example, that Hesiod was the first to distinguish
between the Is, which is determined by natural laws, and the moral-
legal Ought (p. 17; see also pp. 126 ff. and 149 ff. for his use of the
nineteenth-century distinction between sociological and legal doctrine of the state in interpreting Plato and Aristotle). His disregard
of the problem of frame of reference, or of context, leads him to base
his account of the political thought of Thucydides and of the tragic
poets simply and directly on the utterances of the characters presented by these authors (pp. 34 ff. and 55 ff.). Ignoring the context
of the speech which Plato puts in the mouth of Protagoras (see
Protagoras, 317 a4-6 and 319 b3 ff.; compare 316 c5 ff.), Verdross
is led to subscribe to Menzel's view, based chiefly on the same error

of interpretation, that Protagoras was a theoretician of democracy (pp. 41 ff. and 48). His presentation of the doctrines of the sophists is vitiated by the conventional ascription to the sophists of the antithesis between nature and convention, although he quotes a fragment of Heraclitus which implies that very antithesis (pp. 50 ff. and 31). He also says that according to Xenophon's *Memorabilia* the doctrine of unwritten laws, as distinguished from the positive laws, was introduced and developed by Hippias (pp. 53 ff.), though according to the source in question it was Socrates, not Hippias, who introduced this doctrine. Verdross presents Socrates as a teacher of political virtue (p. 61), without mentioning the fact that for Plato "political virtue" is a derogatory term. "For Socrates everything was clear and simple" (p. 70). In accordance with this view, Verdross can rest satisfied with reconciling the Socratic dictum that the just is the legal with Socrates' critical attitude toward the established legal order, by suggesting that the natural law which Socrates recognized legitimates "the state" and acts at the same time as a standard for the gradual improvement of the actual state (pp. 68 ff.).

Since Verdross attaches undue weight to the hypotheses of certain modern philologists, he asserts without any misgivings that the *Protagoras* was written before Socrates' death, that by the aporetic character of the *Protagoras*, the *Laches*, and other dialogues, Plato "obviously" intended to indicate the insufficiency of the Socratic approach, that the first dialogue written after Plato's return from his first Sicilian journey was the *Menexenus*, and that the *Banquet* was "composed in 380" (pp. 70 ff., 74, 76). He is certain that the mature Plato desired to come to power in Athens (pp. 73, 92). It is "obvious" to him that the idea of the good is identical with "the good God" (p. 89). It is equally obvious to him that by speaking in the *Statesman* of the private man who possesses the royal art and who advises the actual ruler, Plato alludes to his own position in Syracuse, and that the divine shepherd mentioned in the myth of the same dialogue is "no one else but the royal philosopher, and hence Plato himself" (pp. 97 ff.). Disregarding the fact that the *Statesman* is based on the explicit distinction between the perfect statesman and the philosopher, Verdross asserts that "in contrast to Plato, Aristotle has separated philosophy from the political art" (p. 122). His interpretation of Aristotle's political teaching depends at the decisive point on the hypothetical distinction between Aristotle's "Urpolitik" and his later political teaching (pp. 122 ff., 137). While he sees more clearly than most other writers that for Plato's fully developed political doctrine we have to turn to the *Laws*, and not to the *Republic* or the *Statesman* (pp. 107, 115), Verdross can still say with reference to the "inquisition" suggested in the tenth book of the *Laws* that "Plato seems to have forgotten completely" the fate of his teacher Socrates (p. 114). He fails to see that Plato replaces the law enforcing belief in the existence of the gods of the city of Athens by a law enforcing belief in the existence of the gods of the universe, thus laying the legal foundation for the freedom of Socratic philosophy, if not for the freedom of philosophy as such.

GRENE, DAVID. *Man in his Pride: A Study in the Political Philosophy of Thucydides and Plato.* Chicago: University of Chicago Press. 1950.

It is difficult to give an adequate notion of this book. The author combines the specific sensitivities of both the historian of culture and the artist with a distrust, not to say contempt, of what is generally known as philosophy. His book vibrates with that "passionate sense of life" which, he feels, contended in Plato's soul with an equally "passionate belief" in ideas. Partly inspired by what Plato suggested about the essential weakness of reasoning and the superiority of indirect communication to direct communication, Grene senses most strongly, deplores most passionately, and avoids most carefully, the pitfalls into which an unbridled concern with conceptual precision and methodic procedure might lead. He is more concerned with bringing to light and to life the hidden drama of the souls of Thucydides and Plato, or the human reality of fifth-century Athens as reflected in Thucydides' and Plato's minds, than with articulating their political philosophies proper, that is, their reasoned views of the nature of political things and the right social order. He thus makes his readers see many things in Thucydides and Plato which would escape the large majority of those whose profession it is to teach philosophy. With gratifying candor he takes the responsibility for his basic premise by using the terms "political philosophy" and "political opinions" or "political beliefs" synonymously.

The book may be said, if not to prove, at any rate to suggest the following thesis. Political philosophy emerged in fifth-century Athens, in a society that was particularly close to our own: both then and now "it is man and man alone, without cosmic or supernatural sanction, who is both the source and the resolution of conflict." In the extreme situation in which man lived in fifth-century Athens, Thucydides and Plato "defined the range within which . . . all political speculation in the West can be seen to move." This would seem to mean that the two classics of political philosophy are opposed to each other; Grene uses the word "polarity." By implication he rejects the accepted view, which may be stated as holding that the Sophists (and not Thucydides) stand at the opposite pole to Plato; and that modern political philosophy has transcended the limits within which all classic political philosophy remained. One might wish that the author had shown why the political teachings of Thucydides and Plato can be said to mark "the limits within which, in its view of political man, our Western tradition has developed." But one could say in defense of Grene's reserve that we are barely beginning to discern the region in which the answer to questions of this kind, nay the proper formulation of questions of this kind, has to be sought.

Grene notes a kinship between Thucydides' opinions and those that Plato attributed to Thrasymachus and Callicles: he speaks of Thucydides' "materialism." But, he adds, Thucydides "may have seen [in certain phenomena] the transcendence of the materialism in which he believed." The phenomena in question are apparently not what one could call the moral phenomena. It is true that Thucydides believed "in the meaningfulness of moral epithets," or he believed that "the old values [decency and nobility] . . . had existed and did in some sense exist, even if human beings no longer paid them their former homage"; but he did not believe "in the actual existence of a genuine power in the moral issues themselves." The phenomenon in which Thucydides "may have seen the transcendence of the materialism in which he believed" was Periclean Athens, or, in general terms, "the great state," which lives "in the radiance of its own beauty and magnitude," which is an end in itself, whose preservation "means more than the happiness or misery of all her inhabitants," and in whose image "the blackest deeds against Greek morality have their place as truly as the love of beauty and wisdom." This solution is based on a number of assumptions, one of them being that the taste of Thucydides was identical with the taste of Pericles. For reasons that I cannot set forth here, I believe that the true solution would require extensive and coherent reflection about what Thucydides indicates in regard to the virtue of moderation. It would require, above all, methodic reflection about that great virtue itself. The fact that Thucydides did not believe in supernatural sanctions does not prove that he was unaware of the "cosmic" or natural sanctions to immoderate courses.

As for Grene's account of Plato's political philosophy, one cannot even attempt to summarize it. Two points in it strike me most. In the first place, Grene, who is keenly aware of the connection between politics and rhetoric on the one hand, and between rhetoric and *eros* on the other, appears to trace the basic difficulty inherent in Plato's political philosophy to the disproportion between the political relationship (that of rulers and ruled) and the "erotic" relationship. I regard this as an important insight. I only wish that it were not blurred by the identification of true rhetoric (the rhetoric adumbrated in the *Phaedrus*) with the art that Plato employed in writing the preambles to laws (in the *Laws*). Secondly, Grene seems to believe that there is in Plato's political philosophy an "inevitable antithesis" between the philosopher and the king, an antithesis that seems to be traceable to the tension between Plato's admiration for "Socrates, the rebel" and his admiration for a "rigid and stratified" or "ritualistic" society. If I am not mistaken, Grene is here again guided by an important insight, and in fact by the same insight as the one referred to before. Yet, to say nothing of other considerations, one cannot accept his contention that according to the *Laws*, and apparently even according to the *Republic*, "in the imitation of the eternal model . . . it is not essential that from moment to moment or generation to generation even the ruler . . . should understand the truth which underlies the organization of the best or second best state." It would be difficult to reconcile this contention with what Plato says about the Nocturnal

Council. But today it is perhaps better thus to overstate Plato's thesis regarding the disproportion between philosophy and politics than to follow the beaten path by failing to see a problem in the relation between philosophy and politics.

GOUGH, J. W. *John Locke's Political Philosophy*. Oxford: The Clarendon Press. 1950.

This volume consists of eight studies which are devoted to the following subjects: the law of nature; the rights of the individual; government by consent; Locke's theory of property; the separation of powers and sovereignty; Locke and the Revolution of 1688; political trusteeship; the development of Locke's belief in toleration.

The author has made use of fresh material (the Lovelace collection of Locke's papers) but one can hardly say that he has made a fresh approach to Locke's political philosophy. He approaches his subject along lines which by now have become conventional. He sees Locke primarily as the mouthpiece of a tradition on the one hand, and of contemporary opinion on the other. The approach might seem to be appropriate to the subject. If we can trust Gough, Locke himself did nothing but follow the beaten path: ". . . what [Locke] was really doing, under the guise of erecting a form of government on the basis of freely consenting individuals, was to describe the operation of the traditional English constitution in terms of the political philosophy current in his age" (p. 71). ". . . practically every feature in Locke's political system . . . was, in fact, a common-place of current English political theory" (p 98; cf. pp. 22, 42, 113, 121, 124, 196). Considering the nature of all "current" political theory, this would explain in a perfectly satisfactory manner why "Locke is full of illogical flaws and inconsistencies" (p. 123), but it would leave one wondering why he achieved a greater fame than the many nonentities whose views he shared. Above all, one would find it hard to understand why "his political doctrines [were] slow at first to win acceptance," even among the Whig leaders (pp. 133, 135).

Gough's view is the outcome of his method. He has tried to

understand Locke historically, but his notion of what "historical" means is much too narrow. His only remark on this subject is to the effect that "it is simply unhistorical to examine [Locke's ideas] in the light of the experience of the nineteenth and twentieth centuries" (pp. 41-42). It is not necessary to discuss whether Gough always obeys this rule and whether, in examining Locke's ideas in the light of the experience of the seventeenth century, he employs the necessary care (cf. p. 35 with p. 189). What is decisive is that by trying to understand Locke's political thought primarily in the light of the political situation of seventeenth century England, he is seduced into understanding Locke's political philosophy as barely more than an ideology of the Revolution of 1688. "He appears to state his political theory in general philosophical terms, as if it were a purely logical deduction from general principles, but if we read between the lines we recognize the historic features of the English seventeenth-century constitution" (p. 70). We may have to read between Locke's lines, but we cannot do this before having laid a solid foundation for it. We would have to know first why he tried "to state his political theory in general philosophical terms." Gough seems to believe that he did this in order to disguise the partisan character of his doctrine (p. 38). The only reasonable explanation, of course, is that it is impossible to approve or disapprove of any actual and hence "individual" constitution without tacit or explicit reference to "universal" principles. To regard Locke's universal principles as secondary in comparison with his acceptance of the English constitution is to put the cart before the horse.

"Political philosophy" is an ambiguous term, but certainly when speaking of the political philosophy of a man like Locke, one must assume that political philosophy is a branch of philosophy. Accordingly, the context within which Locke's political philosophy must be seen primarily is not the political scene of seventeenth century England, but the state of philosophy in seventeenth century Europe. If I am not mistaken, Gough does not even allude to the names of Bacon, Galileo, Descartes and Newton. Seventeenth century philosophy effected, and intended to effect, a break with the philosophic tradition. Locke himself played a leading role in that revolution. It is therefore reasonable to expect that his political philosophy is fundamentally a revolutionary or novel doctrine.

Its revolutionary character is not emphasized by Locke and it is far from being obvious. But this is only what one should expect. The *Civil Government* is meant to serve a dual purpose: to state the eternal principles of politics and to defend a particular political establishment on the basis of those principles. Hence, Locke had to present his principles in a manner which was not merely "philosophical" but at the same time "civil." Gough himself notes that Locke was a cautious man (p. 177). For obvious reasons, Locke had to be much more cautious in the *Civil Government* than in the *Essay*. He had to accommodate, not his thought, but the expression of his thought, to the prejudices of his age. This is the chief reason why one has to read between the lines of the *Civil Government*: one has to distinguish between Locke's universal principles in their undiluted form and the conventional guise in which he chose to present them.

Locke has not made it very difficult for the thinking reader to take his bearings. He indicated his attitude toward the tradition by the way in which he quoted Hooker. He quoted Hooker, as it were, on all occasions when he agreed with him; he practically never noted when he deviated from him. It is the obvious duty of the historian to confront the whole political doctrine of Locke with the whole political doctrine of Hooker. Such a comprehensive confrontation would bring out the fact that a deep and broad gulf separates Locke's political philosophy from traditional political philosophy; it would bring out the revolutionary character of Locke's political philosophy.

From what has been said it follows that the student of the *Civil Government* must pay the greatest attention to the very few passages in which Locke himself states that his doctrine is "strange." Coming across one of these passages, Gough has no other comment to offer than that a certain doctrine which Locke declared to be strange, is not strange any more (p. 88). It is necessary to add that the usual neglect of the *First Treatise* is indefensible. On this subject, Gough merely says: "The *First Treatise*, admittedly, was a controversial work in refutation of Filmer, but this had only a transient interest in its own day and can now be ignored" (p. 122). To mention only one point, one cannot understand the doctrine of the state of nature, if one does not consider its relation to Biblical history; but Locke used much more Biblical material in the *First*

Treatise than in the *Second*. Gough notes a difference between Locke and Rousseau regarding the "historicity" of the state of nature (p. 89), but he does not pay any attention to the fact that Rousseau denied the "historicity" of the state of nature because he saw that the doctrine of the state of nature cannot be reconciled with the Biblical account of the origins of mankind. The bearing of this issue on the question of Locke's relation to "current English political theory" should be obvious.

A typical example of Gough's procedure is his discussion of Locke's doctrine of the law of nature. As Gough notes, Locke rejected the view that there is universal agreement of the nations regarding natural law, or, in other words, he admitted no way, accessible to man as man, of knowing the natural law other than "mathematical" demonstration; furthermore, he tried to give natural law a hedonist foundation. Since Gough believes that Locke's attempt was doomed to failure, he concludes that the real basis of Locke's natural law doctrine was traditional faith (pp. 5-10, 16-17). Whatever might have to be said about this conclusion, it cannot even be considered before one has fully realized the fact that the rejection of the *consensus gentium* and the attempt to combine natural law with hedonism presuppose a radical break with the traditional approach. The least one would have to say is that there was a strong tension between Locke's traditional faith and his effort to think independently. This tension would explain both his caution and his self-contradictions: he may have recoiled from certain consequences of his antitraditional principles. In addition, his attempt to be a rationalist and a hedonist may be deplorable; this does not exclude the possibility that his rationalism and his hedonism had very far-reaching consequences for his political philosophy. Is there no connection between Locke's depreciation of the natural agreement of all men in regard to moral principles and his view that nature, as distinguished from human labor, furnishes "only the almost worthless materials"? Is there no connection between Locke's hedonism and his teaching about the natural law principles that regulate the accumulation and the use of property in civil society? As long as these questions have not been properly discussed, one cannot claim to have understood Locke's doctrine of property and therewith his political philosophy.

SIMON, YVES R. *Philosophy of Democratic Government.* Chicago: University of Chicago Press. 1951.

Simon's philosophy of democratic government is chiefly, not to say exclusively, concerned with modern democracy, *i.e.*, with a kind of democracy which operates within industrial mass society, and which is characterized by the party system. He combines awareness of the dangers inherent in modern democracy—dangers to both democracy itself and to human perfection—with a firm refusal to succumb to the frequently facile despair of "literary men." He tries to show that there is cause for hope. He states the issues with which he deals with uncommon precision and with perfect candor, and he is never for a moment forgetful of the obligations of charity.

Simon prefaces his philosophy of democratic government with a "general theory of government." The problems of democracy in particular are treated in four sections: Democratic Freedom; Sovereignty in Democracy; Democratic Equality; and Democracy and Technology. It is impossible even to enumerate here the many important topics on which his discussion sheds light. Particularly valuable is what he says about the functions of authority (see the summary in 61 n.), about the relation between democracy and liberalism (122-125) and about the proper place of public opinion in democracy (185-190). His discussion of the relation between democracy and liberalism is likely to prove helpful for defining the essential limitations of freedom of speech. His discussion of public opinion lays the foundation for sound judgment on the political dangers inherent in public opinion polls. One must note the absence of a discussion of the manner in which the international situation of our time and of the foreseeable future affects and is likely to affect the character as well as the prospects of modern democracy.

Simon's philosophy of democratic government is based on Thomistic principles. It goes without saying that Thomism is compatible with the view that democracy is just under certain conditions and therefore in particular with the view that at present democracy is the only practicable alternative to various forms of tyranny. But Simon does not leave it at this qualified acceptance of democracy. He expresses his full agreement with what he calls the democratic spirit.

The democratic spirit, as Simon conceives of it, is far remote from doctrinaire democratism. Simon grants "that in certain times and places a quasi-colonial government of the many by the few may be the best arrangement or even the only conceivable one." This could be thought to mean that democracy is simply the best regime and that therefore its actualization depends on particularly favorable conditions, and hence on conditions which are very rarely met. But I am not certain whether this formulation does justice to Simon's intention. He indicates what he understands by the democratic spirit by opposing it to the "conservative" spirit. He understands by conservatism the view "that, so long as men are what they always have been, nothing will be better for the many than paternal domination by the few." Conservatism would thus be identical with the doctrinaire view that democracy is illegitimate or at any rate undesirable under all circumstances. But doctrinairism cannot be said to be of the essence of conservatism. If one wants to speak at all of conservatism in this context, one would have to say that the reasonable conservative would prefer in doubtful cases non-democratic non-tyrannical regimes whereas the reasonable democrat would prefer democracy in doubtful cases. Simon describes the character of the democratic spirit as follows: "Besides its willingness and anxiousness to declare that there are cases, whether frequent or not, in which the many do not need to be ruled paternalistically, the democratic spirit is characterized by a certain sort of audacity highly uncongenial to conservatives." Since, as we have seen, the "willingness and anxiousness" in question is not peculiar to democrats, the distinctive feature of the democratic spirit would then be "a certain sort of audacity," the willingness "to accept a risk" from which the conservative recoils: "democracy increases enormously the demand for heroism" (16-17). The term "audacity," which reminds one, not only of Danton and Machiavelli but, above all, of Pericles' Funeral Speech itself, points to the basic problem.

Simon's attempt to combine the Thomistic principles with the democratic spirit presupposes that the Thomistic principles can be divorced from the "conservative" context within which they occur in Thomas' writings. Simon starts from an examination of the view that Thomas himself conceived of the multitude as the essential transmitter of governmental authority. He reaches the conclusion that "to state with no qualification that the transmission theory is that of Aquinas would perhaps be more than the texts warrant" (158-160). In addition to what Simon says on the subject one could perhaps remark that "multitude" does not necessarily designate a democratically ordered multitude. It is true that the constituent multitude must be understood as a democracy if the assumption is made that all men are by nature equal in the politically relevant respects, but this assumption is rejected by the Aristotelian Thomas. Simon turns then to the doctrines of Cajetan, Bellarmine and Suarez. Bellarmine conceives of the constituent multitude as consisting of equals (166) and according to Suarez "democracy comes into existence *by nature* as opposed to monarchy and aristocracy which cannot come into existence except by positive disposition" (172-176). Yet, as Simon points out, "neither of these thinkers meant to recommend democracy"; "the transmission theory is not understood by its proponents to be distinctly democratic" (177). That is to say, the classical exponents of Thomism did not go beyond admitting that democracy is one among a number of legitimate regimes. They did not agree with what Simon calls the democratic spirit. But, he goes on to say, "it is hardly possible to give much thought to [the common right of deposition which is implied in the transmission theory] without inclining toward the establishment of [the democratic right of control]"; "the concept of popular control inherent in the transmission theory and inseparable from it favors the promotion of democracy" (180-181). Here the question arises why this democratic implication escaped the notice of the classical Thomistic writers.

Simon seems to suggest an answer when speaking of a crucial premise of modern democracy, "the universalism of the rights of man." "If theoretical ideas were always allowed to unfold their consequences in the actual course of events, the universalism of the rights of man would not have come into historical existence at a time that was the golden age of nominalism [the seventeenth and eighteenth centuries]. But the tendencies of a theory may be held in check by a conflicting moral environment" (201). If one may utilize this remark for an answer to our question, one would arrive at the following conclusion: the theory which is in conformity with the democratic spirit ought to have come into existence in the golden age of realism but historical accident (the moral environment of that age) prevented it; through historical accident (the moral environment of the age of Enlightenment) the theory in question emerged only, say, in the eighteenth century. Very much would then depend on a clear grasp of the difference between the moral environments of the two ages. However this may be, Simon believes that a bias in favor of democracy is the necessary consequence of the transmission theory, *i.e.*, that we understand the meaning of that theory better than did its most illustrious proponents. Or, to apply to this subject what Simon says in regard to a related subject, *viz.*, the changed attitude toward "man-killing economic inequalities": "on this subject our conscience has changed and, no doubt, improved" (205). I confess to a great reluctance to believe that "our conscience has improved" on any important subject or that we understand great thinkers of the past better than they understood themselves. I am inclined to assume that the classics of Thomism have given sufficient thought to the transmission theory to bring out all its necessary implications. I would therefore regard it as wise to assume that the democratic spirit is a possible, but not a necessary, development of the transmission theory, a development favored by extraneous or accidental circumstances.

Simon speaks in the same breath of "the equalitarian dynamics of *human nature*" and the equalitarian dynamics of *"modern societies"* (206-207; my italics). Neither his argument nor his authorities seem to warrant the first contention, but many observers would agree with the second contention. The transition from the second contention to the first would be permissible if one could assume the existence of a law of progress or of manifest wisdom in historical change. Simon does not believe in such a law (286-287). He does not say that the time "when it was possible to believe that the destiny of the common man was safely entrusted to the wisdom of the upper class" is gone forever; he merely says that "that time is gone, apparently, forever" (98-99). Being a political philosopher and not a philosopher of history or a pseudo prophet, he obviously feels that no one can know whether mankind will not go through a period of atomic wars (*cf.* 273) and whether after such a period non-democratic regimes, which today are regarded as altogether obsolete, may not become again "the best arrangements or even the only conceivable ones."

Simon can trace the equalitarian dynamics of modern societies to an equalitarian dynamics of human nature because he regards the modern situation (let us say the situation that exists or is emerging since the middle of the nineteenth century) as the normal situation. ". . . under certain conditions the genuine life of the city is better expressed by restricted than by universal vote—this happens as a result of such abnormalities as widespread ignorance. . . . Such situations are not so rare in our time; in the history of mankind considered as a whole their frequency is such as to conceal their purely accidental character." ". . . the participation of all in political elections is a normal condition for the integrally political character of elections. The qualification needed concerns situations in which the suffrage of all is, by accident, incapable of exercising its normal function as expressive of the entire life of the community" (87). This amounts to saying that the conditions required for democracy are the normal conditions, the conditions required by human nature. To judge of the validity of that contention, one must look at an example which Simon discusses when speaking of democratic equality, *viz.*, the "equal right to protection against the risk of dying prematurely." "It is human nature which demands that human life be protected by the efforts of human society; this demand holds equally for all the bearers of human nature." But, as Simon notes, this demand of human nature approximates the status of a genuine right of all only by virtue of the modern technological development (205). One is forced to wonder whether what is true of this particular right, is not likewise true, *mutatis mutandis*, of the abolition of "widespread ignorance" in a number of countries in the recent past (*cf.* 206-207). To express this generally, Simon does not show whether what he regards as the normal condition is not a condition which presupposes modern technology. He does not show, that is, whether what he regards as an improvement of our conscience is not the inevitable consequence of the application of an unchanged conscience to a situation, or an opportunity, created by modern technology.

The condition created by modern technology would be the normal condition if modern technology itself were normal. It is then for a very good reason that Simon's book culminates in a discussion of "Democracy and Technology." Just as democracy, technological society is rooted in human nature: "domination of physical nature is part of the vocation of man. . . . In the fulfillment of his vocation it was normal that man, after having used empirical procedures for many generations, should develop scientific methods and put them to use." But "this does not mean that the process by which societies became technological was governed by strict necessity." Above all, it does not mean that this process is normal or that the situation created by it is the normal situation of man: "out of a sense of danger, men might have decided to observe moderation in the conquest of nature." Man can choose between moderation and audacity. But, "as a matter of fact, restraining factors were defeated in the long run" (273). We have no right to applaud a situation that was created by a decision which, however well intentioned, was not evidently virtuous and wise. But we cannot escape from that situation; it is our duty to act virtuously and wisely in it. We must beware of the danger which is now becoming greater than it ever was before, of trying to escape "into anti-social dreams" (273). One cannot but agree with this sober and manly conclusion.

INDEX OF NAMES

Northern Michigan University

3 1854 001 659 237

EZNO
JA71 S795 1973
What is political philosophy? and other